GW01145924

Democratic Extremism in Theory and Practice

Democracy and extremism are usually considered as opposites. We assume that our system (in the UK, the USA, the Netherlands, etc.) is democratic, and that extremists aim to destroy our system and introduce some kind of dictatorship, if not chaos and anarchy. Yet, in many cases, the extremists seem sincere in their attempt to construct a more democratic polity. Hence, they can be called democrats and yet also extremists, in so far as they strive for a regime with characteristics that are more extreme in a significant sense.

This book analyses radical and extreme democratic theories and ideas in their historical context, interlocked with critical descriptions of historical institutions and experiments that help to evaluate the theories. Cases range from ancient Athens to recent experiments with citizen juries and citizen assemblies, from the time-honoured Swiss Landsgemeinde to contemporary (and controversial) workers' councils in Venezuela and participatory budgeting in Porto Alegre. Among the theorists discussed here are familiar names as well as relatively unknown persons: Jean-Jacques Rousseau and Karl Marx, Murray Bookchin and John Burnheim, William Godwin and Barbara Goodwin, Anton Pannekoek and Heinz Dieterich. Whereas the extreme ideas do not seem to work very well in practice, they do indicate ways by which we could make existing political systems more democratic.

This book will be of interest to students of Politics and Current Affairs, as well as an inspiration to political activists and reformists.

Paul Lucardie was affiliated with the Documentation Centre on Dutch Political Parties at the University of Groningen, the Netherlands, from 1979 till 2011. He has done research on Dutch parties, especially new and extreme parties, as well as on ideologies.

Routledge studies in extremism and democracy
Series Editors: Roger Eatwell
University of Bath
and
Matthew Goodwin
University of Nottingham.

Founding Series Editors:
Roger Eatwell
University of Bath
and
Cas Mudde
University of Antwerp-UFSIA.

This new series encompasses academic studies within the broad fields of 'extremism' and 'democracy'. These topics have traditionally been considered largely in isolation by academics. A key focus of the series, therefore, is the (inter-)*relation* between extremism and democracy. Works will seek to answer questions such as to what extent 'extremist' groups pose a major threat to democratic parties, or how democracy can respond to extremism without undermining its own democratic credentials.

The books encompass two strands:
Routledge Studies in Extremism and Democracy includes books with an introductory and broad focus which are aimed at students and teachers. These books will be available in hardback and paperback. Titles include:

Understanding Terrorism in America
From the Klan to al Qaeda
Christopher Hewitt

Fascism and the Extreme Right
Roger Eatwell

Racist Extremism in Central and Eastern Europe
Edited by Cas Mudde

Political Parties and Terrorist Groups (2nd Edition)
Leonard Weinberg, Ami Pedahzur and Arie Perliger

The New Extremism in 21st Century Britain
Edited by Roger Eatwell and Matthew Goodwin

New British Fascism
Rise of the British National Party
Matthew Goodwin

The End of Terrorism?
Leonard Weinberg

Mapping the Extreme Right in Contemporary Europe
From local to transnational
Edited by Andrea Mammone, Emmanuel Godin and Brian Jenkins

Varieties of Right-Wing Extremism in Europe
Edited by Andrea Mammone, Emmanuel Godin and Brian Jenkins

Routledge Research in Extremism and Democracy offers a forum for innovative new research intended for a more specialist readership. These books will be in hardback only. Titles include:

1 **Uncivil Society?**
   Contentious politics in post-Communist Europe
   Edited by Petr Kopecky and Cas Mudde

2 **Political Parties and Terrorist Groups**
   Leonard Weinberg and Ami Pedahzur

3 **Western Democracies and the New Extreme Right Challenge**
   Edited by Roger Eatwell and Cas Mudde

4 **Confronting Right Wing Extremism and Terrorism in the USA**
   George Michael

5 **Anti-Political Establishment Parties**
   A comparative analysis
   Amir Abedi

6 **American Extremism**
   History, politics and the militia
   D. J. Mulloy

7 **The Scope of Tolerance**
   Studies on the costs of free expression and freedom of the press
   Raphael Cohen-Almagor

8 **Extreme Right Activists in Europe**
   Through the magnifying glass
   Bert Klandermans and Nonna Mayer

9 **Ecological Politics and Democratic Theory**
   Mathew Humphrey

10 **Reinventing the Italian Right**
    Territorial politics, populism and 'post-Fascism'
    Carlo Ruzza and Stefano Fella

11 **Political Extremes**
An investigation into the history of terms and concepts from antiquity to the present
Uwe Backes

12 **The Populist Radical Right in Poland**
The patriots
Rafal Pankowski

13 **Social and Political Thought of Julius Evola**
Paul Furlong

14 **Radical Left Parties in Europe**
Luke March

15 **Counterterrorism in Turkey**
Policy choices and policy effects toward the Kurdistan workers' party (PKK)
Mustafa Coşar Ünal

16 **Class Politics and the Radical Right**
Edited by Jens Rydgren

17 **Rethinking the French New Right**
Alternatives to modernity
Tamir Bar-On

18 **Ending Terrorism in Italy**
Anna Bull and Philip Cooke

19 **Politics of Eugenics**
Productionism, population, and national welfare
Alberto Spektorowski and Liza Saban

20 **Democratic Extremism in Theory and Practice**
All power to the people
Paul Lucardie

Democratic Extremism in Theory and Practice

All power to the people

Paul Lucardie

Routledge
Taylor & Francis Group

LONDON AND NEW YORK

First published 2014
by Routledge
2 Park Square, Milton Park, Abingdon, Oxon OX14 4RN

and by Routledge
711 Third Avenue, New York, NY 10017

Routledge is an imprint of the Taylor & Francis Group, an informa business

© 2014 Paul Lucardie

The right of Paul Lucardie to be identified as author of this work has been asserted by him in accordance with sections 77 and 78 of the Copyright, Designs and Patents Act 1988.

All rights reserved. No part of this book may be reprinted or reproduced or utilised in any form or by any electronic, mechanical, or other means, now known or hereafter invented, including photocopying and recording, or in any information storage or retrieval system, without permission in writing from the publishers.

Trademark notice: Product or corporate names may be trademarks or registered trademarks, and are used only for identification and explanation without intent to infringe.

British Library Cataloguing in Publication Data
A catalogue record for this book is available from the British Library

Library of Congress Cataloging in Publication Data
Lucardie, Paul, Democratic extremism in theory and practice: all power to the people / Paul Lucardie.
  pages cm. – (Extremism and democracy)
  Includes bibliographical references and index.
  1. Democracy–History. 2. Radicalism–History. I. Title.
  JC421.L79 2013
  321.8–dc23
                                                                    2013022935

ISBN: 978-0-415-60312-6 (hbk)
ISBN: 978-1-315-85755-8 (ebk)

Typeset in Times New Roman
by Wearset Ltd, Boldon, Tyne and Wear

Printed and bound in Great Britain by
TJ International Ltd, Padstow, Cornwall

Contents

Preface		ix
Acknowledgements		xi
1	**Introduction**	1
	Three theoretical perspectives 3	
	Purpose and content of the book 6	
2	**Extremism**	11
	Conceptual problems 11	
	Othmar Spann and aristocratic conservatism 15	
	Fascism and National Socialism 17	
	Stalinism and Marxism–Leninism 19	
	Theocratic extremism 22	
	Murray Rothbard and libertarianism 25	
	Conclusion 28	
3	**Neathena: assembly democracy**	32
	Theory 34	
	Bookchin's libertarian municipalism 37	
	Practice 44	
	The power of the ekklèsia in Athens 44	
	The longevity of the Landsgemeinde in Switzerland 48	
	Town Meeting in New England 50	
	The Orçamento Participativo in Porto Alegre 52	
	Assembly democracy in political movements 54	
	Evaluation 56	
4	**Jacobinland: bounded-delegate democracy**	61
	Theory 63	
	Jacobins and sans-culottes: disciples of Rousseau? 63	

Neo-Jacobins and other democratic radicals in the nineteenth
  century 71
The Paris Commune and Karl Marx 75
Soviet democracy and Lenin 78
Council-democracy and Pannekoek 81
The New Left, 'autogestion' and council-democracy 87
Populist democracy: Torbjörn Tännsjö and Heinz Dieterich 95
Practice 99
Populist democracy in Venezuela? 99
Plebiscitary democracy in Switzerland and the United States 101
Evaluation 108

5 **Aleatoria: sortitionist democracy** 114
   Theory 117
   Barbara Goodwin's House of Lots 117
   John Burnheim's demarchy 118
   Strong sortitionism: the citizen juries of Simon Threlkeld 124
   Strong sortitionism: the Partido Azar 125
   Sortitionism balanced with electoralism: Callenbach and
     Phillips 126
   Sortitionism balanced with electoralism: Sutherland and the
     Kleroterians 129
   Sortitionism subordinated to electoralism: Zakaras, O'Leary and
     Leib 132
   Pros and cons of sortitionism 134
   Practice 137
   The Council and the courts in Athens 137
   Sortition and the jury system 140
   Opinion polls, citizen assemblies and juries 141
   Evaluation 148

6 **Conclusion: extremist theories and radical practices** 154

   References 165
   Index 191

Preface

My first conscious encounter with power was probably when I was ten years old. I was lying with my face in the snow, a boy who was a bit older and stronger than me was sitting on my back. That was bad enough, but worse, I felt, was that he was acting under the command of a girl from my class. She obviously had power over him – and over a large part of our class, too. I hated her, and felt utterly powerless.

At that youthful age, I often fantasised that I became emperor of the world – obviously a compensation for my lack of real power. Yet later, when I did taste a little real power – in a modest way, for instance as president of a student society – I did not enjoy it. In high school, I was moved by a novel by Stefan Zweig which we read in our German class, entitled 'The eyes of my eternal brother' (*Die Augen des ewigen Bruders*). The hero, Virata, is a warrior in an ancient Indian kingdom. When the King was about to lose a war against a pretender – his own brother-in-law – Virata saved his lord. Yet in the decisive battle, Virata killed his own brother, who had sided with the pretender. The eyes of his slain brother haunted him. He threw away his sword and accepted a position as a judge. Yet when he condemned a violent criminal to a long prison sentence, he recognised his brother in the eyes of the prisoner, and so he resigned and refused to accept another official position:

> Do not give me power, King, as power provokes action; and which action is just, my King, and not against a fate?[1]

Renouncing all power, Virata ends up as keeper of the King's dogs, the lowliest position in the kingdom.

I did not follow Virata's example, but remained ambivalent about power, both fascinated and repelled at the same time. One way to deal with an ambivalent feeling is to study it from a distance. So I studied sociology, Critical Theory (the Frankfurt School) and political science.

Meanwhile, my fantasies changed. The hierarchical and skewed power distribution of a world empire made way for a more egalitarian dream of radical democracy. Like many other baby-boomers, I became increasingly critical of the idea that the Netherlands, the United States and other countries around the

Atlantic Ocean had established real democracy, rule by the people, as opinion leaders, politicians and academics claimed. Though I was never a leader or full-time activist, I took part in demonstrations and meetings of various New Left organisations, such as the *Sozialistische Deutsche Studentenbund* (SDS) in Frankfurt on Main and the New Left wing of the Dutch Labour Party in Groningen. In Frankfurt, I also discovered the darker, intolerant and violent side of the New Left – which would later manifest itself in the terrorism of the Red Army Faction. Puzzled, I decided to write my PhD thesis about the New Left and its ideas.

After completion of the thesis, the ideal of radical democracy seemed to disappear behind my horizon. In 1979 I became a researcher at the Documentation Centre on Dutch Political Parties at the University of Groningen. Yet twenty years later, at a conference celebrating the twenty-fifth birthday of the Centre, the old question came back to me in a different garb. I presented a paper about political representation without political parties – just to do something different. The topic titillated my imagination and, after the conference, I decided to develop some of the ideas into a book. Towards the end of my academic career I returned to the questions that had motivated me to study politics in the first place: how to distribute power while preventing domination and repression. They were also (largely) the questions that had inspired the New Left: how come our political system claims to be democratic, yet most decisions are taken by a political elite? Can we realise those claims and make democracy work? Are radical and extreme ideas about democracy dangerous dreams or sources of inspiration for a better future?

I do not pretend to give a definite answer to any of those questions. In fact, I am afraid I remain somewhat ambivalent. When invited to present my ideas, I was asked quite often by people in the audience: what is the purpose? What do you want with all these ideas? Are you a democratic extremist yourself? The anwer I give here is no, I am not an extremist; but I am a democratic radical. Whether the reader will accept this answer, or not, is up to her or him.

Note

1 My translation from the German: 'Nicht Macht gib mir, König, denn Macht reizt zur Tat, und welche Tat, mein König, ist gerecht und nicht wider ein Schicksal?' (Stefan Zweig, *Die Augen des ewigen Bruders*, Frankfurt on Main/Zürich: Insel Verlag/Williams Verlag, 1922, p. 36).

Acknowledgements

Though I cherish the illusion that one or two of the ideas in this book are original, I realise the rest has been adapted or borrowed (if not stolen) from others. The list of references is quite long, but probably not long enough: sometimes I may have forgotten where an idea came from. A few people are not quoted but have inspired, encouraged and assisted me in different ways. I would like to thank them here.

I extend special thanks to the colleagues who have read (parts of) the manuscript and provided constructive criticisms and useful suggestions: Uwe Backes, Jan Willem Burgers, Marius De Geus, Cas Mudde, Marc Pauly and Keith Sutherland. Though I followed most of their suggestions, I cannot, of course, blame them for any mistakes I made. I also appreciated very much the suggestions and advice given by Kristof Jacobs, Cristóbal Rovira Kaltwasser, Ted Loewenberg, Nikolaus Werz and Evert van der Zweerde. I am equally grateful to the people who allowed me to present my ideas in workshops, seminars and conferences they organised – Bob Brecher, Joris Gijsenbergh, Saskia Hollander, Joop van Holsteijn, Tim Houwen, Wim de Jong, Steffen Kailitz, Cas Mudde, Gerrit Voerman and Phil Wood. Some of the ideas in this book were anticipated in my contribution to the volume edited by Gijsenbergh, Hollander, Houwen and De Jong.[1]

Cas Mudde strongly encouraged me to proceed with the book, as a friend but also as editor of the Routledge series Extremism and Democracy. I am also grateful to the other editors, Roger Eatwell and Matthew Goodwin (who has succeeded Cas), as well as to the editorial staff, first Nicola Parkin, then Peter Harris and Craig Fowlie, and to the anonymous reviewers. The text has been corrected by Christoph Mehrlein, often at short notice, which I appreciate very much.

Last, but not least, I would like to express my gratitude to three very special people who have stimulated and helped me in a more indirect way. First of all Yvonne, my wife: she not only encouraged me to complete the book, even when she suffered a nasty accident and had to spend several months in a wheelchair, but she also showed me how democracy can be practiced at the micro-level. She developed the 'two-minute method', which allows all participants two minutes to express their feelings at that moment, free from external pressure. We apply it almost every day. Moreover, Yvonne tries to redistribute power in daily life, while coaching and counselling her clients who often feel powerless to change their situation. Second, I would like to thank my mother for her active support, her interest in the book and the liberal way she raised me (in co-operation with my father). And third, I would like to mention my cat, Piepje, who often tried to distract me, miaowing, sitting on my books, walking over the keyboard and tearing up my notes. She made me realise there are other things in life than books – and also that the book is not about animals at all (perhaps my next book should be).

Note

1 'From Crisis to Democracy? An Exercise in Political Imagination', in: Joris Gijsenbergh, Saskia Hollander, Tim Houwen and Wim de Jong (eds) *Creative Crises of Democracy*, Brussels: P.I.E. Peter Lang, 2012, pp. 47–59.

1 Introduction

Politics is about power. 'Who gets what, when, how', in the succinct definition of the British political scientist Harold Lasswell (1950).[1] Students of politics have always pondered how power is distributed in the world they know – and how it should be distributed in an ideal world.

In one of the first classical texts on politics, written presumably around 380 BCE, the Greek political philosopher Plato argues – through the mouth of his teacher Socrates – that ideally political power should be put in the hands of a select group of philosophers ([Lee] 1955: 233). These philosophers should be educated and trained in a rigorous mental and physical discipline in order to serve and guard the common interest of the community. Other citizens should not worry about politics, but instead confine themselves to their own trade or profession. For Plato, the exercise of political power was clearly a profession, and one not to be trusted to laymen. Unfortunately, he observed that philosophers did not rule any of the states he was familiar with. They were imperfect societies, governed by military aristocracies, monarchs, propertied oligarchies or – even worse – the common people.

In Plato's eyes, rule by the people – *demokratia* – as practiced in his native Athens, was a degenerated regime: an anarchic society where everyone did as they pleased, and where the poor reigned at the expense of the rich. Officials were selected by lot rather than by merit or noble birth. A few decades later, Plato's student Aristotle gave a similar description of democracy: 'the system of all ruling over each, and each, in his turn, over all', where all important decisions are taken by a popular assembly of citizens, rather than by elected officials or hereditary rulers ([Barker] 1958: 258). Aristotle (and probably most of his contemporaries) regarded rule by elected officials as a form of aristocracy. After all, *aristokratia* means rule by the best (*aristoi*), and people should elect the best possible leaders, at least in their own opinion. Aristotle, who was not an Athenian citizen and did not share Plato's utopian ideal of a philosophical elite, preferred a mixture of democracy and aristocracy.

By the time Aristotle died in 322 BCE Athens had just lost her independence. Like other Greek city-states it was absorbed first into the Macedonian kingdom, then later into the Roman Empire. Democratic practices may have survived in other parts of the world, such as in the Persian city of Susa and, to some extent, in Arab towns (Sen, 2006: 52–53; Keane, 2009: 126–153). Indeed, Phoenician and Mesopotamian city-states might even have practiced democracy long before the Greeks (Hornblower, 1993: 2; Keane, 2009: 104–126). Unfortunately, these experiences are not very well documented. The writings of Plato and Aristotle, on the other hand, have resisted the ravages of time, thanks to Arabic and Latin translations. Therefore, the classical Greek conception of democracy as rule by a popular assembly survived the death of the democratic city-state in Greece and has continued to inspire political theory as well as practice into today.

In the modern era, however, city-states have become quite scarce. Most of them were gradually swallowed up by nation-states. The size of the latter made it practically impossible to gather all citizens in an assembly. For aristocrats and monarchists this fact merely confirmed that democracy was an outdated and unrealistic ideal in the modern era. They believed that large states should be ruled by either an (elected or hereditary) elite or by a single person. People with democratic sympathies, therefore, had to invent something new. The result was 'representation ingrafted upon democracy', in the apt phrase of Thomas Paine, the English artisan who helped to trigger the American Revolution with his pamphlets ([1792] 1989: 170). Citizens should elect delegates who would serve their interest and implement their demands.

In a similar vein, the French revolutionary leader Robespierre defined his ideal democracy as 'a state in which the people, as sovereign, guided by laws of its own making, does for itself all that it can do well, and by its delegates what it cannot' (Robespierre, 1967: 352–353; see also: Hobson, 2008: 461, 463; Palmer, 1953: 215).[2] Though Christopher Hobson praises the Jacobin leader for making the break with the classical notion of direct democracy, one cannot help but detect a certain ambivalence in the definition (see also Fontana, 1993: 112). Popular participation remained an important ideal for Robespierre and other Jacobins. In the French constitution that was approved by the revolutionary parliament in 1793 – but never implemented because of the civil war that was ravaging several parts of the country – citizens should take part in 'primary assemblies' at the local level, not only to elect delegates to parliament, but also to approve or initiate legislation (Tønneson, 1988). Some revolutionaries, nicknamed the *sans-culottes* because they could not afford the knee-breeches (*culottes*) worn by the more well-to-do citizens, wanted to go even further and give specific instructions or a binding mandate to the delegates (more about this in Chapter 4).

More moderate French revolutionaries preferred a government by representatives who were elected but not controlled by the people – representative democracy in the contemporary sense, but in those days usually called 'republican', 'mixed government' or 'mixed constitution' (Fontana, 1993: 117; Rosanvallon, 2000: 9–17; Urbinati, 2008: 1–3; Wood, 1993a: 92–94). The moderates lost the struggle against the Jacobins in the 1790s, but would prevail in the long run – not only in France, but also in most other parts of the modern world. In America, similar ideas had already triumphed a decade earlier, when the United States gained independence and adopted its own constitution (Wood, 1993a). Alexander

Hamilton, a rather moderate leader of that revolution, had argued for 'representative democracy' as early as 1777 or 1788 (according to Christophersen, 1968: 287, or Wood, 1993a: 98, respectively). Most of his contemporaries still shunned the term, but from 1800 'democracy' began to lose its pejorative meaning and gained acceptance as a description of the American regime.

However, by the nineteenth century this 'representative democracy' had itself changed. By 1825 practically all white American men had the right to vote, but the candidates they could vote for were usually professional politicians affiliated with organised political parties. Politics was no longer the province of gentlemen-farmers and other amateurs (Wood, 1993b: 287–305). The Jacksonian Democrats that ruled the US at that time used democratic rhetoric, but also monarchist practices such as patronage. Similar changes took place in Europe, though much later. In many countries universal suffrage (for men and women) was introduced around 1918. By then, the ruling classes no longer associated 'democracy' with revolution, anarchy and domination by the poor masses, but with regular elections and competition between political parties (Maier, 1993; Maier, 1972; see also Christophersen, 1968: 287–290; Nordmann, 1974: 77). However, this competition involved divergent world views, not merely rivalry between ambitious politicians. Citizens could have some impact upon the policies decided by their delegates by voting for a party, and even more by joining that party and taking part in meetings, nominating candidates and drafting programmes. They could also join a pressure group or movement, such as a trade union or a farmers' league, which would articulate their collective interests and influence public opinion, the political parties and the government and its policies.

Three theoretical perspectives

Modern representative democracy, therefore, is more than electoral democracy, the Italian-born political theorist Nadia Urbinati argues. It implies the active involvement of citizens as well as interaction between representatives and electors (Urbinati, 2008: 4, 5, 44). She realises that existing states do not always measure up to this ideal and worries about the rise of populism and the influence of money in politics (Landemore, 2007). She also favours institutions such as referendum and recall, in order to give more power to voters, provided that representatives retain substantial autonomy and do not have to carry out instructions from their constituents (Urbinati, 2008: 29). Urbinati belongs (in her own words) to a 'tiny minority of theorists' who argue that 'representation is not an alternative to but in fact supports democratic participation' (2008: 3). Hanna Pitkin had already blazed this trail, as Urbinati acknowledges, in her pioneering work on representation (1967). The Australian-born political theorist Michael Saward follows a similar trail, while arguing that even 'pure' direct democracy requires representative politics (2010: 160–164). Representation is not 'second best', but indispensable in any democratic system. Representative claims are not only made by elected politicians, but also by political activists, lobbyists and 'ordinary' citizens participating in a public meeting (see also Saward, 2012).

4 Introduction

Perhaps Urbinati exaggerates her minoritarian position; certainly, if we go beyond the realm of political theory. Her view of representative democracy as 'real' democracy rather than a substitute for direct rule by the people seems far from rare or uncommon among political scientists, politicians or journalists, and probably also many ordinary voters (see also Näsström, 2011: 509). Robert Dahl, an influential American academic, defined the democratic process by five criteria: opportunities for effective citizen participation, equal voting rights, enlightened understanding of alternatives by the citizens, control of the agenda by the people and equal opportunities to acquire resources (1989: 106–118). He admits these conditions are not always met in real life, hence he prefers the term 'polyarchy' to 'democracy'. Yet even in polyarchies elections insure at the very least that 'political leaders will be somewhat responsive to the preferences of some ordinary citizens' (Dahl, 1956: 131).

Quite a few scholarly observers question even this cautious liberal description of the present political systems in Europe and North America, however. The Italian historian Luciano Canfora regards the present regime in France, Italy and similar countries as a modern 'mixed system': 'a little democracy, and a great deal of oligarchy' (2006: 216). People can freely express their views, but decisions are taken by an oligarchy that eludes the control of elected bodies. Voters are manipulated by mass media and can only elect politicians who belong to the same (middle) class and adhere to the same ideology: 'the plebiscite of the market' and 'the worship of wealth' (Canfora, 2006: 214–232). His conception of democracy seems close to the classical one, even if he is not uncritical about Athenian democracy. Rather than a 'people's government', it was, in his eyes, a regime controlled by a section of the 'rich' and the 'gentry' that 'had mastered the art of speaking' and was willing to accommodate the mass of poor citizens to some extent (Canfora, 2006: 21–34). Even so, he considers the values cherished by the Athenians – liberty and equality – to still be relevant and inspiring.

The French-born political scientist Bernard Manin and the Swiss constitutionalist Alois Riklin also describe the prevailing political systems in the Western world as 'mixed constitutions'. Election is 'an aristocratic or oligarchic procedure in that it reserves public office for eminent individuals whom their fellow citizens deem superior to others', Manin writes (1997: 238). Moreover, in a modern system the elected representatives are not bound by imperative mandates or pledges and cannot be recalled, so they remain independent from their electors; this independence separates representation from 'popular rule' (Manin, 1997: 237). Yet representative government has a democratic dimension, too, as representatives are (usually) subject to re-election and will be held to account by their voters. Riklin points out that modern mixed constitutions (in German: *Mischverfassungen*) suffer more from plutocratic tendencies within the (professionalised) political elite than their ancient predecessors, but also contain stronger democratic elements because of universal suffrage (2006: 406–408). The German political scientist Uwe Backes defends a similar position in his study of political extremism (2006: 240–241).

The Dutch historian and philosopher Frank Ankersmit seemed more negative in his farewell lecture: what most of us call 'representative democracy' is really 'elective aristocracy' (2010). In his opinion, Urbinati ignores the real gap between the political elite and the people and has dissolved the notion of sovereignty into a meaningless abstraction (Ankersmit, 2010: 8–11).

Other scholars refer to the existing system as 'post-democracy' (Crouch, 2004), incomplete democracy (Arblaster, 1987), 'thin democracy' (Barber, [1984] 1990) or 'elite-managed democracy' (Wolin, 2008). According to the American political philosopher Sheldon Wolin, citizens in his country are not represented by politicians, but politics is re-presented to the citizens (2008: 261). Citizens have been made 'as predictable as consumers' and no longer question the regime ideology (Wolin, 2008: 47). The regime has become totalitarian in a subtle, almost gentle way, without the brutal repression that characterised earlier totalitarian regimes.

Ankersmit, Canfora and most other critical observers of the prevailing system seem to adhere to a classical conception of democracy, centred on popular participation in decision-making – whether through popular assemblies or other forms. Although their interpretation of the system as elitist may not be shared by Urbinati and Dahl, it does resemble the view of a third category of scholars who are often called 'elitist democrats' or 'democratic elitists'. The political economist Joseph Schumpeter is usually seen as the founding father of this school. Schumpeter, who was born in Austria but moved to the US in 1932, defined democracy as 'the institutional arrangement for arriving at political decisions in which individuals acquire the power to decide by means of a competitive struggle for the people's vote' (1976: 269). In other words, the people can vote for one of two or more competing elites, but cannot take any other decisions. Schumpeter's definition became quite influential among sociologists and political scientists, for example Seymour Martin Lipset (1963: 27; see also Pateman, 1970: 3–5). Public choice theorists such as William Riker argue on similar lines: democracy means 'a popular veto', not 'popular rule' (1982: 244). Riker shows in detail that the outcome of a popular vote can never be interpreted unambiguously as 'the will of the people', as it is always dependent upon the way in which alternatives are presented and votes are counted. He considers the theory of a 'responsible party system' where political parties offer voters a clear choice between policies – more or less what Urbinati argues for – to be a 'populist illusion' (Riker, 1982: 63). Voters cannot choose policies, only policy-makers. Even then, they may not have sufficient information (and commitment) to make a reasonable choice, but at least they exercise a veto 'by which it is sometimes possible to restrain official tyranny' (Riker, 1982: 244). Though Riker prefers to call his theory 'liberal democracy', critics consider it neither liberal nor democratic and compare it to Plato's rule by philosopher-guardians (Gilley, 2009: 116).

The word 'democracy' may have hundreds of meanings, yet in simplifying the scholarly debate we can distinguish three theoretical perspectives or schools which differ not only in terms of semantics, but also on substance and often also take different normative positions.

6 *Introduction*

First there is the **classical school**, which has basically retained the definition of Plato and Aristotle. In a democracy, all (or at least most) important decisions should be taken by the people, as directly as possible. In the eyes of classical democrats, the United States and most European states are at best 'incomplete', 'thin' or 'weak' democracies; or, more accurately, mixed regimes; or, worse, elective aristocracies, ruled by elites that may be elected but are not controlled by the people. Whereas Plato and (to a lesser extent) Aristotle held a rather negative opinion about rule by the people and preferred an aristocracy or a 'mixed regime', their modern heirs usually value democracy very positively and often regret that contemporary political systems do not measure up to it. There are exceptions, such as Manin, who seems quite content with the prevailing 'mixed constitution' (1997: 238; see also Landemore, 2007).

Second, the **elitist school** agrees (more or less) with this analysis of Western regimes but considers them worthy of the term 'democracy', with all the positive connotations the term entails. Real rule by the people is, in the eyes of the elitists, an impossible pipedream. And if it were possible at all, it would not even be desirable: it would probably end in chaos. Competition between elites is the best a democrat can hope for. Democracy means free elections, nothing more.

A third position in between these two schools has been defended by Urbinati, Saward and, in a different context, also by Dahl. They argue that the existing system does allow people considerable influence upon policy-making, through elections, direct political action and the pressure of public opinion. Decisions are taken in a kind of dialogue between politicians and citizens; hence, I would refer to this school as '**dialectical democrats**', yet without the Hegelian connotations of the term 'dialectical'. The dialectical democrats do not idealise the existing system and often advocate reforms, but deny that direct democracy may be a realistic or desirable alternative.

The debate between the three schools is not just academic, but also political in every sense of the word. Whereas the elitist perspective and to a lesser extent the dialectical view might be used by established parties and political leaders to defend the status quo, many protest movements of different colours use (implicitly or explicitly) the classical perspective. Groups such as the *Front National* in France, the *Partij voor de Vrijheid* of Geert Wilders in the Netherlands, the *Chavistas* in Venezuela, the Zapatistas in Mexico, the Global Justice Movement, the Spanish *indignados* and the Occupy Wall Street movement may have divergent origins, goals and social backgrounds, but practically all of them demand 'power to the people!'.

Purpose and content of the book

The main purpose of this book is to contribute to the debate about democracy by investigating the claims of the classical school. Does it offer an alternative (or a number of alternatives) to the prevailing system that is feasible, coherent and desirable? Feasibility will be determined by analysing the institutional designs proposed by the classical democrats, as well as by examining historical examples or practical experiments that appear to meet the criteria of classical democracy.

Desirability will be evaluated by internal criteria, i.e. democratic values and principles. Though internal criteria allow for more objectivity than external criteria, they are still a minefield wherein subjective biases and partisan prejudices lurk. In a minefield it seems wise to follow in the footsteps of predecessors who have managed to pass through it alive. In this case, the predecessors are David Beetham, Graham Smith and John Dryzek. In his analysis of discursive or deliberative democracy, Dryzek refers to three dimensions of democratisation: the number of people participating in collective decisions, the scope of the decisions, and the authenticity and effectiveness of the control (2002: 29). Beetham uses three slightly different criteria in his evaluation of democratic practices: the participatory range (inclusiveness and numbers involved), the deliberative mode, and the impact upon participants, the public debate and policy outcomes (2012: 59; see also 1994). Smith proposes four criteria: inclusiveness, popular control, considered judgment and transparency (2009: 12–13). These criteria are all of primary importance. Yet one should also consider the social and cultural conditions necessary for the survival of a democratic regime in the long run, as suggested by Dahl (1989: 322–341). This criterion is secondary, yet relevant when one wants to evaluate a complete political regime and not just a particular democratic innovation, as Beetham and Smith are doing, or democratisation as a process, as Dryzek sets out to do.

Combining these elements, we could use five criteria to evaluate democratic projects, theories and practices:

1   Do they offer people substantial opportunities to take all or most decisions on important matters?
2   Are decisions taken after sufficient public deliberation, without manipulation by elites or demagogues and in accordance with the needs and interests of the people?
3   Are decisions implemented?
4   Is 'the people' defined in a more or less inclusive way – e.g. all mentally sane adult residents of a country – or are dissidents, ethnic minorities, immigrants or other groups explicitly or implicitly excluded?[3]
5   What impact does the theory or practice have on the social and cultural conditions of democracy, such as fundamental freedoms, equal rights, social equality, a sense of citizenship and efficacy?

To apply these criteria to all political theories and practices that might fit the label of classical democracy would be too ambitious and time-consuming – there are too many of them. Also, it seems impossible to construct one ideal type or model of classical democracy, as there is too much diversity here. One has to make a selection somehow. As the title indicates, this book will concentrate on extremists, i.e. classical democrats who reject the prevailing 'mixed systems' completely and want to hand all power to the people (more about this notion in Chapter 2).

The book offers a little more than the title suggests, however. Democratic extremism turns out to be a relatively scarce commodity, both in theory and in practice. Most classical democrats stay away from extremism and seem willing to compromise. Even in a classical democracy, the people may have to share power with a political elite that takes some important decisions, too. In other words, a mixed regime might be inevitable. Even so, these classical democrats will argue, in a real democracy the most important decisions will be taken by the people. Of course, one can quibble over what is important. If a classical democrat considers important only those decisions that affect the basic structure of the socio-economic and political order – such as nationalisation or privatisation of all means of production – then she may be practically indistinguishable from a dialectical democrat like Urbinati or Saward. Her theoretical framework, however, will be different. In the context of this study, any classical democratic theory that is not extremist will be called 'democratic radicalism' and the corresponding practice 'radical democracy'.

Admittedly, these may be confusing terms. On the one hand, 'radicalism' (with or without the adjective 'democratic') may refer to political parties and currents in the nineteenth century that stood for universal franchise, direct elections of public officials, and often for referendums as well as for economic liberalism (Mayer, 1969; Von Beyme, 1982: 47–57; Nicolet, 1961; Nordmann, 1974; Lucardie, 1994). They often referred to themselves as 'Radicals' (in the UK), 'Radicaux' (in France) or 'Radikalen' (in Switzerland). In the course of the nineteenth century, most of them merged with or evolved into more conservative Liberal parties. On the other hand, many scholars use the terms 'radical' and 'radicalism' as synonyms for 'extreme' and 'extremism', or at least as very closely related concepts (see Backes, 2006: 217–222). Radicals may pursue less extreme goals than extremists, but apply similar violent methods, for example. In order to avoid confusion as much as possible, I will attach the adjective 'democratic' – perhaps *ad nauseam* – to the words 'radical' and 'radicalism', and use a capital R when referring to the Radical parties of the nineteenth century and their Radicalism. The democratic radicalism in this book overlaps with but does not coincide with the Radicalism of the nineteenth century.

The distinction made here between radical and extreme democracy resembles Benjamin Barber's distinction between 'strong' and 'unitary' democracy (1984: 139–162). The latter is based on collectivism, presupposes an organic community with a collective will, and aims at consensus. Strong democracy is based on individual participation and creation of a political community. The term 'unitary democracy' is also used by Jane Mansbridge to refer to consensual politics, but for her, it is the opposite of 'adversary democracy' (1983). The two cover the whole area of democracy and should be balanced, somehow. In her eyes, 'unitary democracy' is not necessarily a bad thing under certain conditions – when there are no conflicting interests or when the conflicts are worked out rather than covered up (Mansbridge, 1983: 270–277). In Barber's framework, strong democracy stands between thin and unitary democracy – which may appear a little confusing, as he also uses 'thin' and 'strong' democracy as

Introduction 9

opposites. This is one reason why his terminology has not been adopted here. To sum up: this book is a critical study of both extremist and radical democratic projects, in a classical democratic perspective.

Arguably, all classical democratic projects (whether extremist or radical) could be divided analytically into three categories. Logically, the three models exhaust all possible democratic alternatives to the prevailing representative system. Let me explain. Decisions have to be taken either directly, by the people in a popular assembly, or indirectly, by their representatives. In the latter case, the representatives have to be selected either by elections or by sortition. Other selection procedures such as appointment by a committee or other authority are, by definition, not democratic. If representatives are elected by the people, they should be prevented from dominating their constituents; this can be done by giving them a binding mandate or recalling them if they do not follow the instructions from the people, or by circumventing them through popular initiative and referendum. Thus the representatives would be relatively powerless 'bounded delegates' carrying out the demands of the people. If representatives are randomly selected – in a statistically adequate way – their opinions and needs will automatically reflect those of the people. Other forms of representation can be imagined and have been practiced – in corporatist arrangements, for instance (see the next chapter) – but it seems to me they would not leave sufficient power in the hands of the represented to satisfy the classical democrats. Therefore, it may be hard to imagine another form or model of democracy apart from the direct assembly democracy, representation by bounded delegates, or representation by a random sample from the population.

Thus, the three basic alternatives mentioned here provide the structure for the book. The assembly model will be discussed in Chapter 3, the 'bounded delegate' systems and practices in Chapter 4 and sortitionist democracy in Chapter 5. Each of these chapters contains a section on theories or utopias and on historical institutions or practices that may illustrate (and qualify or disqualify) the theories. Thus the book offers a combination of political theory, the history of ideas, and political or institutional history, with a little political fiction thrown in as well. Chapter 3 deals with the 'libertarian municipalism' of Murray Bookchin, and with institutions such as the Athenian *ekklèsia*, the Swiss *Landsgemeinde*, the American Town Meeting and the participatory budgeting that has spread from Porto Alegre in Brazil to hundreds of towns across the world. In Chapter 4 the ideas about democracy of Rousseau, Marx and Lenin will be briefly discussed, as well as Anton Pannekoek's theory of workers' councils and its influence on New Left groups, but also the plebiscitary democracy practiced in California, Switzerland and perhaps in Venezuela. Chapter 5 contains a critical analysis of John Burnheim's 'demarchy' and of various sortitionist proposals developed by American and British scholars, as well as a summary of experiments with citizen panels and deliberative opinion polls. Chapter 6 provides a comparative evaluation of the three models and a few speculations about their relevance in the future.

Prior to all of that, I propose an excursion in the opposite direction: to non-democratic varieties of extremism. In Chapter 2 the concept of 'extremism' will be analysed and illustrated with short descriptions of Fascism, National Socialism, Marxism–Leninism, clerical or theocratic extremism, and Libertarianism. Readers with little time or with limited interest in that subject may skip the chapter. However, it may be useful to clarify the notion of extremism used in a book with this noun in the title. The term extremism is often used in political debates, but rarely clarified. Moreover, a short survey of non-democratic extremist theories and practices might throw light on the 'mixed regime' which classical democrats are trying to change. After all, these regimes are mixtures of democratic and non-democratic (aristocratic or monarchist) elements, so some understanding of the latter may be helpful for a better insight into the nature of the mixed regime and its alternatives. And, finally, some of the democratic models that will be investigated later in this study show an uncanny resemblance to types of non-democratic regimes – which may tell us something about the desirability and feasibility of the former.

The book is written not only for specialists in democratic theory, political history and philosophy, but also for political amateurs and activists, and all citizens concerned about democracy. After all, democracy should be a concern of the people, wherever they are and whatever they do.

Notes

1 In his book with the same title, Lasswell used the term 'influence' more often than 'power', but did not seem to distinguish the terms clearly (1950: 24). Georges Burdeau – another classical author though perhaps not very well known outside of France – regarded politics as the activity that defines and exercises power: 'la politique est l'activité qui consiste à définer le Pouvoir et à en exercer les prérogatives' (1980: 148). The German scholar Max Weber wrote that all political institutions are based on power: 'Alle politischen Gebilde sind Gewaltgebilde' (1968: 80).

2 In French:

> La démocratie n'est pas un état où le peuple, continuellement assemblé, règle par lui-même toutes les affaires publiques.... La démocratie est un état où le peuple souverain, guidé par des lois qui sont son ouvrage, fait par lui-même tout ce qu'il peut bien faire, et par des délégués tout ce qu'il ne peut faire lui-même.
>
> (Robespierre, 1967: 352–353)

3 With apologies to ecocentrists and animalists: it is assumed that the *demos* can include only human beings.

2 Extremism

> I would remind you that extremism in the defense of liberty is no vice.
> (Barry Goldwater, 1964)

When US Senator Goldwater spoke these words at the Republican convention of 1964 that had just nominated him for the presidency, his supporters cheered. However, some of his advisors and other Republican leaders could not disguise their disgust. Media and commentators jumped on his statement with biting criticisms. 'The race to calumniate Barry Goldwater was on' (Perlstein, 2001: 392). It would lead to the largest landslide victory in the history of American Presidential elections for his Democratic opponent, Lyndon B. Johnson. Obviously, 'extremism' was a notion Presidential candidates should not identify with. As a matter of fact, practically all politicians, not only in the USA but also in Europe, might harm their careers if they claimed the label 'extremist'.

Conceptual problems

The German political scientist Uwe Backes explains very well why the term has predominantly negative connotations (2006: 27–53). It has been derived from the Greek notion of *eschatos*, translated into the Latin word *extremis*, which was contrasted by philosophers such as Aristotle with notions like stability, moderation and the virtuous 'middle way'. However, one does not have to be a Greek philosopher to think critically of extremes. Few people like extreme cold or extreme heat, extreme noise or extreme silence. Aristotle also applied this common-sense aversion to extremes to politics, preferring a moderate or mixed constitution to the extremes of despotism and democracy.

The conception of 'extremism' as an ideology or political belief system is much more recent. Backes has traced the word back to the 1830s, a period when many '-isms' were invented (2006: 109–136). Yet it was used rarely in the nineteenth century. The Bolshevik Revolution of 1917 changed this: 'extremists' had captured power in Russia, at least in the eyes of their enemies. Over the next two decades, other 'extremists' seized power in Italy and Germany. Leftwing extremism was compared with rightwing extremism by political scientists and philosophers, especially after the Second World War. Thus, an analytical concept of 'extremism' was constructed, from elements common to both Bolshevism and Fascism or National Socialism, which would be used in the Cold War against Soviet Russia and its allies.

After the collapse of the Soviet regime, 'extremism' continued to be associated with violence and terror – especially after the terrorist attacks of 11 September 2001, in a new Cold War against Islamic extremism. At the same time, social scientists who try to purge all scientific notions from normative elements – and stay out of all wars, whether 'hot' or 'cold' – have tried to define extremism in a more neutral 'value-free' sense, relating it to a psychological disposition or to tensions in the social and political systems.

Simplifying slightly, at present we can distinguish three different approaches to extremism. The first approach is instrumental or psychological: extremists are rigid, inflexible and passionate people who use violence to achieve their political ends – whatever those are. Mary Kaldor and Diego Muro refer to violence, exclusiveness and fundamentalist doctrines as characteristics of extremists (2003: 152). The philosopher Robert Nozick lists eight characteristics of what he regards as the extremist syndrome: doctrines that claim an impersonal validity; goals that should be realised immediately and in full; the view of opponents as evil; unwillingness to compromise; willingness to use violence; some form of organisation; trying to surpass competitors in extremism; and a certain type of personality (1997: 296–299). In the French *Dictionnaire de politique* extremism is circumscribed in psychological terms such as intransigence, passion and inflexibility: '*idées, opinions, attitudes déterminées par un attachement intransigeant, irréductible et passionné à un programme ou à une doctrine défendus dans leurs aspects les plus avancés*' ('ideas, opinions, attitudes determined by an intransigent, uncompromising and passionate commitment to a programme or doctrine [which are] defended in their most extreme aspects') (Akoun *et al.*, 1979: 132). This may be a useful definition for practical purposes, such as the maintenance of law and order and the investigation of (potential) political crimes, but not for political theorists interested in the content of ideologies. As the economist Ronald Wintrobe points out, some groups might apply extremist methods (such as bombings, terrorist activity or inflammatory language) in order to achieve moderate, centrist goals such as national independence or liberal democracy (2002). Under extreme circumstances, even moderate people may use violence, for example to defend their country against foreign invaders or colonial powers. Moreover, one might add, groups with extremist goals (anarchists or neo-fascists, for example) might use moderate, peaceful and legal methods, whether as a matter of principle or for opportunistic reasons. For analytical purposes it does not make much sense to define the moderate patriots fighting the Nazi occupation of France, Belgium or Norway in 1940–1945 as 'extremists' and peaceful anarchists or neo-fascists in the post-war period as 'moderates' or 'centrists'.

A second approach would seem more convenient for our purpose, as it leaves open what the substantive goals and methods of extremists are: they want to change the dominant system, whatever that may be – a liberal multi-party system or a totalitarian one-party state or a military dictatorship. If the system prevents gradual change, tensions might grow and lead to more extreme opposition. In the words of Gianluigi Galeotti: 'Extremism, interpreted as a challenge to the existing rules and values of politics, is a phenomenon that features in any constitutional order, democratic or non-democratic alike, and its evolution' (2002: 122). The Slovakian political scientist Josef Smolik defines extremism as 'the rejection of the basic values, norms and behaviour prevalent in current society' (2011: 101). A German political dictionary identifies extremism with radicalism and defines the latter as the pursuit of a totally different and new political, social and economic order, usually via violent methods (Beck, 1977: 690). The Italian political scientist Piero Ignazi refers to 'anti-system value sets' (2003: 30). This relativistic type of definition may be free from normative connotations, but it creates other problems. To classify liberal opposition against a military dictatorship, such as the movement led by Aung San Suu Kyi in Myanmar (Burma), as 'extremist' goes against our intuition.[1] If we do so, we seem to play into the hands of the dictators, in a sense. Thus even this approach could be accused of an implicit ideological bias – conservative with a small 'c', protecting the status quo against any fundamental change.

A third approach also concentrates on the goals of extremists rather than their means, but is more specific and more often normative. Quite succinctly, the Israeli political scientist Daphna Canetti-Nisim defines extremism as 'attitudes in favour of anti-democratic world views' (2004: 40). The British author John Tomlinson gives a more elaborate description: 'the extremist subscribes to and promotes a social critique the end of which, and often the means also, is implicitly anti-democratic within the understanding of the liberal tradition and its prevailing institutions' (1981: 11). The Dutch political scientist Cas Mudde suggests a similar definition: 'opposition, in terms of ideas or actions, to the fundamental values or institutions of the democratic regime ... that is, democracy as it exists within the country or region of the extreme actor' (2002: 135). The American scholars Seymour M. Lipset and Earl Raab follow the same pattern, adding more elements:

> The basic ideology of extremism is contained in the model of monism. Extremism describes the violation, through action or advocacy, of the democratic political process. The democratic political process refers fundamentally to democratic political pluralism: an open democratic market place for ideas, speech and consonant political action. Monism amounts to the closing down of the democratic market place, whether by a massive majority or by a preemptive minority.
>
> (1971: 428)

In a similar vein, the German political scientists Uwe Backes and Eckhard Jesse define extremism as the antithesis of liberal democracy (*'Extremismus ist der Gegenbegriff zur freiheitlichen Demokratie*' (1987: 19)). They do not deny that it is a value-laden notion, but disagree with German colleagues who reject the whole notion because it is used as a political weapon (*politischer Kampfbegriff*) rather than an analytical construct (Backes and Jesse, 1985: 21). Even if extremists claim to be democrats, they subvert democracy and secretly plan for dictatorship.

Of course, as we have seen in Chapter 1, democracy is a contested concept with a strong normative value. 'You don't need to be a student of political philosophy to know what a multitude of meanings and nuance those words [democracy and freedom] have gathered over the last 2500 years', writes the language specialist John Humphrys, adding that they 'have become zombified words ... mantras to be chanted' and 'the ultimate hurrah words' (2004: 312, 313). Nowadays it is hard to find anyone, even at the fringes of the political systems of Europe or North America, who rejects 'democracy'. Yet there are intellectuals as well as political movements that propose a more democratic system – as will be shown below. Some of these people appear quite extreme, and yet sincere in their democratic beliefs. However, according to the advocates of the third approach, 'democratic extremism' must be a contradiction in terms (*contradictio in adiecto*, lovers of Latin might say). Obviously, it is rather inconvenient if one wants to write about a phenomenon that by definition cannot exist.

So, none of the three most common approaches to extremism will serve our purpose, namely to understand democratic extremism. Fortunately, a more adequate approach has been suggested by Uwe Backes in his penetrating monograph, while borrowing elements from the definitions mentioned above – and moving beyond the definition advocated by Backes and Jesse (1985 and 1987).

Backes starts from the assumption that most constitutional states in the world are best understood as mixtures of aristocracy, monarchy and democracy. The classical term 'mixed constitution' or 'mixed regime' (in Latin: *regimen mixtum*; in German: *Mischverfassung*), which has been resuscitated and elaborated by the Swiss constitutional expert Alois Riklin, seems still relevant to the current political systems of countries such as the US, Britain, France, Germany and The Netherlands (Riklin, 2006; Backes, 2006: 240–241).[2] In a mixed regime, most political decisions are taken by elites, some by a single person like an elected president or prime minister, and a few by the people (in elections or referendums). Modern aristocrats are no longer noblemen or landowners, but mainly professional politicians, senior civil servants, lawyers and possibly corporate managers, capitalists and bankers. Yet the people enjoy some influence by electing at least some of the decision-makers – others may be appointed – and by expressing their opinion in various ways. Moreover, competition between elites may result in checks and balances, pluralism of interests and values, tolerance, and the rule of law.

Most mixed regimes are accepted and supported by a very broad majority of citizens, yet they can be (and have been) attacked from various sides: by classical democrats (as defined in Chapter 1) as well as libertarians, religious fundamentalists and neo-fascists. In recent years, populists of different shades and movements such as Occupy Wall Street, *Indignados* and Zapatistas have called for 'real' democracy. If critics try to replace a mixed regime with pure democracy, they will be considered democratic extremists, in this study. Alternatively, if they wished to replace it with pure aristocracy, they would be classified as aristocratic extremists.

A pure aristocracy can be defined as a political regime where most (if not all) decisions are taken by a selected minority or elite – whether selected by birth or by wealth, by (positions in) political parties or by other criteria – that is not responsible or accountable to the majority. In a pure monarchy or autocracy, most decisions are taken by one person (a hereditary monarch, an elected president or a military dictator).[3] In a pure democracy all important decisions are taken by the people, either directly or indirectly. In all pure regimes, ideological homogeneity has replaced pluralism and absolute power has eliminated checks and balances. This definition of extremism – a slightly simplified version of the one developed by Backes in his recent work – will serve as a guideline in this book (see Backes, 2006: 240–250).

Democracy and extremism are obviously not seen as opposites here. Extremists oppose a mixed regime, yet they also oppose each other. If autocratic or aristocratic extremists gain power, they will probably eliminate, imprison or exile the democratic extremists – and vice versa. Autocratic and aristocratic extremists may be occasional allies against the common democratic enemy. In a modern society, autocracy and aristocracy are often hard to distinguish, as even the most autocratic dictator has to delegate quite a few decisions to civil servants or military officers – in other words, to some kind of aristocracy. Mixtures of autocracy and aristocracy are not 'mixed regimes', however, as defined here: they are extreme in comparison with pluralist mixed regimes that contain at least some democratic elements. Most (but not all) of them tend to be authoritarian regimes. Rejecting political equality and participation, they favour forms of guardianship, to use the term introduced by Robert Dahl (1989).

Whereas the remaining chapters of the book deal with different varieties of democratic extremism, the rest of this chapter will be devoted to five varieties of aristocratic and/or autocratic extremism: aristocratic conservatism; Fascism and National Socialism; Stalinism or Marxism–Leninism; theocratic extremism; and the rather singular case of libertarian extremism. By looking at them, we may better understand the properties of their opposite, i.e. democratic extremism.

However, it is not always easy to distinguish the latter from the former, given the popularity of the term 'democratic'. Nowadays, hardly any political group, even at the fringes of the system, dares to denounce democracy, and even fewer openly advocate aristocracy or autocracy. To meet overt and unqualified aristocrats and autocrats, we have to go back in time a bit.

Othmar Spann and aristocratic conservatism

A good example of an aristocratic theorist may be the Austrian sociologist Othmar Spann, who lived from 1878 to 1950. He started from a holistic theory of society (he preferred the term 'universalism'). Society, in his eyes, was a 'superorganism', even more interdependent and integrated than a biological organism (Spann, 1972: 211). Individualism was his main enemy, and one which he fought in every area: in science and ethics, as well as in politics. Individuals exist merely as parts of society: '*der Einzelne ist nur als Bestandteil des Ganzen vorhanden, er ist daher Abgeleitete*' (Spann, 1972: 36). Individual members of society had to perform different functions and should not claim equality. Society should be organised around the main socio-economic functions, as it was in the Middle Ages. Spann suggested a corporatist hierarchy of strata or estates (in German: *Stände*), ranging from manual workers in agriculture and industry through artisans, clerical workers, intellectual workers and entrepreneurs to the supreme estate (*Höchststand*) of political, military and religious leaders. Whereas every estate should enjoy some autonomy in the management of its affairs, the supreme estate is sovereign in its own right. It decides on internal and external affairs and defence. Spann regarded the mass of people as incompetent and incapable of electing good leaders, hence leaders should not be elected – or, at best, elected indirectly – and should represent an idea rather than an electorate ('*Der Führer wird dem Wesen der Sache nach nicht gewählt, sondern vertritt einen Gedanken*' (1930: 495)). Decisions are taken not by majorities who delegate authority upwards, but by 'the best', who delegate authority downwards. The truth cannot be discovered by a majority vote, only by wise rulers: '*Nicht die Mehrheit von unten her soll über die Wahrheit abstimmen, sondern das Beste von oben her soll herrschen*' (Spann, 1972: 118). Democracy, in the long run, is impossible, according to Spann: it will inevitably result in rule by demagogues or wealthy plutocrats.

While Spann's utopia of a 'true state' and an organic society may sound vague and unpractical to modern ears, it did inspire quite a few Austrian and German Conservatives in the 1920s and 1930s. The Austrian constitution of 1934 reflected his authoritarian and corporatist ideas, at least to a large extent (Tálos and Manoschek, 1988: 77; Carsten, 1977: 236–237; Schneller, 1970: 110). Some of Spann's followers played a role in the German Nazi movement, but only for a short period. Spann himself admired Hitler, and is alleged to have opened a bottle of champagne when German troops invaded Austria in 1938 (Schneller, 1970: 18). However, the admiration was not mutual. On the same day, Spann was arrested and sent into exile. His aristocratic (and to a lesser extent autocratic) conservatism did not suit the Nazi leaders, who pursued another (more plebeian, racist and totalitarian) variety of extremism.

German conservatives may have been more hostile towards democracy than Conservatives elsewhere in Western Europe, but their ideas were not unique. In the Netherlands, William Westerman, who represented the small Association for National Reconstruction (*Verbond voor Nationaal Herstel*) in parliament from 1933 to 1937, had argued for a modest parliament, elected only by well-educated and well-to-do citizens (1925: 59–64, 87).[4] Aristocratic extremism was also *en vogue* in France throughout the nineteenth century, usually in connection with monarchism. Not only the monarchy, but also every public office should be hereditary, argued Joseph de Maistre in 1821 ([1821] 1960: 267–268). His reactionary ideas lost support in the following decades, but were not forgotten. The political scientist René Rémond shows considerable continuity in the development of *la droite légitimiste*, as he described the aristocratic and monarchist conservative tradition, from 1815 until the New Right of the 1980s (1982: 274–289). The authoritarian regime of Pétain in Vichy (1940–1944) to a large extent realised the aristocratic ideal in a modern context, as most decisions were taken by an elite – mainly civil servants – without responsibility to any representative body (Paxton, 1972: 193–198; Rémond, 1982: 231–238).

In Britain a similar bureaucratic regime was advocated by James Fitzjames Stephen in 1873 (O'Sullivan, 1976: 112–115). Aristocratic conservatism of a more romantic colour could be found in the work of Thomas Carlyle, who wished to replace parliamentary government with rule by 'heroes', titular and natural aristocrats (O'Sullivan, 1976: 92–98). However, most British Conservatives rejected extremism, preferring a 'balanced constitution' or mixed regime by way of a compromise between aristocracy and democracy.

After the Second World War, practically all Conservatives in Europe and North America made peace with the mixed regime that was now (re)defined as liberal or parliamentary democracy. Even if they disliked the democratic and egalitarian tendencies in the mixed regime, the Conservatives realised that it could not be replaced by pure aristocracy or autocracy without some kind of revolution, counter-revolution or a coup d'état – and Conservatives generally abhor radical change, whether revolutionary or counter-revolutionary.

Fascism and National Socialism

Fascism can be regarded as a hybrid ideology, mixing autocratic and aristocratic ideals with a radical appeal to the people. Or, as Roger Griffin put it: 'it is populist in intent and rhetoric, yet elitist in practice' (1993: 41). Fascists wanted to create – or recreate – an organic and classless national community without the inequities of capitalism, yet ruled by a new elite. The elite, and in particular its leader, would represent or even incarnate the true will of the people.

Enrico Corradini, one of the main ideologues of the Italian Fascist Party (*Partito Nazionale Fascista*), called for a corporatist and authoritarian state controlled by the productive bourgeoisie, 'the aristocrats of the modern epoch' (Marsella, 2004: 214). Before joining the Fascist Party, Corradini had founded the Italian Nationalist Association (*Associazione Nazionalista Italiana*, ANI). Though he realised that modern nationalism needed some participation by the masses, he failed to turn the ANI into a real mass movement. Hence he used the opportunity to join forces with Mussolini, who had already proven his talent in mobilising the masses, in 1923.

Mussolini had started his political career as a revolutionary Socialist with elitist ideas – an *elite proletaria* should lead the masses in revolutionary action. Yet gradually he evolved into a national fascist with (some) socialist ideas (Nolte, [1963] 1971: 200–307). He came to reject democracy, in theory as well as in practice, as a dangerous illusion based on the erroneous principle of political equality (Mussolini, [1932] 1961: 125–126). It was dangerous because, in his opinion, it led to collective irresponsibility. Responsibility required authoritarian leadership. In a fascist state, authoritarian leaders would take individual responsibility while serving the interests of the people. Insofar as 'the people' were incarnated in an elite or in one person, even Fascism could be regarded as democratic – '*una democrazia organizzata, centralizzata, autoritaria*' ('an organised, centralised and authoritarian [type of] democracy') (Mussolini, [1932] 1961: 127). Once appointed Leader (*Duce*) by the king, however, Mussolini was responsible only to the king and not to the people or parliament (Mussolini, [1932] 1961: 191–194). The people would merely be allowed to approve or disapprove the list of candidates for parliament nominated by the Great Council of Fascism – a body largely appointed by the Leader. And even this parliament did not have much power (Mussolini, [1932] 1961: 198–207; see also Eatwell, 1995: 78).

Hitler was even less ambiguous about democracy. He regarded it as degeneration of the political system caused by Jews and Marxists (the two categories were almost indistinguishable in his eyes). If the 'masses' prevailed over 'the brains', and the will of the majority became more important than the principles of authority and personality, the national community (*Volksgemeinschaft*) would begin to disintegrate (Hitler, [1925] 1941: 497–498). Equality led to racial impurity and degeneration, in his opinion. Mankind would lose its culture and, in the end, even its life. Nature required inequality and hierarchy, both between nations and within each nation. History was made by elites, but only if the elite incarnated the will of the majority: '*Weltgeschichte wird durch Minoritäten gemacht dann, wenn sich in dieser Minorität der Zahl die Majorität des Willens und der Entschlußkraft verkörpert*' ('World history is made by minorities, when a numerical minority incarnates the will and determination of the majority') (Hitler, [1925] 1941: 441). Thus Hitler added a populist element to the aristocratic idea. The national state should be ruled by 'natural leaders', who would 'emerge from below' rather than be selected from above. The leaders have to be elected; but once elected, they are not responsible to their electors any more but should only consult them when they want advice: '*der völkische Staat hat, angefangen bei der Gemeinde bis hinauf zur Leitung des Reiches, keinen Vertretungskörper, der etwas durch Majorität beschließt, sondern nur Beratungskörper, die dem jeweilig gewählten Führer zur Seite stehen*' ('from the municipality up to the leadership of the Empire, the people's state does not have representative bodies but only advisory bodies which assist the elected leaders at every level') (Hitler, [1925] 1941: 501). The leaders would be creative, intelligent and racially pure – the latter being perhaps the most important quality in Hitler's eyes, but related to the other two. A good leader would recruit a racially pure elite and purge the nation of impure elements. Thus a new 'plebeian' aristocracy would emerge, based on race rather than birth. Hitler would offer even a garbage collector a chance to join the elite – provided he was a pure Aryan German, of course (Nolte, 1971: 498).

Though few aristocratic Conservatives in Germany seem to have agreed with Hitler's racist utopianism and totalitarian fantasies, many sided with him in the struggle against the liberal republic and the Communist movement (Nolte, 1971: 416–418). Once they had helped Hitler to become chancellor, most of them were quickly shunted aside and deprived of power and privileges. National Socialism should not be confused with conservatism, even if both cherished values such as authority and hierarchy. The Nazis did not try to restore the Hohenzollern monarchy or feudal estates; they wanted to create a New Order – a New Man, even – based on (relatively) new racist ideas (Griffin, 1993: 104–106). In this respect they were radical rather than conservative. The *völkische Staat* was a totalitarian state that tried to control every nook and cranny of society, changing the way people worked, played and reared their children (see also Eatwell, 1995: 150–167).

Though Fascism and National Socialism suffered a bloody and absolute defeat in 1945, they did not disappear completely from the minds of people. After the war, small groups sprang up which revived and propagated similar elitist and racist ideas, not only in Germany and Italy, but in practically all other European countries too (Griffin, 1993: 161–174; Eatwell, 1995: 245–347). Some even venerated Hitler as the messiah of a new pagan religion (Ginzel, 1981: 94–100). Others strove for a new European order, *Nation Europa* or *Ordine Nuovo*, led by an Aryan elite (Ferraresi, 1996: 30–50). These groups tended to remain quite small and generally ineffective, apart from some bloody terrorist actions. A few moved away from Fascism and came to accept and even favour democracy, mixing it with a little autocracy. The *Movimento Sociale Italiano* (MSI), for example, founded by supporters of Mussolini, did not want to abolish the Italian republic, but only to have the president elected directly by the people – and to give him executive powers (Caciagli, 1988: 29). In a similar vein, the leader of the *Front National* in France, Jean-Marie Le Pen, called for a stronger presidential regime in France in the 1980s (Le Pen, 1984: 182). Even the National Front in Britain, described by Roger Eatwell as racial populist as well as neo-fascist, claimed to be 'the most democratic of all parties', promising to 'empower the people' and also to increase the powers of the House of Commons (National Front, 2004; see Eatwell, 1995: 335–342).

Stalinism and Marxism-Leninism

Karl Marx and his friend and benefactor Friedrich Engels belonged to the radical wing of the German democratic movement in the 1840s (Lichtheim, 1967: 76–77; Rosenberg, 1938: 61–77). Unlike liberal democrats they did not regard a parliamentary republic and universal suffrage as a final political goal, but only as a transitional stage (see, for example, Marx, 1972: 33–34). In this stage, the class struggle between the bourgeoisie and the proletariat would reach a climax. In the end, they expected that the workers would win and establish a 'dictatorship of the proletariat'. The term 'dictatorship' created considerable confusion among Marxists in the nineteenth and twentieth century (Lichtheim, 1967: 118–121, 232–233). Some interpreted it as a more or less peaceful and democratic conquest of power by the proletarian majority of society; others as dictatorship by a revolutionary minority. Marx and Engels themselves did give a concrete example, however, of such a regime: the Paris Commune of 1871 (Marx, [1871] 1972). As will be argued in Chapter 4, the Commune could be seen as a cruelly suppressed experiment with pure or classical democracy. Elected representatives were expected to act as 'mandatories, referring matters back to the local population in their clubs and National Guard battalions' (Edwards, 1971: 359). The Commune did not try to rule over the rest of France, but aimed at a federal system of autonomous communes all over the country.

Russian Marxists such as Vladimir Lenin and Leon Trotsky shared Marx's admiration for the Commune (Lichtheim, 1967: 340–351). In August 1917, while leading a revolutionary party not yet in power, Lenin defined the dictatorship of the proletariat as 'the organisation of the vanguard of the oppressed as the ruling class for the purpose of suppressing the oppressors' ([1917] 1964: 466). He did not immediately explain exactly what he meant by 'vanguard of the oppressed', but became more specific at the end of the text:

> the entire class-conscious proletariat will be with us in the fight ... to overthrow the bourgeoisie, to destroy bourgeois parliamentarism, for a democratic republic after the type of the Commune, or a republic of Soviets of Workers' and Soldiers' Deputies, for the revolutionary dictatorship of the proletariat.
> (Lenin, [1917] 1964: 495)

This was only a transition towards socialism, when

> the mass of the population will rise to taking an independent part, not only in voting and elections, but also in the everyday administration of the state. Under socialism, all will govern in turn and will soon become accustomed to no one governing.
> (Lenin, [1917] 1964: 492–493)

Clearly, Lenin argued like a democratic extremist here.

The Soviets of Workers' Deputies (*sovety rabotsjich deputatov*) had sprung up spontaneously at the end of the First World War, when the Russian economy was in serious crisis. Workers would meet in their factory to elect delegates and give them a binding mandate to negotiate with management, but also with local political authorities. In turn, the councils would elect deputies to regional and indirectly to national conferences of workers', peasants' and soldiers' deputies. Delegates could be recalled by their electors at any time (Anweiler, 1958: 45–61). Bolsheviks played an active part in the Soviets, especially in the two most important cities, Moscow and Petrograd. With the slogan 'All power to the Soviets!', they conquered those two cities and dissolved the Constituent Assembly that had just been elected (Carr, 1966: I, 81–133). Within a few years the Bolsheviks had disempowered the councils and established a party dictatorship instead of a dictatorship of the proletariat – against resistance from dissidents in their own ranks who would later develop 'Council-Communism' as a new ideology (see Chapter 4). In 1920, Lenin summed it up quite well:

> the dictatorship is exercised by the proletariat organised in the Soviets; the proletariat is guided by the Communist Party of the Bolsheviks.... No important political or organisational question is decided by any state institution in our republic without the guidance of the party's Central Committee.
> ([1920] 1970: 40–41)

The party was really a centralised oligarchy with iron discipline, yet it should 'observe the temper of the masses' (Lenin, [1920] 1970: 43).

Lenin's successor as party leader, Joseph Stalin, used similar (though usually less concise and clear) terms to justify the party dictatorship: 'the leader of the state, the leader in the system of the dictatorship of the proletariat is one party, the party of the proletariat, the party of the Communists, which cannot and does not share leadership with other parties' (1954: 160). The party 'draws into its ranks all the best elements of the proletariat' (Stalin, 1954: 166). In other words, a new aristocracy was ruling Russia: no longer the aristocracy of blood and landed property, but an aristocracy of class-conscious and disciplined proletarians, guided by Marxist-Leninist theory. As Neil Harding shows, the Bolshevik leadership justified its dictatorship in terms of objective knowledge, based on a 'scientific' theory – dialectical materialism (1993: 169–173). Of course, the party 'must closely heed the voice of the masses' (Stalin, 1954: 174). However, the masses are often ignorant and wrong, hence they have to be corrected and guided by the party. At the same time, Stalin claimed that the Soviet Union was the most democratic state in the world. In 1936, when his opponents within the party had been exiled, imprisoned or murdered, he introduced a new constitution which would guarantee 'consistent and thoroughgoing democratism' in Russia – while preserving the 'present leading position of the Communist Party' (Stalin, 1954: 691, 699). This may look like an extreme perversion of the word democracy; however, Harding points out that 'democratism' is defined as 'participation of all, of every citizen, in the process' (1993: 180). Soviet citizens were expected to take an active role in the political process, in a wide variety of elected bodies in factories and collective farms, villages and regions. Moreover, social equality remained the supreme ideological goal.

These two characteristics in particular – active political participation and the pursuit of social equality – distinguished Marxist-Leninism from Fascism and National Socialism.[5] While the latter two movements approved of elitism and dictatorship as a perfect and permanent state of affairs, the Marxism–Leninist movement justified it as instrumental and transitional. In theory, at least, the dictatorship of the proletariat (and of the party) would eventually give way to a classless society and the state would start 'withering away'. In practice, the two types of dictatorship may not have been very different, in terms of brutal power and repression (Cassinelli, 1976: 225–244). Both were aristocratic, in a sense – even if to impartial outsiders the term 'cheiristocracy' (rule by the worst) might be more appropriate than 'rule by the best'.

With the disintegration of the Soviet Union, Marxism–Leninism also seemed to disintegrate as an ideology. In the twenty-first century it is still used to justify the dictatorship of Fidel Castro in Cuba, of the Kim family in North Korea, and to some extent the party aristocracy in China, but it may have lost its universalist ambition and is mixed (increasingly) with nationalism. Several experts agree that the ideology is in crisis, even in China where the regime has benefited from spectacular economic growth – quite unlike Cuba and North Korea (Domes, 1990: 195–201; Linden, 1990: 20; Michael, 1990). Marxist-Leninist parties advocating the Soviet model have survived in most parts of the world, but mainly in the margins of the political systems. Of hardly more importance are Trotskyite groups, which go back to the revolutionary ideas about workers' councils in 1917, as glorified later by Leon Trotsky in his struggle against Stalin. Their ideas will be discussed briefly in Chapter 4.

Theocratic extremism

If China and the Soviet Union can be regarded as aristocratic regimes of a special kind, so too can Iran and other theocratic regimes. In both types of regimes, power is monopolised by an elite claiming absolute truth. In Soviet-style regimes the truth is defined in secular terms – 'scientific socialism' or dialectical materialism – while it is defined in religious terms in theocratic regimes. Theocracy should not be taken literally: God does not rule directly, but His Word (the Scriptures or the Qoran) is used to legitimate rule by priests, ministers or mullahs.

Not all theocrats are extremists. The Dutch Calvinist Party (*Staatkundig Gereformeerde Partij*, SGP), possibly one of the few parties in Europe that advocates 'theocratic politics', does not argue for government by theologians or Protestant ministers (Massink *et al.*, 1994; Slagboom, 1996: 43). In practice, it has accepted the parliamentary system, while admonishing the government to heed the word of God and criticising the democratic doctrine of political equality and the sovereignty of the people.

Many Islamists do the same. 'Islamism' will be used here as an umbrella term. Islam is a religion, rather than a political ideology, as most – though not all – scholars seem to agree (Waardenburg, 2002: 331).[6] The religion has inspired a variety of political ideologies, which are usually labelled 'political Islam', 'Islamic fundamentalism' or 'Islamism'. It may be misleading to put them all into one box. Some Islamists call for 'Islamic democracy' and advocate a pluralist, parliamentary system not very different from most European or American polities (Fuller, 2003: 47–67; Sadiki, 2004: 242–245). The Malaysian scholar Hussein Alatas, for example, argued in the 1950s that Islam combined the best of liberalism and socialism (1956: 38). In an Islamic state, 'rulers are to be elected from among the people in a democratic manner', according to him (Alatas, 1956: 45).

Yet other Islamists, such as the Egyptian Sayyid Qutb (1906–1966) and the Pakistani Abul Ala Mawdudi (1903–1979), rejected 'Western' notions of democracy and parliamentarian institutions (Moussalli, 1992: 157–168; Choueiri,

1997: 111, 114–115; see also Sadiki, 2004: 238–242). Even if they refrained from elaborating an alternative system, arguing that 'the Quran is our constitution', they seem to agree about one thing: sovereignty rests with Allah (God) (Roy, 1994: 42). Sovereignty may be delegated to a ruler, the *amir* or *Khaleefah* (caliph) – literally 'successor' of Mohammed, God's Messenger. It may also involve some kind of parliament or council (*shura*). According to Mawdudi, this council should advise rather than check or veto the caliph (Nasr, 1996: 91–95). Both the caliph and the council might be elected by the people, but probably without competition between parties or individual candidates. The Islamic state would most likely have a one-party system and dispense with political pluralism (Nasr, 1996: 99). Mawdudi defined this regime as 'theo-democracy' (Nasr, 1996: 84). The first four 'just caliphs' who succeeded the Prophet Mohammed are generally seen as examples of ideal rulers of the Muslim community (*Ummah*). In practice, however, the caliphs may not have consulted any elected body, as Bassam Tibi argues, but ruled in a rather autocratic style (1998: 173–175; 2000: 73–86). Some Islamists accept this implicitly, or even explicitly. According to Sheikh Omar Bakri Mohammed, leader of the international Islamist Muhajiroun movement in the 1990s,

> the job of managing the affairs of the Ummah is restricted to the Khaleefah (head of state). […] The main officials of the state are appointed by the Khaleefah. Every decision must emanate from the head of state. This negates any corruption or confusion within the ruling system. The Khaleefah is ultimately responsible.
>
> (OBM Network, no date: 1–2)[7]

Somewhat similar ideas may have been expressed in the 1990s by leaders of the Algerian Islamic Salvation Front (*Front Islamique du Salut*, FIS), such as Ali Benhadj (Zoubir, 1998: 149).

The ideologue of Iranian Islamists, Ayatollah Ruhollah Khomeyni (1900–1989), advocated almost a pure theocracy. In an Islamic state sovereignty belonged to the *faqih*, the learned men of religion, who had inherited the right (and duty) to govern from the prophets, Muhammed, Ali and their successors (Khomeyni, 1979: 49, 58–64; see also Roy, 1994: 172). The clerical government would be assisted and advised by a 'planning assembly' (Khomeyni, 1979: 44). Unlike most other Islamist ideologues, Khomeyni obtained the chance to implement his ideas. After the revolution of 1979, he became the supreme guardian of religious law or *valiye faqih* in the Islamic Republic of Iran (Moslem, 2002: 26). He could dismiss the president, even if the latter was elected by the people – and he did, in 1981 (Kamrava, 1992: 94). He appointed a Council of Guardians (*shouraye negahban*) – consisting of theologians and legal experts – who would be able to veto legislation passed by parliament and veto candidates for parliamentary elections. Though not a one-party state, the Islamic Republic of Iran does not favour liberal pluralism, let alone democracy, but may be regarded as a mixture of clerical autocracy and (partly elective, partly clerical) aristocracy.

The Taliban regime in Afghanistan seems to have been a slightly different mixture. The Taliban leader Mohammed Omar Mujahed was regarded as *amir* and *khalifah* by his followers (Nojumi, 2002: 152). His charismatic leadership did not require legitimation by a popular election, according to the Taliban. They rejected the 'modern Islam' advocated by Mawdudi and his followers in Pakistan (Nojumi, 2002: 153–154). Their semi-traditional regime lacked the formal institutional structure of the Islamic Republic of Iran (Maley, 2001).

The Kingdom of Saudi Arabia may be more institutionalised, but it is not necessarily more modern than the Taliban regime. The kingdom was established by the Saudi family in co-operation with religious leaders (*ulama*) and is still ruled by the family in an autocratic, patriarchal style. All power rests with the King, according to Article 44 of the constitution (Twal, 2003: 163). The King appoints and chairs the cabinet. The King consults a council (*majalis al-shura*) which is appointed by himself; if the council disagrees with the cabinet, the King decides (Nehme, 1998: 286–287; Twal, 2003: 187–196). Political parties are forbidden. Although the *ulama* do not control the government directly, as they do in Iran, they exercise considerable influence through the educational system and the Islamic legal system (*shari'a*).

While we should not generalise about all Islamists, we can conclude that at least some of them can be qualified as theocratic, autocratic or aristocratic extremists, while the *aristoi* are in their eyes the religious elites, *ulama* or *faqih*.

Other religions have also inspired theocratic regimes, though few of them have survived until today. Tibet was ruled (mainly) by Buddhist monks (*lamas*) for four centuries, from 1642 until the Chinese invasion in 1950. Religion and political affairs were 'joined together' (*chösi nyitrel*) (Goldstein, 1989: 2). Monks would assist or supervise lay officials in central bureaucracy as well as at the district level (Kapstein, 2006: 188–194). From the late nineteenth century the national government would consult a National Assembly, but this body could hardly be regarded as a democratic element in the constitution, as it consisted mainly of abbots, former abbots and lay officials (Goldstein, 1989: 19–20). Some lay officials, managers and aristocratic families could exercise substantial influence, yet ultimate authority was in the hands of the Dalai Lama, who would appoint secular ministers as well as religious leaders, like the abbots of the large monasteries in the central part of Tibet (Goldstein, 1989: 11, 31; Kapstein, 2006: 188–194). The Dalai Lama was considered to be the reincarnation of the Boddhisattva Avalokitésvara – a divine being, one might say, though this notion may not really chime with the originally atheist character of Buddhism. His office was neither elective nor hereditary. When a Dalai Lama died, senior monks would go searching for his successor among recently born boys (Kapstein, 2006: 109). Relying on paranormal signs as well as practical tests to see if the boy recognised certain objects of the deceased, they would claim – after some time – to have found the next reincarnation (*trülku*, translated by Kapstein as 'reborn emanational embodiment') of the Boddhisattva.

This procedure suggests more divine intervention than the selection of a new Pope – who, after all, is elected by the college of cardinals. In other respects, the

Dalai Lama and the Pope may have exercised similar powers within their polity. The Holy Father governs the Vatican like an absolute monarch (Poulat, 1981: 38). Nowadays, the Vatican state is a micro-state with limited power, but before 1870 its territory covered a large part of central Italy. Today, however, few Catholics seem to look at the Vatican state as a model political system. Theocratic extremism probably does not appeal to significant numbers of Christians any more. It may be more popular among (some) Islamists and Tibetan Buddhists, even if one should not exaggerate its significance there either.

Murray Rothbard and libertarianism

Libertarians claim to be the radical heirs of classical liberalism, regarding liberty as the supreme good (Rothbard, 1978: 1–19; see also Barry, 1986). Individuals have an absolute right to life, liberty and property. If government has any function at all, it is to protect these rights against those (individuals or other governments) that infringe upon them (Hospers, 1974). Yet many libertarians would rather do without a government; governments infringe upon human rights by collecting taxes and fines, confiscating property, and banning pornography and drugs. Parliamentary democracy does not prevent this. Initially it may have served the cause of freedom, but it 'ended as parliament being the essential part of the state', breaking all constitutional limits (Rothbard, 1974a: 77–80). In the words of the Canadian libertarians Richard and Ernestine Perkins, the difference between dictatorship and democracy is comparable to the difference 'between a lone armed robber and a gang of armed robbers' (1971: 60). Democracy 'would have nearly everyone involved in the game of aggression' (Perkins and Perkins, 1971: 60). Another Canadian libertarian defines democracy as 'the dictatorship of the majority' (Narveson, 2002: 173). Democracy is essentially incompatible with liberalism, as many classical liberals have realised (Gottfried, 1996). In fact, even 'dictatorship of the majority' may be a euphemism, as well-organised minorities tend to manipulate the amorphous majority. Sooner or later, practically every government will pursue the interests of its agents and serve special interests instead of the public interest (Barry, 1986: 190–196).

Libertarians believe that all human relations should be based on voluntary co-operation and exchange between individuals, rather than on laws enforced by a coercive body named 'government'. Their trust in the market also earns Libertarians the label of 'market anarchists', or 'anarchist capitalists', and distinguishes them from social anarchists or anarchist Socialists. While the latter want to replace the state with collective organisations – municipal communes, trade union 'syndicates' or workers' councils – the former prefer individual initiatives and private enterprise (Sheehan, 2003: 48–49). The social anarchists also reject representative government, but usually favour direct or participatory democracy – 'to allow sovereignty to return to the primal units of society' (Woodcock, 1963: 24–25). Hence their ideas will not be discussed here, but elsewhere in this book (see Chapter 3). Here we deal only with the market anarchists or libertarians.

Extreme libertarians want to privatise the public sector completely: not only banks, schools and hospitals, but also the courts, army and police should be run as private businesses – or maybe as co-operatives. Citizens who want to settle a conflict will agree to go to a mediator or arbitrator. In case of violent aggression, they would hire a mercenary army. Not all libertarians go quite as far: moderates are willing to accept a minimal kind of government that protects citizens against violent aggression from others (Hospers, 1974: 11–13). They agree, however, that the government should not interfere with the economy and should not provide services, education, welfare, or social security to its citizens. Citizens should look for private insurance against illness, unemployment and old age. Public utilities become private utilities, even if individuals in a certain area form voluntary associations to construct roads, distribute water and electricity, and collect garbage and treat sewage. If the air or water is polluted by a company or an individual, the neighbours might take him to court; alternatively, they might organise a boycott of the company's products or block access roads.

Unlike Fascists, Marxist-Leninists and Islamists, libertarians have never had a chance to realise their political dreams. The Libertarian Party may have become the largest third party in the USA soon after it was founded in 1971, and has won seats in legislatures of states such as Alaska, New Hampshire and Vermont, but it did not come close to power anywhere at any time (Libertarian Party, 2005). In other countries, such as Canada and the Netherlands, Libertarian parties did not do any better.[8] Yet Murray Rothbard, the main ideologue of the American Libertarian Party, claims he found a model in ancient Ireland, in the era before the English conquest. The emerald island was divided into many small kingdoms (*túath* in Irish) ruled by a king (*rí*), but territorial boundaries were not very important and the king's powers were limited to military and (in pagan times) religious functions. The king neither made the law nor enforced public or private justice (Ó Corráin, 1972: 28). The law was not supposed to be 'made by man', but maintained first by the druids and later by the caste of secular lawyers (*brehon*) who could refer to immemorial customs, preserved orally by poets and written down in the sixth or seventh century (Ó Corráin, 1972: 75). As central authority was weak or non-existent, interaction between families, clans and kingdoms was based on customs, mutual obligations and contracts. Sureties were taken to maintain the contract. In case of conflict, people would consult a lawyer or *brehon*. The authority of the *brehon*, as well as fosterage and family relations, would help to moderate conflicts. Even so, some arguments were settled by violent combat. Medieval Ireland was not a pacifist's paradise, even if all-out wars may have been rare (Otway-Ruthven, 1968). It was a feudal, hierarchical society which cherished honour and privilege as much as (if not more than) individual freedom. Commoners enjoyed the protection of noblemen in exchange for services.

Egalitarian liberals would not feel at home in medieval Ireland. In our terms, the Irish regime should be considered an aristocracy rather than a democracy. Libertarians tend to frown on egalitarianism (Narveson, 2002: 49–62). Governments, as far as they have any legitimacy at all, should not interfere with the unequal distribution of wealth produced by the market. The market rewards individual achievement, based on talent, effort and fortune. If the market creates an aristocracy of talented entrepreneurs, libertarians would not object. They might not like the term 'aristocracy' because it contains the word 'cratos' ('power'), arguing that even the most successful entrepreneurs do not exercise power in a market economy. However, this argument seems rather naïve. In a capitalist society, wealth entails power. In most existing capitalist societies, power is based not only on wealth but also on bureaucratic position or political popularity, but libertarians would do away with practically all bureaucracy and reduce the power of elected politicians to a minimum. Thus, wealth would remain about the only access to power. Talented and fortunate individuals will own the means of production, and thus will employ less talented or less fortunate individuals. If the latter obey the orders given by their employers, they will be rewarded (by a wage increase or a promotion, for example), and if they disobey they will be demoted or fired. Wealthy and smart individuals will be able to hire skilful lawyers, public relations specialists and, if necessary, a private militia in order to get what they want. Smart, courageous and good-looking entrepreneurs are the heroes in the novels of Ayn Rand, another ideologue of the American Libertarian movement. In her novel *Atlas Shrugged*, the entrepreneurial individualists are rational and autonomous, talented, honest, purposeful, brave, and usually beautiful people, whereas the others who depend on government support tend to be passive and lazy, insecure, devious or dumb (Rand, 1957; see also Bertonneau, 2004: 305).

As a consequence, pluralism may be rather superficial and fragile in a libertarian society. Non-conformists can survive only if they adapt to the market – and to the demands of the rich in particular. Moreover, the libertarian society may be fragile and defenceless if attacked by well-organised thugs or aggressive neighbouring states.

The hidden aristocratic and monistic tendencies of libertarianism became explicit in more extreme groups in the US such as the Militia of Montana, Posse Comitatus and Aryan Nations (Stern, 1996). In the latter, libertarianism is combined with a racist and nationalist, if not National-Socialist, interpretation of Christianity (Aryan Nations, no date). The Militia movement tends to focus more on practical issues like gun ownership and protection of the autonomy of counties and states against federal interference, but most militias predominantly recruit white Christian men (Stern, 1996: 246). Liberal pluralists will probably not feel very comfortable in their midst – if they would be accepted at all.

While libertarians share with conservative extremists the elitist contempt of democracy, they agree with radicals on the potential of man to control his own destiny (see also Rothbard, 1974b). However, while democratic radicals and mainstream anarchists view this control as a collective decision-making process, libertarians see collectivities as irrational and erratic. Only individuals can control their own destiny – provided they are sufficiently endowed with reason and will power. Collective attempts to change the world inevitably turn into disasters: at best, bureaucratic mismanagement and economic decline; at worst, civil war and mass murder. Man should not tinker with the social order once a market economy has been established (or perhaps one should say 'emerged', as 'established' suggests some kind of collective action anyway). In their defence of a more or less natural social order, libertarians again resemble conservatives.

Conclusion

Five varieties of extremism have been described in this chapter. They have only one thing in common with each other and with democratic extremism: all reject the mixed regime that passes for democracy in most parts of the world. The quest for a more pure regime is, in my view, the defining characteristic of political extremism.

The extremists differ, however, as to the type of regime they like to substitute for the mixed polity. Modern aristocratic conservatives such as Othmar Spann envisaged a new kind of elite, based not on family ties and landownership – as with traditional aristocrats – but on intelligence, education and talent for leadership. Fascists and National Socialists also favoured a new elite, but gave priority to autocratic leadership – modernising traditional monarchist ideas, in a way. In fact, they turned autocratic leadership into an ideological principle. The nation should be led not so much by a hereditary monarch as by a charismatic leader elected by (or at least emanating from) the people. *Il Duce* or *Der Führer* incarnated the will of the people, and might occasionally confirm this by organising (and manipulating) a plebiscite. The autocratic leader took the most important decisions himself and delegated the rest to his officials. Theocratic extremists agree with this idea, provided the leader is sent by God and applies the divine laws. Some Buddhists, as well as some Islamists and Christians, might belong to this category. Other Islamists prefer a clerical aristocracy: rule by religious scholars, *ulama* or *faqih*. Again, other Islamists reject all clerical rule and argue for a mixed regime, similar to Christian Democracy – naturally, they belong to the 'moderate centre' and should not be regarded as extremists. Fascists, Nazis and the more extreme Islamists favour an authoritarian and monist regime that does not tolerate dissent and opposition. As they believe in absolute truth, they see no need for a competition of ideas.

Libertarians are a very different brand. Like Fascists, Islamists and aristocratic conservatives they disapprove of democracy and egalitarianism, yet they detest authoritarianism even more. Competition and freedom are sacred to them. Social and political inequality are not explicit goals, but logical consequences of their policies of privatisation and elimination of a public sector. Libertarians are aristocrats by implication, and perhaps unwillingly. As talents and opportunities are generally distributed unequally, competition will result in inequality – in politics as well as in business.

Marxist-Leninists – especially of the Stalinist variety – are, in my opinion, also aristocrats by implication, even if they would not happily accept this qualification. In theory, they favour political equality and even radical democracy, binding mandates and recall of representatives, yet in practice they created a new, proletarian aristocracy of party bosses and bureaucrats. Stalin and his Asian imitators added autocracy to aristocracy and destroyed pluralism and opposition with as much cruelty and violence as Hitler and Mussolini had done. Like Fascists and theocratic extremists, Marxist-Leninists can be considered extremist because they reject not only political equality and a mixed polity, but also pluralism. Libertarians are extreme in the opposite direction, asking for more freedom than the moderate centrists are willing to grant; though they favour pluralism in theory, one may wonder if it would survive libertarian practice.

These two dimensions – political equality versus inequality, and authoritarian versus libertarian – allow us to map the ideologies discussed here in a two-dimensional space (see Figure 2.1). The various types of extremism surround, as it were, a moderate centre dominated by ideologies such as social democracy, liberalism, Christian democracy and moderate conservatism. The aristocratic and autocratic varieties of extremism are positioned to the right, as they favour political inequality – in politics, the term 'right' is usually associated with inequality, as shown by scholars like Jean Laponce (1981) and Norberto Bobbio (1996). Democratic extremism is positioned to the left, as it favours political equality.

To some extent, the picture is symmetrical: certain varieties of democratic extremism mirror types of aristocratic or autocratic extremism. Anarchism and libertarianism are almost identical twins, as we have seen already. Both try to maximise freedom, but they disagree about the value of equality (more about Anarchism in Chapter 3). Council-communism resembles Marxist-Leninism, at least in its origins: when Lenin and his followers betrayed and disempowered the workers' councils in revolutionary Russia, dissidents broke with the Communist party and tried to set up council-communist organisations. In Russia their attempts were nipped in the bud, but in Germany and a few other European countries they were more successful – even if their organisations remained weak and usually short-lived (see Chapter 4). Democratic radicalism emerged during the democratic revolution in France and inspired aristocratic Conservatism as its negative counterpart, one could argue (see O'Sullivan, 1976: 9); Sabine and Thorson trace its origins back to the Levellers in the English Revolution, between 1647 and 1650 (Sabine and Thorson, 1973: 442). Both radicalism and conservatism have remained fairly diffuse and under-developed ideologies, taking different forms depending upon the circumstances and the dominant ideologies at the time, such as liberalism or socialism. This is even more true of populism, which seems to exist only in hyphenated form, i.e. combined with other ideologies such as nationalism, socialism or liberalism (Mudde, 2004). Populism and democratic radicalism are not necessarily extremist – on the contrary: they often shade into moderate centrism – yet both favour forms of direct democracy with extremist potential, as will be argued in Chapter 4. Sortitionism, finally, may not be considered to be an ideology by most scholars – or not yet, anyway. So far, it is an idea advocated by intellectuals and a few very small groups, as we will see in Chapter 5, but it is hardly a comprehensive utopian design of a

30 *Extremism*

```
                          Authoritarian
                               ▲
        Marxist–Leninism –     |---▶
        Council–Communism              Fascism
                          Populism                    Islamism*

                    ┌──────────┼──────────┐
'Left'      Democratic│         │  Aristocratic      'Right'
Political           │   Moderate│                    Political
equality   ◀────────┼   centre  ┼────────────────▶  inequality
                    │           │
            Radicalism│         │  Conservatism
                    └──────────┼──────────┘
                       Sortitionism
              Anarchism        Libertariansim
                               │
                               ▼
                          Libertarian
```

Moderate centre:

```
┌─────────────────────────────────────────────┐
│                                             │
│          Christian democracy                │
│                                             │
│                       Moderate              │
│                       conservatism          │
│                                             │
│        Social                               │
│        democracy                            │
│                    Liberalism               │
│                                             │
└─────────────────────────────────────────────┘
```

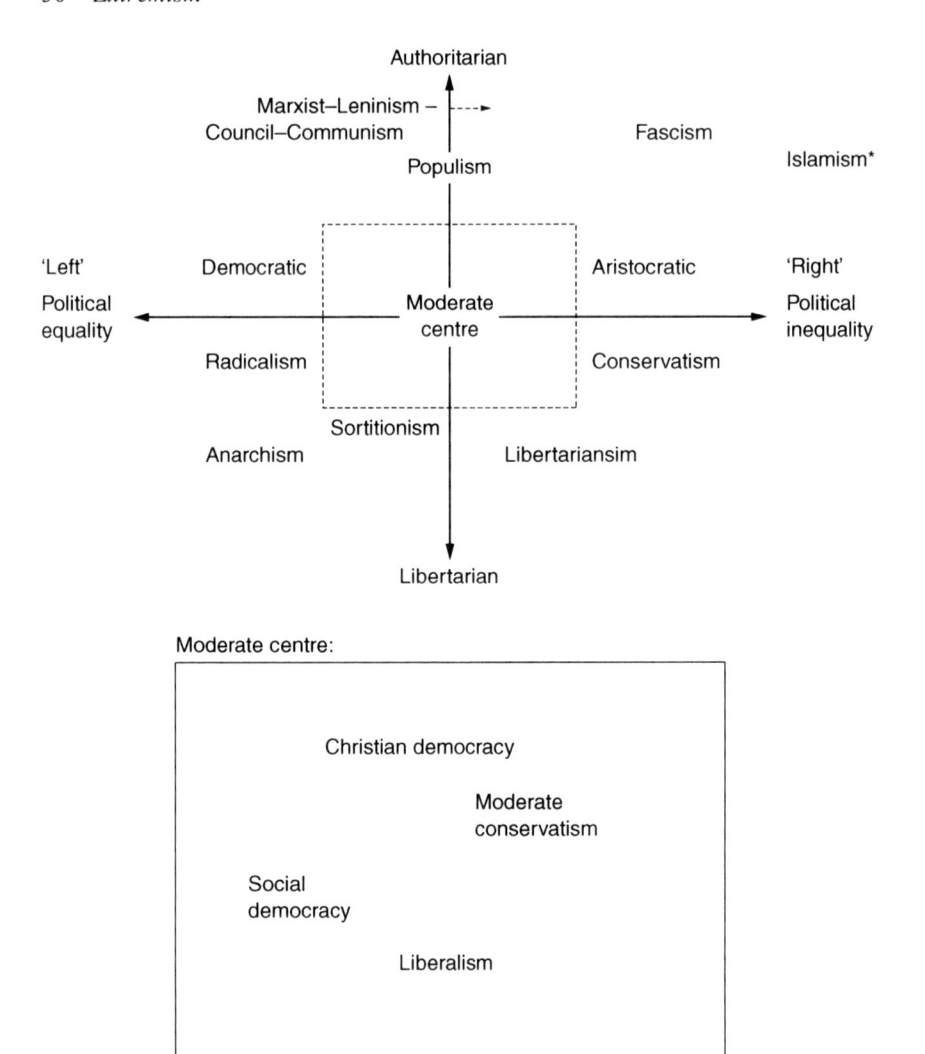

Figure 2.1 Varieties of political extremism.

Note
* Islamism is a broader category which may belong (in part) to the Moderate Centre.

different society, nor a broad political movement. However, in recent years the idea has spread and attracted more attention, so eventually a comprehensive and coherent sortitionist ideology might develop and perhaps even inspire a mass movement.

To most readers, the democratic extremist ideologies will be less familiar than their aristocratic and autocratic counterparts. The latter have attracted a larger following and have had a stronger impact on human history. Apart from libertarianism, all of them have inspired political regimes in the world. Yet their influence seems to have waned since 1945 – except for Islamism. Perhaps the time has come for radical and extreme democratic projects? As I hope to show in the remaining chapters of this book, democratic extremists and radical democrats have developed a wealth of interesting ideas, even if history has rarely been very kind to them.

Notes

1 According to Tin Maung Maung Than, the fairly heterogeneous coalition (National League for Democracy) led by the Nobel Prize winner Aung San Suu Kyi agreed on 'Western notions of liberal democracy and a market economy with an independent monetary authority. They emphasised liberty, individual rights, freedom of the press, rule of law, equal opportunity for all, social justice, and leaned towards a federalist state system' (Maung Maung Than, 2001: 230).
2 Others might prefer the term 'polyarchy' introduced by Ronald Dahl in the 1950s; yet his term seems to require more explanation and has never caught on – possibly for that very reason (1956: 63–89).
3 As many readers might associate the term 'monarchy' with a hereditary kingdom I will use 'autocracy' as a broader term here, even if both terms mean practically the same in ancient Greek.
4 The League for National Reconstruction (*Verbond voor Nationaal Herstel*) called for a corporatist parliament and more powers for the executive branch of government (De Jonge, 1968: 185–186, 265–269).
5 One might object that even Fascism and National Socialism cultivated mass participation – but it was a more passive participation in mass rallies and marches, rather than active participation in elections and committees.
6 In the Netherlands this became a controversial issue around 2007 when Geert Wilders, leader of the Freedom Party, denounced Islam as a political ideology and referred to a few scholars who supported this claim.
7 Omar Bakri Mohammed fled Britain in 2005 when he expected to be charged with treason (Raymond, 2010: 6–8).
8 In Canada, the Libertarian Party obtained 0.3 per cent of the popular vote at federal elections in 1988, but 0.0 per cent in 2011; the Dutch *Libertarische Partij* received less than 0.1 per cent in 1994 and again in 2012.

3 Neathena
Assembly democracy

When I left my apartment and entered the courtyard, most of my neighbours were already there, engaged in a lively discussion. Only the students who lived on the top floor were absent.

'Good morning!' I said, 'I assume you are all going to the assembly today?'

'Yes of course,' answered Mrs Rabinda, a retired schoolteacher, 'it is our citizen duty, isn't it? I go every month.'

'Well, I try to go too. I would not want to forego the tax credit we all get when we go, even if it is only twenty-five dollars' said Mr. Wong, who owned a small shop not far from our condominium. 'Last month I had to meet a representative from one of my wholesale suppliers, he could not come any other day, he said. Fortunately today I have a bit more time.'

'Come on, let's go!' admonished Mr. Lopez Estado, who worked for the communal government. 'It is an important meeting today, you know, we have to take decisions on the new city theatre and on the brewery!'

While we started walking towards the bus that would take us to the city plaza, Mr. Lopez tried to persuade us that we should vote for the theatre proposed – and designed – by his colleagues. Mrs Rabinda nodded in agreement, but Mr. Wong shook his greying head:

'It may be a nice plan, but far too expensive! We have to economise, Mr. Lopez! Don't you think so, Mr. Ahmed?'

'Oh, I don't know,' I admitted, 'after all, I am new here. I only received my citizenship card in January! This is the first assembly where I am allowed to vote.'

'But you have been there at least three times!' remarked Mrs Rabinda, rather severely. 'You had to, in order to pass your citizen's test!'

'True, Mrs Rabinda', I admitted, 'But it is different on the visitor's gallery, you see, I tried to understand what was being said and what happened, but did not form an opinion of my own.'

'You could have attended a preparatory meeting in our neighbourhood centre, Mr. Ahmed,' the retired schoolteacher persisted. 'However, I must admit I rarely go there myself. There are simply too many meetings! I go to one meeting a week, usually the local board of education, and of course the jury. That is enough.'

We boarded the bus, where others were engaged in similar discussions – or chatted about the weather or a recent baseball match. By the time we entered the assembly hall – which was also used for musicals and other shows – I felt even more confused than before, so I stayed close to my neighbours. I carefully watched how they put their citizen cards in the slot before pushing the turnstile open. Mr. Lopez Estado helped me, and pointed out where the people of our neighbourhood would normally sit.

'It is just a habit, you are free to sit anywhere, but people usually sit in their neighbourhood area,' he explained.

We sat down, and he showed me how to operate the microphone and the voting machine that were built into the seat. They worked only when you pushed your citizen card into the slot, and went dead as soon as you pulled it out. Once installed, I looked around me. The assembly hall was filling up quickly, though the upper rows remained largely empty. I guess there were several thousand people there when the meeting was opened by the mayor. The mayor was a purely ceremonial figurehead, a comedian who would entertain us with jokes and songs during intervals. He gave a short rousing speech about the importance of today's meeting before giving the floor to the assembly president, who had been elected at the end of last month's meeting.

'I am glad it is Mrs. Smyth, my former principal who chairs this meeting,' Mrs Rabinda whispered to me. 'She is very strict and fair, you know.'

The president spoke slowly and articulated very well. 'Please be ready to vote. We will vote first on today's agenda. There are two options, really: one, we start with the city brewery, then go to the new theatre, or two, we start with the theatre and go to the brewery afterwards. In both cases, we will end with appointments and other business. Clear? Yes? Alright! If you prefer option one, push button one, and if you prefer two, press two. Oh yes, if you don't care either way, better press three'. Her words appeared on a huge screen behind her so that even deaf citizens could follow her. I did not care and pressed button three, but the majority voted for the second option.

The plan for the theatre was presented and defended by two architects, in about twenty minutes. Opponents of the proposal were invited to express their opinion, also in twenty minutes. Ten people made themselves known. Two minutes each? No, three withdrew, so the others had almost three minutes each. Some complained about the costs of the new building and argued that the level of taxation was already too high in our commune; others suggested alternative locations for the theatre. The advocates of the proposal reacted briefly to the criticisms, then the floor was open to anyone waiting to comment or to suggest a compromise. All sorts of arguments were presented; some seemed rather irrelevant to me – like one young man who kept rambling on about his rather unsuccessful attempts to stop drinking, until his time was up and his microphone was switched off. At last, what a relief: we could vote. The proposal was approved by a narrow margin. While everywhere people began commenting – some applauding and others booing – the president's voice boomed: 'Fifteen minute break? We start again at 11 am sharp!' Many people *rushed towards the machines that offered coffee, tea and mineral water – for free, of course.*

After the break, the question of whether the city should continue to run its own brewery or sell it to an international company was discussed. The two options were defended by speakers who both claimed to represent brewery workers, but the second one added 'and beer drinkers! Because beer will become cheaper when we sell the brewery.' 'But the quality will go down!' his opponent replied. The discussion soon acquired ideological overtones, when members of the Free Enterprise Club, the Workers' Solidarity Club and the Communal Independence Society began to debate the virtues of international free trade versus autarchy and workers' rights.

'The first speaker seems very eloquent,' I whispered.

'Of course!' Mr. Lopez Estado scowled, 'he has been trained very well, the Free Enterprise Club has lots of money! Very dangerous, those political clubs, we should ban them, if you ask me.'

He stopped short when Mrs Rabinda started hissing again. Other people in the audience became a bit restless too. The chairwoman called for silence and politeness, with moderate success. The vote was close: a narrow majority refused to sell the brewery.

'Okay, let's have a beer now,' sighed Mr. Wong, with a wry smile. Yet there were a few minor matters to be decided, including some official appointments, before the meeting was closed. Some people rushed home, a few insisted on going to work, but many filled the bars and restaurants around the assembly hall.

The description above is political science fiction: Neathena does not exist – not yet, anyway. Of course, it is inspired by classical Athens. Like the ancient city-state, its imaginary counterpart is governed directly by the people. Yet 'the people' was defined in a much more restrictive and exclusive manner in ancient Athens than in Neathena. An immigrant like Mr. Ahmed would not be eligible for citizenship in Athens. In both cities, however, important decisions are taken by the popular assembly, after some deliberation, through a majority vote. The city is a sovereign community, possibly allied with similar cities in loose confederations.

THEORY

This seems to be the most direct and extreme type of democracy one can imagine. It is a type of democracy that appeals even to anarchists, who generally distrust any form of government, democratic or otherwise. For instance, it appealed to William Godwin (1756–1836), a Protestant English minister who became an atheist, and who is the author of what is generally considered to be the first theoretical exposition of anarchism – *avant la lettre*, as the term had not been invented yet (Carter, 1971: 1). In his *Enquiry Concerning Political Justice*, he argues that 'democracy with all the disadvantages that were ever annexed to it ... would still be preferable to the exclusive system of other forms' (Godwin, [1798] 1971: 203). He admitted that popular assemblies in Athens were 'somewhat tumultuous' and liable to vices such as demagogy and sophistry, the incapacity of the multitude, the envy of superior merit and 'the rude dictates of savage folly' (Godwin, [1798] 1971: 202). Even so, he preferred them to a representative assembly, as representation 'removes the power of making regulations, one step further from the people whose lot it is to obey them' (Godwin, [1798] 1971: 205).

Godwin agreed that representative assemblies might be needed occasionally, e.g. to deal with serious conflicts between local communities or parishes, but they should not be held regularly. Preferably, decisions should be taken at the local (parish) level, by people's assemblies and juries. Official secretaries and clerks acting on behalf of the people should be 'subject to their revisal, and renewable at their pleasure' (Godwin, [1798] 1971: 235). Yet even those institutions restrict individual freedom, which was the supreme good in Godwin's eyes. Hence, he looked forward to the day when 'juries themselves, and every other species of public institution, may be laid aside as unnecessary'; in other words, to 'the dissolution of political government' (Godwin, [1798] 1971: 222). Thus, one might regard Godwin as a reluctant democratic extremist (as defined in the first chapter of this book): his extreme democracy seemed a necessary step towards a completely free or anarchic society. To be sure, he influenced not only anarchists, but also utopian socialists and the democratic radicals of the Chartist movement in nineteenth century Britain (Marshall, 1992: 192).

Anarchism should not be seen as an extreme form of democracy, according to one of anarchisms most famous historians, George Woodcock (1963: 30). Whereas democrats advocate the sovereignty of the people, Anarchists advocate the sovereignty of the individual. Nonetheless, Woodcock also points out that anarchists want to 'allow sovereignty to return to the intimate primal units of society' (1962: 24–25). For some anarchists the primal unit might be the individual, but for many others it is the local community, the collective farm or workshop, or another economic unit (see also Carter, 1971: 58–59; Freeden, 1998a: 311–314). As long as the local community remains small and independent, it could do without a professional and hierarchical state apparatus – probably the main enemy of all anarchists, in the eyes of most experts. The well-known political philosopher Michael Freeden defines anarchism by three core concepts: antagonism to power, which is 'decontested as centralized and hierarchical and manifested above all, though not exclusively, in the state' (Freeden, 1998a: 312); a belief in liberty, decontested as spontaneous voluntarism; and the postulation of natural human harmony. Benjamin Franks wants to replace the latter two concepts with 'anti-mediation' (rejection of representative democracy and a preference for direct action) and 'privileging prefigurative methods' (means should be consistent with ends); but in his view, above all anarchists are 'contesting hierarchies of power', whether based on capitalist relations of production or on gender or ethnic prejudice (Franks, 2012: 216). So, anarchists need not reject all forms of power, only centralised and hierarchical power.

If the community allows all members an equal share in collective decision-making, no man or woman can rule over another, so there is no 'rule' or *archè* (αρχή) – hence 'anarchy'. For most people 'anarchy' has negative connotations and implies chaos and lawlessness, but anarchists imbued the term with positive values.[1] The absence of a state apparatus – i.e. policemen, prison wardens and lawyers trying to force people to comply with laws they did not make themselves – would allow people freedom, but not licence to harm each other. All Anarchists seem to agree on this, yet they prefer different means of preventing chaos and violence. Some reject all institutionalised restrictions of individual freedom and expect individuals to solve their disagreements through negotiation and arbitration, whereas others rely more on social control, mutual co-operation and, if necessary, communal sanctions against anti-social behaviour. The sanctions might be imposed by the communal assembly or by a jury elected or selected by lot from the community (see also Carter, 1971: 80–83). Thus, *pace* Woodcock, the autonomy and sovereignty of the individual cannot be absolute in an anarchist community. Both anarchists and democratic extremists might fight for sovereign communities ruled by popular assemblies; they might disagree about the limits of individual freedom within the community, but they would agree that there must be limits. In fact, one could argue that 'anarchism' and 'democratic extremism' are overlapping concepts: some Anarchists, such as Godwin, are (possibly reluctant) democratic extremists, and some democratic extremists are in fact anarchists – even if historically anarchists have often criticised the concept of democracy, associating it with a hierarchical state (see also Dahl, 1989: 37–51).[2]

The next section of this chapter will focus on a modern anarchist who is also an extreme democrat (cf. Biehl, 1998: 145–146). Murray Bookchin (1921–2006) may have articulated and developed the ideal of a direct democracy based on popular assemblies more explicitly and coherently than any other contemporary thinker (White, 2008: 155–178). Hence 'libertarian municipalism', as he preferred to call his political project, deserves serious attention here, as it seems the most extreme articulation of the assembly model. In fact, ancient Athens came close to this ideal, but differed in important respects, as will subsequently become clear. The cantons in Eastern Switzerland that hold annual assemblies and the towns in New England that continue to have town meetings do not enjoy full sovereignty and autonomy as they have to defer to higher authorities in their polities. The powers of local assemblies in Porto Alegre and other Brazilian cities and their European counterparts seem even more limited. Yet all these cases will throw more light on the advantages and disadvantages of the assembly model in different historical, geographical and institutional contexts. Moving from the most extreme to the most modest implementation of the assembly model, one might gain insight into its practical possibilities and 'best practices': where feasibility meets desirability, perhaps somewhere between the extreme ideal and the muddled reality of mixed regimes.

Bookchin's libertarian municipalism

Murray Bookchin was born in 1921 in a working-class family of Russian descent in New York. While working as a foundryman and later as an autoworker, he steeped himself in Marxist theory (White, 2008: 12–28; Biehl, 1998: vii). He joined the Communist party at an early age, but left it in the late 1930s. Afterwards, he flirted with Trotskyism until he developed his own brand of libertarian socialism or eco-anarchism in the 1950s and 1960s. Continuing his work in industry, he began writing. Presciently, in the 1950s he warned about the use of too many chemicals in food and other pollution problems. In the early 1970s he switched to an academic career without relinquishing his political activism. He combined the two by founding the Institute of Social Ecology (with Dan Chodorkoff) at a scenic location in Vermont. This small institute would offer interdisciplinary courses and workshops on environmental and social issues, as well as facilitate action. Students were invited 'to not only remake themselves but remake society as well' (Institute for Social Ecology, 2012).

As Peter Marshall, the very knowledgeable historian of anarchism, concluded, Bookchin 'has brilliantly renewed anarchist theory and practice by combining libertarian and utopian ideas with ecological principles in the creative synthesis of social ecology' (1992: 622). His ideas inspired activists in the Students for a Democratic Society (SDS) in the late 1960s. In the 1980s he played a leading role in the Left Green Network, a faction within the US Greens (White, 2008: 203; see also Rensenbrink, 1992: 186–187, 252–271).

While influential (in the 1980s) among many green activists and in Europe also, Bookchin remained sceptical about the potential of green parties to solve the ecological crisis facing humanity (Biehl, 1998: 127–129, 140). By taking part in national elections, the Greens in fact accepted the centralised nation-state, which in his eyes was one of the major agents causing the ecological crisis. The nation-state serves capital, and capital needs growth (Biehl, 1998: 148). If capital cannot grow, it will die. So, in the long run, capitalism will destroy the biosphere and mankind, by global warming or exhausting the earth, wasting raw materials, polluting air, land and water, or other ways (Bookchin, 1980: 35–44, 293). Capitalism is 'a parasite on the future' (Bookchin, 1971: 347). This claim seems to be one of the most persistent themes in Bookchin's mature work (White, 2008: 84).

Bookchin's work is too rich and sophisticated to deal with here *in extenso*, but a short summary may help to put his ideas about assembly democracy into context. For him and his associates – most prominently his partner, Janet Biehl – libertarian municipalism is more than an attractive ideal, or a way to achieve political equality, freedom and justice. It is 'a precondition for our survival as a species' (Biehl, 1998: 140). Bookchin does not perceive any alternative between his 'ecotopia' and the destruction of the biosphere (1980: 70–71). In his view, replacing capitalism with statism or state socialism (Soviet style) would not stop ecological devastation (Biehl, 1998: 117–118). Shifting power from capitalists to state bureaucrats would not go to the roots of the ecological crisis, which are hierarchy and domination, of man over nature as well as of man over woman and man over man. Bookchin's central thesis runs as follows:

> the conception that humanity must dominate and exploit nature stems from the domination and exploitation of man by man. Indeed, this conception goes back earlier to a time when men began to dominate and exploit women in the patriarchal family.
>
> (1980: 40)

i.e. at the dawn of civilisation. Capitalism merely represents the highest stage in this development of domination over nature and over man. At the same time, he argues that the material abundance and technology created by capitalist society would allow mankind to break its chains and establish a sustainable society without hierarchy and domination (Bookchin, 1971).

This sustainable society would consist of sovereign and almost self-supporting and ecologically balanced communities, called 'municipalities' or 'eco-communities' by Bookchin and his followers.[3] They would be 'large enough so that its citizens could meet most of their material needs, yet not so large that they were unable to gain a familiarity with each other and make policy decisions in open, face-to-face discourse' (Bookchin, 1990a: 180). Decisions should be made by a popular assembly, accessible to all inhabitants over a certain age, by a majority vote after a thorough deliberation (Biehl, 1998: 56–59, 158). The communal assembly would meet regularly, say once a week. If the community were too large for all citizens to meet in one place and have a reasonable discussion, it would have to be broken up into neighbourhoods or even city blocks which would have their own assemblies and elect delegates to a central assembly. These delegates would have to act as 'walking mandates of the local assemblies': they would rotate and could be recalled whenever they failed to carry out their mandate (Bookchin, 1990a: 175; Biehl, 1998: 58). The same principles of strict mandates and recall would apply to officials elected by the assembly to carry out its decisions, and to delegates at inter-municipal meetings or confederal councils.

Preferably, citizens would volunteer to carry out important tasks, such as the maintenance of public order and safety. They should control the militia or civic guard that would protect them from criminals as well as foreign invaders (Bookchin, 1995). Municipalities could cooperate with each other within a confederation, without giving up their sovereignty: delegates would negotiate and co-ordinate with each other but not take any decisions without the approval of their own municipal assembly (Biehl, 1998: 101–102, 105–110). At most, municipalities within a confederation could hold a referendum in order to put pressure on a municipality which violated important agreements, e.g. by dumping waste in a river or denying basic human rights to parts of its own population (Biehl, 1998: 108–109).

Through the popular assembly, the citizens should control not only the political but also the economic affairs of the community. The economy should be 'municipalised': i.e. land, industrial entreprises and banks placed in the custody of the citizens of the municipality (Bookchin, 1991; Biehl, 1998: 118–120). Large corporations and factories should be broken up into smaller units. Production should become small-scale and more artisan-based. Repetitive routine work should be left to machines, creative work to human beings. New 'soft' technology would make this possible (Bookchin, 1971: 351–355; Biehl, 1998: 132–137).

Bookchin severely criticised neo-Marxists and syndicalists who called for workers' control or self-management of large factories without paying attention to technology and decentralisation – though he would not favour the latter without the former either (1980: 115–132, 52–53). He agreed that workers should participate in the management of their workshop, but final decisions about production and distribution would be best left to the municipal assembly, in order to prevent particular interests prevailing over universal (communal) interests. Without municipal control, even a factory managed by workers might decide to dump its waste in a river or wreak other ecological mayhem (Biehl, 1998: 120, 161–163). Control by the municipal assembly would be real public control, very different from the pseudo-public control exercised in the Soviet Union and similar socialist states over the means of production in the interest of their elites (Biehl, 1998: 116–118).

A municipalised economy would not aim at maximal growth and profit, but at the satisfaction of the needs and desires of its citizens. For this reason, it would also respect ecological boundaries. Bookchin did not believe that human needs would expand *ad infinitum* in a libertarian municipalist society. Present tendencies to constantly increase mass consumption are produced and manipulated by the capitalist system. Once people had again learned to take control of their collective destiny and decide what they wanted to produce and consume, Bookchin trusted that they would develop a different value system and a different set of ethics, based on ecological principles, solidarity and moral responsibility, rather than material greed and ambition (Bookchin, 1990b: 118–125).

Thus, all elements in Bookchin's theory are intricately connected. Political and economic decentralisation – or rather, municipalisation – are required not only to maximise human freedom and self-realisation, and to restore social and political equality, but also to save the biosphere from the destructive forces of capitalism and statism. Yet even a coherent theory may suffer from inconsistencies and ambiguities, as several critical readers of Bookchin have argued. Bookchin's libertarian municipalism has been attacked on three levels: its theoretical assumptions, its internal contradictions or unsolved problems, and the revolutionary strategy he advocated.

For the purpose of this study, the latter two areas of criticism seem more important than the first one. Bookchin's thesis about the intimate connection between the domination of nature and the domination of man (and, even more, of woman) seems questionable, even in the eyes of sympathising critics such as Damian White (2008: 50–55) and Marius De Geus (1999: 201). Bookchin may have idealised the 'organic' and libertarian character of prehistorical societies, as well as their benign relationship with their ecosystems, as anthropological studies suggest (White, 2008: 42–50). Yet even if he were completely wrong here, his moral and ecological arguments in favour of radical decentralisation and 'municipalisation' may still stand. More damaging might be the criticism that his ideas about capitalism and the state are too dogmatic and rigid – and too reminiscent of the Marxism-Leninism Bookchin claimed to have left behind (White, 2008: 88–98). Bookchin cannot really prove that capitalism will inevitably destroy the ecosystem sooner or later or that green reformism or even green capitalism could never work. Moreover, he fails to convince his critics that decentralised and 'municipalised' economies will always be ecologically more efficient than centralised market or state economies (De Geus, 1999: 201–202; Gundersen, 1998: 199–202). True, decentralisation will reduce transportation costs (and thus save fossil fuel), but it will not necessarily restrict pollution or prevent the extermination of animal and plant species.

Never mind the ecological effects of municipalisation, a libertarian municipalist might argue that her project deserves our support because it will create more liberty and equality for all. Yet critics have questioned this argument as well. They perceive a tension between individual freedom and social control or conformism in small and relatively closed communities (De Geus, 1999: 224–225; White, 2008: 169–171). Citizens depend on each other, politically as well as economically – as the municipal assembly also controls the local economy. Hence, they might be afraid to deviate from public opinion and make enemies in the municipal assembly. Moreover, verbal skills, reasoning, and intelligence are not distributed equally. Surely, this criticism applies not only to Bookchin's utopia, but to all proposals for deliberative democracy (see Cohen and Rogers, 2003). Assemblies can be manipulated by eloquent demagogues who may serve private interests disguised as public interests – for example, they might persuade the assembly to close a small factory that supposedly pollutes the environment because this would create more space to build houses, thus benefitting their friends in the construction industry.

Even worse, a municipal assembly might decide to restrict individual freedom by passing repressive laws – such as banning abortion or euthanasia, disallowing gay marriages, or even expelling all Muslims or another religious minority. According to Bookchin and Biehl, a municipality that infringes upon basic human rights would be pressured by other municipalities in its confederacy to change its policy – but they fail to explain how this could be done, without some kind of supra-municipal authority that could impose economic or even military sanctions on the evil-doer. Of course, other municipalities might decide to boycott the repressive municipality and stop buying its products – but recent history has shown that repressive regimes can easily survive trade boycotts and even drastic economic sanctions. Both White and James Clark (another relatively mild critic of Bookchin) fear that the libertarian municipalists may rely too much on the civic education and democratic experience that should make citizens more tolerant and enlightened than they are at present (White, 2008: 171–174; Clark, 1998: 159).

At any rate, it is difficult to deny the potential tension between libertarian values and municipalism. One way out of this diabolic dilemma might be to accept that some municipalities – probably a minority – will adhere to conservative values and restrict the individual freedom of their citizens. As long as they do not prevent dissidents from migrating to more libertarian municipalities, one might argue that the problem will solve itself in the long run: municipalities will become homogeneous in terms of values – some will be dominated by Christian conservatives, others by libertarian atheists or progressive Buddhists. Some might even decide to abolish democracy and elect a dictator.

Of course, libertarian municipalists might be filled with disgust by this possibility, but would be compelled by their own principles to tolerate it. Actually, it seems rather naïve to assume that all people would opt for libertarian municipal democracy all of the time. Yet to tolerate inequality does undermine the core values of libertarian municipalism – Bookchin was well aware of this basic dilemma. Within the municipality, the dilemma can be dealt with by a majority vote of the assembly – which has the power to distribute and redistribute income, wealth and other assets and values. Inequality between municipalities cannot be reduced by a simple vote, however, given the sovereignty of the municipality. Some may possess scarce resources, others may suffer from famine, drought, or other natural disasters.[4] Obviously, solidarity has its limits, also within a confederacy.

This leads, almost logically, to the third set of questions: how coherent and feasible is the project? How could a municipalised economy work? As Clark has pointed out, Bookchin and Biehl remain quite vague about its organisation and operation (1998: 170–175). Presumably it would be a democratic small-scale command economy – if that is not a contradiction in terms. The municipal assembly decides how much grain, steel or computing equipment should be produced and how much could be exported, and in exchange for what other goods, allocating the remaining products to its citizens. It is not clear how goods will be distributed 'to each according to needs' (Biehl, 1998: 120). Even within a small community socio-economic interests may clash. It seems unlikely that a weekly assembly could iron out all differences, reconcile conflicts and solve all practical problems (see also White, 2008: 175–176). More frequent assemblies would probably be counter-productive in more than one sense: attendance might drop, people may lose interest and productive work might be neglected. So, in order to avoid democratic overload decisions might increasingly be delegated to managers of workshops and other production units, to traders or brokers dealing with trade relations with other municipalities, engineers and other specialists – thus undermining the power of the assembly. Alternatively, decisions could be left to workers' councils running the various workshops – but this might undermine the assembly as well, and would eventually meet with resistance from the libertarian municipalists too (see Biehl, 1998: 161–163).

It will be hard to maintain libertarian municipalism – but even harder to establish it in the first place. At least two formidable barriers will have to be negotiated. Many municipalities are, at present, far too large to allow face-to-face assemblies and would have to be cut up into smaller units. Clark calculated that Paris should be divided into about 340 sections, each containing about

25,000 citizens (1998: 178–179). Assemblies of 25,000 people would be rather cumbersome, though, and would allow people only to listen to a few selected speakers and then vote for or against a proposal, rather than seriously debating different alternatives and amendments. So the chair of a committee should make a selection of the most relevant proposals and amendments – which might invite manipulation. Alternatively, the assembly would have to make a selection itself, which might lead to cyclical voting.

The latter is a fatal weakness of any assembly democracy, in the eyes of public choice theorists such as Riker (1982). Once an assembly considers more than two options, quite likely not one of them may receive the support from a clear majority. Say, option A appeals to 40 per cent, B to 35 per cent and C to 25 per cent; first A will be defeated by a coalition of supporters of B and C; then B will be rejected by advocates of A and C; and finally C will be voted down by supporters of A and B. So deadlock will result (for a succinct and clear analysis of the problem, see Dahl, 1970: 34–54; more elaborate is Riker, 1982: 65–113). This will happen especially when the majority prefers A to B and B to C, but not necessarily A to C. In other words, transitive individual preferences result in an intransitive collective preference. However, even if a compromise would be reached (say, between supporters of B and C), a substantial minority may leave the assembly frustrated and disillusioned. If this happens only once every so often, it may be considered part of the deal – you win some, you lose some. But suppose that supporters of A are all blacks, or Catholics, or farmers; and, worse, they discover that they are often defeated by a similar coalition of whites, Protestants, or city-folk. Democracy might degenerate into the tyranny of a majority, as many philosophers have warned. As a consequence, the minority might boycott the assembly and find other ways to fulfil its vital demands, such as secession or a *coup d'etat*. Theoretically, cyclical voting could also occur in smaller assemblies and in elected legislatures, but it is usually prevented by rules and procedures. As Benjamin Radcliff and Ed Wingenbach argue, participatory institutions tend to encourage sophisticated and value-restricted preference formation, which renders cycles improbable or even impossible (2000: 993). This may be more complicated in very large assemblies, however.

Yet dividing a large city into sovereign smaller political and economic units will create all kinds of political and logistical problems. So, a trade-off between small size and sovereignty seems inevitable: one could imagine cities such as Paris, London or New York governing themselves and municipalising their economies, but not having regular popular assemblies; or one could imagine the citizens of Montmartre, Greenwich or the Lower East Side of Manhattan deliberating in weekly assemblies about the planning of their neighbourhood, but perhaps not regulating the economy to the full or deciding on immigration policies.

The final and most vital obstacle, however, may be the lack of interest and sympathy most people have shown for libertarian municipalism so far. Bookchin and his Institute for Social Ecology have been propagating it for several decades now, but their influence seems to be waning rather than waxing. 'Locked in a series of bitter and ever more unhelpful squabbles with former colleagues and allies, from the mid-1990s onwards Bookchin became an increasingly isolated figure', according to White (2008: 186). In line with this, Clark commented sarcastically: 'this aspiring anarchist Lenin has been left stranded at the Finland Station along with his ideological baggage' (1998: 188). One might blame this on his stubborn personality, growing with age, or on an increasingly hostile, conservative or neo-liberal *zeitgeist*, dominant rightwing media or growing apathy among hedonistic youth. Yet one could also argue that the project, analysis and strategy of the libertarian municipalists have actually been proven wrong by history, insofar as they failed to convince the public – students, readers of the books and papers of Bookchin and Biehl – of the validity of their theories and the attractiveness of their ideal. Though maximising freedom and equality in an abstract sense, libertarian municipalism could be perceived as a basic threat to the freedom of the small businessmen, professionals and farmers who would have to donate their private enterprise, no matter how small, to the municipality. It would also threaten the jobs of many (if not most) employees of the national or federal state. Perhaps even manual workers and engineers in large factories would worry about municipalisation destroying their companies and endangering their jobs.

Bookchin, of course, refused to address all of these specific interests, referring only to universal interests, the survival of the planet and 'individuation', 'the rounded man', self-liberation (1971: 353, 355, 361). In a revolutionary process, people may transcend their particular interests, at least temporarily. Revolutionary moments do occur, even today – in Egypt, Libya and Tunisia in 2011, for example. Liberty and equality also continue to inspire rebels in European cities such as Athens, Barcelona and Madrid. Yet so far no municipalities have declared their independence. Since 1871, few (if any) communes have tried to follow the example of Paris; perhaps the defeat and repression of the Paris Commune has been too gruesome to be ignored (see Castells, 1983: 15–26). One may have to agree with the pessimistic conclusions of Manuel Castells in his fascinating study of urban movements – which he looked at with some obvious sympathy. He wrote that 'they are unable to put forward any historically feasible project of economic production, communication, or government', and therefore 'they are not agents of structural social change, but symptoms of resistance to the social domination even if, in their effort to resist, they do have major effects on cities and societies' (Castells, 1983: 329).

Having digested this cascade of criticisms, the reader might easily be tempted to do away with libertarian municipalism altogether and forever. Yet even a project with some problematic assumptions, some inconsistent and ambiguous goals, and a not very realistic strategy might inspire others, willing to blunt its extreme and sharp edges and apply some of the ideas in a more moderate setting. Indeed, as will be argued below, in the remaining part of this chapter, various forms of assembly democracy have been tried throughout history. Admittedly, few of the polities described here qualify as pure examples of libertarian municipalism as they either restricted individual liberty or enjoyed limited autonomy rather than complete sovereignty. They will be analysed in more or less historical order, starting with the Athenian *polis* of more than 2000 years ago that inspired (among many others) Bookchin. Moving through the Swiss *Landsgemeinden* that date back to the late Middle Ages and the American Town Meetings established in the seventeenth century we will arrive at the *orçamento participativo* (participatory budgeting) introduced in some Brazilian cities in the late twentieth century, but also in European towns such as Hoogeveen in The Netherlands, while making short stops at the anarchistic Spanish village Marinaleda, the Orange Free State in Amsterdam, and a few other experiments.

PRACTICE

The power of the ekklèsia in Athens

Assemblies of all able-bodied men or warriors may have existed in many prehistoric societies, as Jane Mansbridge suggests (1983: 11–13). Yet most societies that entered documented history seem to have been ruled by kings, priests or wealthy landowners of noble birth rather than by popular assemblies. If the latter existed at all, they would probably serve symbolic or ritual functions, like shouting approval or listening to speeches from the rulers. Ancient Greece was no exception, probably until the sixth century BCE (Hornblower, 1993: 2–3). Around 600 BCE this began to change, at least in Athens and a fewer other city-states that had developed in fertile and maritime areas. The legendary Solon, an aristocrat himself, seems to have given more power to the popular assembly (*ekklèsia*, ἐκκλησια) in order to reconcile a dangerous conflict between landowners and heavily indebted peasants (Hornblower, 1993: 3–5). About a hundred years later another aristocrat, Kleisthenes, mobilised the peasants against his rival and turned the assembly into the locus of power in Athens (Hansen, 1991: 27–54; Stockton, 1990: 19–56).

During the fifth century BCE the assembly must have held supreme power. Most experts seem to agree on this, on the basis of the available evidence: inscriptions and other archeological findings, as well as speeches and references in ancient Greek texts that have survived over two millennia (see Hansen, 1991: 4–26, 140, 287; Jones, 1957: 111, 118; Sinclair, 1988: 67, 83–4; Starr, 1990: 29; Thorley, 2004: 32). The assembly passed laws and decrees, declared war and peace – very important in this warlike era – and elected the military leaders (*stratègoi*) as well as other professional public officials such as the city architect or the superintendent of the water supply, while other officials were selected by lot (Hansen, 1984: 95–122; Hansen, 1991: 140; Starr, 1990: 39–48). In fact, the *ekklèsia* was as much an executive as a legislative agent. It passed decrees on matters that would be decided in modern states by senior or even junior civil servants – for example, the design for the door of a new temple of Athena (Starr, 1990: 40). The Athenian state, however, employed hardly any civil servants.

In the fourth century, the legislative power of the assembly seems to have been more restrained, though it still remained substantial. In 402 BCE, a new institution was created: the legislators (*nomothetai*, νομοθέται) – a commission selected (probably also by lot) from the pool of jurors to draft new laws, if required (Hansen, 1991: 161–77). As a consequence, the assembly could no longer pass new laws but only decrees (i.e. decisions on particular cases), according to Mogens Hansen, the Danish expert on ancient Athens. Sinclair, however, qualifies the power of the legislators and argues that the assembly could instruct them to change the law or prevent them from doing so (1988: 84).

Even in the fifth century, the assembly shared power with two other institutions: the Council of 500 (*boulè*, βουλή), and the popular juries that filled the law-courts or *dikastèria* (δικαστήρια). The Council of 500 prepared and subsequently executed the decisions taken by the assembly. Formally, the assembly could only vote on decrees prepared and discussed by the Council, though it could amend them or vote for alternative proposals. The available sources suggest that the Council tended to play a modest, mainly administrative role, rather than trying to manipulate the assembly (Hansen, 1991: 140; Hornblower, 1993: 15; Jones, 1957: 105–108; Sinclair, 1988: 84–105). The *dikastèria*, however, could quash decrees passed by the assembly that were denounced as illegal or invalid by citizens (Hansen, 1991: 178–224; Hornblower, 1993: 13; Jones, 1957: 123). Officials elected by the assembly could be deposed and impeached by the courts (Sinclair, 1988: 146–152). Therefore, Hansen argued, the court might have been as important as the assembly (1991: 178). The courts consisted of citizens, selected by lot, who had sworn a solemn oath – like jurors in Anglo-American courts. However, as Raphael Sealey has pointed out, the latter decide questions of fact and leave the legal decisions to professional judges, which did not exist in ancient Athens. The Athenian *dikastai* simply passed a verdict by voting, after listening to prosecution and defence – again, citizens rather than professional lawyers (Sealey, 1987: 54). At any rate, the bodies of *ekklèsia*, *boulè* and *dikastèria* overlapped. All three can be considered as assemblies of citizens, rather than bodies of elected politicians (Hansen, 1991: 304). The juries consisted usually of 201, 501 or 1001 citizens.

All citizens who met certain basic conditions could take part in the assembly, and be selected (by lot) for Council or jury duty. The conditions were rather strict: full citizenship was reserved only for free adult males born from two Athenian parents. Freed slaves and alien residents (both called *metoikoi*) and women could own property, but could not take part in an assembly, Council of 500 or law court. Slaves did not even own themselves. Though reliable figures cannot be provided, most scholars estimate that slaves and *metoikoi* outnumbered citizens, possibly by 4:1 or even by 8:1 or more (Jones, 1957: 10–17; Sealey, 1987: 7–9; Sinclair, 1988: 9–10; yet cf. Starr, 1990: 33). Between 15,000 and 40,000 Athenians might have qualified for full citizenship in the fifth and fourth centuries BCE.

Not all of them went to the assembly every time. Excavations have shown that the Pnyx, the hill where most assemblies met, could not hold many more than 6,000 people (Hansen, 1984: 24–27). One might expect that casual labourers and peasants could rarely afford the time to attend a meeting that took place about once a week, that might last half a day or more, and that required perhaps a day's travel for citizens living in the rural areas far from the city. However, in the fourth century attendance was rewarded with a modest sum of money, almost a day's wage, which must have fostered the participation of the poorer citizens (Hansen, 1984: 51–53; Jones, 1957: 5).

The assembly meetings were prepared by the Council, and specifically by the standing committee of the month (*prytaneis*), 50 members belonging to one tribe. They would draft the agenda and post it four days before the meeting. However, the assembly could alter the agenda, amend proposals or instruct the Council to elaborate a proposal (Jones, 1957: 111–123). Thus, it seems unlikely that the Council could easily manipulate the assembly. Many proposals of the Council may have been rubber-stamped without debate and vote, but sometimes debates were long and heated. The Council would also provide a chairman for the assembly, selected by lot (Hansen, 1984: 43–44; Starr, 1990: 50–51). An elected secretary would read out the proposals drafted by the Council and record the decisions taken. A herald would then ask who wanted to speak – priority being given to senior citizens, at least in the fifth century (Starr, 1990: 50). A speaker should not address the same issue twice, but was not restricted in the time he used – at least not formally. Informally the audience might enforce restrictions by heckling and shouting at long-winded speakers (Starr, 1990: 51–52). The number of speakers was not limited either – occasionally it may have been over a hundred (Hansen, 1991: 140–144). Votes were usually by show of hands, rarely by ballot (pebbles) (Hansen, 1984: 46–49). So, arguably most conditions for reasonable deliberation must have been met.

Though Athens cultivated equality, informal leaders inevitably emerged. During the fifth century the military leaders (*stratègoi*) – elected by the assembly for one year, but frequently re-elected if successful – seem to have dominated the assembly quite easily. Yet they often did not agree among themselves (Jones, 1957: 124–126). In the fourth century, military and political leadership began to diverge, as both were to some extent professionalised. Well-trained public speakers (*rhètores*) such as Demosthenes may have exercised substantial influence (Hansen, 1991: 266–276); however, their position was never secure. Rivals might rouse the meeting against them, accusing them of unconstitutional behaviour, and have them fined, exiled or even executed. In the fifth century, even very popular leaders such as Themistocles could be ostracised, i.e. forced into exile by a vote of the assembly, when a majority would write the name of the unfortunate leader on a potsherd (*ostraka*) (Starr, 1990: 16, 23). In other words, the people did hold power: they could carry through and enforce decisions against the will of formal or informal leaders, and did so repeatedly (see also Stolz, 1968: 60–66).

An informal political leader could mobilise supporters, who cheered him on and would sometimes advocate proposals drafted by him – thus reducing for him the risk of prosecution for submitting unconstitutional proposals (*graphè paranomôn*). As far as we know, these informal groupings were probably not very stable and did not develop into political parties in the modern sense (Hansen, 1984: 75–89). Formal and informal associations did exist, but served mainly social and religious functions. Some may have articulated local interests, particularly in rural areas far from the city (Jones, 1999: 288–306). Only extreme circumstances such as the defeat in the Peloponnesian War gave birth to a political party, in a sense: the oligarchs who seized power in 411 BCE. and again in 404 BCE. Yet in both cases the oligarchs lost power within a short time.

Democracy survived for about 180 years, from its establishment around 500 BCE until the end of Athenian independence in 322 BCE. Its longevity has surprised and impressed historians and political scientists for centuries since. After all, assembly democracy could easily have degenerated into anarchy and chaos, or tyranny – as Plato had predicted. Law and order had to be maintained by a weak police force – mainly Scythian slaves – and an unruly army that elected its own commanders. As practically all citizens were trained soldiers, civil war could be expected to break out frequently. Yet it did so only twice, in the shadows of military defeat and Spartan interference. Apparently, citizens were able to discipline themselves and accept majority decisions (most of the time), regardless of the consequences for their particular interests. Decisions could be reversed, either by the assembly itself or by the courts, when they were persuaded by the force of better arguments. In a sense, Athens was a democracy where the rule of law applied and checks and balances existed, as Sealey has argued (1987). Moreover, its society and culture reflected egalitarian, democratic values, but also aristocratic values like competition and a strong sense of honour. Wealth was not distributed equally, but the poor were guaranteed a relatively secure existence (Pabst, 2003: 44). Individual freedom was limited, in the eyes of modern liberals, by laws and moral traditions, but much less so than in comparable societies at the time. Even if Plato exaggerated when he wrote that 'every individual is free to do as he likes' and that there is no need to submit to authority in a democracy, he was probably not wide of the mark (1955: 329–330).

However, the assembly democracy required a considerable effort from a great many people. The average citizen might devote two full years of his (usually not very long) life to political deliberation and public administration (Ferguson, [1913] 1967: 15). Of course, this applied only to the minority of the population that enjoyed full citizenship. In a sense it was an elite, relatively privileged and educated, even if most of them were probably not men of leisure but had to work for their living (Jones, 1957: 3–20). The wealth produced by slaves (mining silver in the hills), by the trade and commerce centred in Athens, and the tributes paid by her colonies and allies created a surplus that did allow the citizens some leisure.

Yet in spite of its elitist aspects the Athenian *polis* could be considered an extreme type of democracy, at least in the late fifth century. Most important decisions were taken by the popular assembly, or by assembled jurors. The municipality enjoyed complete sovereignty. Though the economy had not been municipalised the way Bookchin advocated, it was not a capitalist market economy either; private property could be confiscated fairly easily by the city-state. It remains to be seen whether a similar system could survive under different conditions. The Swiss experience might throw some light on this question.

The longevity of the Landsgemeinde in Switzerland

An assembly democracy somewhat different from the Athenian system has survived in two Swiss cantons for more than 500 years. When the German Empire began to decline in the thirteenth century, the Swiss mountain cantons developed into sovereign states, while co-operating with each other in a loose confederacy. The people's assembly, or *Landsgemeinde*, that may previously have performed more limited functions then acquired supreme power in most cantons (Möckli, 1987: 16–24; Carlen, 1976: 5–11). In 1798 it had to cede supremacy to the Helvetian Republic, and subsequently to the Swiss federation, but maintained substantial autonomy (Gerstein, 1969: 9–25). Not only cantonal legislation, but also the application of federal laws and constitutional amendments, still have to be approved by the *Landsgemeinde*, as well as cantonal tax rates and expenditures above a certain amount (Möckli, 1987: 27–30; Stauffacher, 1962: 83–102; Kriesi, 1995: 53–55; Kanton Appenzell Innerrhoden, 2013: 1, 4, 7–8).

However, in the twenty-first century the tradition has survived merely in two cantons: Appenzell Inner Rhoden (strictly speaking a half-canton) and Glarus. Municipal assemblies (*Gemeindeversammlungen*) are more common in Switzerland, but do not have as much power (Gerstein, 1969: 310–314). On the last Sunday of April and the first Sunday of May thousands of citizens still gather on the 'Landsgemeindeplatz' of Appenzell and Glarus (respectively). Extra-ordinary meetings may take place at another date, but this is quite rare.[5] Thus the assembly meetings are much less frequent in the Swiss cantons than they were in the Athenian city-state. As in Athens, foreigners and non-residents (whether Swiss or foreign) are not allowed to participate, but women (if residents) are no longer barred.

The *Landsgemeinde* is the supreme authority in the canton, but it shares power with other institutions: the cantonal court (*Kantonsgericht*), the cantonal parliament (*Landrat* in Glarus, *Grosse Rat* in Appenzell) and the government (*Regierungsrat* in Glarus, *Standeskommission* in Appenzell). The courts seem to be less involved in political decisions than the Athenian *dikastèria*. Its members are elected by the *Landsgemeinde*, rather than selected by lot. The law has been professionalised in Switzerland as in other European countries, even if judges can be laymen (as in Athens). In 2008, for example, the *Landsgemeinde* of Appenzell elected a museum director as president of the cantonal court (König, 2008). The cantonal government and cantonal parliament prepare the meetings of the *Landsgemeinde*, they set the agenda and formulate proposals and bills (Möckli, 1987: 35–37; Stauffacher, 1962: 52–80, 219–264). Moreover, they execute the decisions taken by the assembly.

When citizens initiate a proposal, it will either be taken over (and possibly reformulated) by the cantonal parliament or it will be presented as such but accompanied by an alternative proposal drafted by the parliament (Kanton Appenzell Inner Rhoden, 2013: 3, Article 7bis12). In this respect the cantonal parliament and government, taken together, resemble the Athenian Council of 500, even if both Swiss councils are elected by the people rather than selected by lot. The *Standeskommission* of Appenzell is elected by the *Landsgemeinde*, by a show of hands, the *Grosse Rat* by the six municipalities of the canton (Kanton Appenzell Innerrhoden, 2013: 7–8, Articles 20 and 22; Kanton Appenzell Innerrhoden, 2008).[6] The procedures are somewhat similar in Glarus (Stauffacher, 1962: 52–80). In both cantons the president or *Landammann* is elected by the *Landsgemeinde*. Given the rare frequency of the assembly meetings, the cantonal parliament and government are bound to exercise more influence than the Athenian *boulè*. They take administrative decisions and pass by-laws and ordinances (Möckli, 1987: 27–30; Stauffacher, 1962: 83–165). Expenditures under a certain amount – in 2008: under a million Swiss francs – do not need approval from the *Landsgemeinde* unless this is requested by at least 200 citizens (Kanton Appenzell Innerrhoden, 2013: 4, Article 7ter). The cantonal government is assisted by professional civil servants – about 500 in Glarus – which hardly existed in Athens (Glarner Kantonalbank, 2006: 11). The *Landammann* presides over the *Landsgemeinde* as well as over the government, and is generally considered to be a powerful figure (Möckli, 1987: 32–35).

The *Landammann* and his (or her) government produce most – but certainly not all – proposals for the *Landsgemeinde*. Werner Stauffacher calculated that almost half of the proposals discussed in Glarus from 1887 to 1961 had been drafted by the *Regierungsrat* or *Landrat*, about a quarter by political parties and pressure groups, and the remaining quarter by private citizens (Stauffacher, 1962: 235–64). Even the latter are often reformulated and commented on by the *Landrat*. A negative recommendation from the cantonal parliament reduces the chances of a proposal being approved by the *Landsgemeinde*. However, even proposals that were frowned upon by both government and parliament have occasionally been accepted by the *Landsgemeinde*, and vice versa: proposals endorsed by parliament have been rejected by the assembly. In Glarus a proposal from a citizen to reduce the size of the cantonal parliament (from 80 to 60 seats) won a very narrow majority in 2008, against opposition from the parliament and most political parties, though with support from the government (Kock Marti, 2008). Even more surprising was the defeat of a government proposal concerning education, which was supported by all political parties – and had already been approved by practically all other Swiss cantons – in Appenzell in 2008. The speech of a (self-proclaimed) housewife and mother of six children against the obligation to send four-year-olds to kindergarten may have turned the tide in the assembly (Dörig, 2008). Similar defeats of the government have occurred in the past. The sociologist Peter Stolz relates in some detail how a working-class majority in Glarus imposed its will on rather recalcitrant capitalists and the dominant bourgeois parties in 1864 and 1871–1872, even if only to introduce modest reforms such as a working day of no more than eleven hours instead of twelve or thirteen (1968: 108–132). These reforms were not only decided, but also implemented. This does indicate that the people could carry through decisions against the will of the political elite.

From the perspective of rational government, the somewhat erratic and unpredictable outcome of a popular assembly can be seen as a disadvantage. Already in the nineteenth century, Swiss scholars complained about the 'moods and selfish passions' that could swing the *Landsgemeinde* (Riklin and Möckli, 1983: 53). Demagogues might abuse and manipulate the people. At the same time, this unpredictability may contribute to liveliness and raise participation. The two rather surprising meetings of the *Landsgemeinde* in 2008 were well-attended, according to comments in local newspapers and personal observation by the author. Even so, a lot of citizens did not attend because they had other obligations (work, care for relatives), had lost interest, or were too ill or weak to stand for several hours on a square. It is impossible to send a substitute or vote by proxy at a *Landsgemeinde*. Hence, turnout is often modest: of the 30,000–40,000 (Swiss) inhabitants of Glarus only about 5,000 or 6,000 tend to show up at the *Landsgemeinde* (Stauffacher, 1962: 35–39, 286–298; Gerstein, 1969: 33). In Appenzell turnout may not be much higher than 20 per cent. This is one of the reasons why several cantons have replaced the *Landsgemeinde* by the ballot box (Möckli, 1987: 55). Another important reason for abolishing the tradition is its open and public character: votes are never secret. At the same time, this may be considered an advantage: the vote on the square is preceded by public deliberation, whereas anonymous voters in the polling station do not have to listen to any arguments at all (Stauffacher, 1962: 18–30).

Moreover, in Glarus and Appenzell the *Landsgemeinde* is no despot; it shares power with the cantonal parliament and government and has no judiciary power – restrictions which Bookchin would probably frown upon. There may be subtle pressures for conformity, especially in a rural and almost homogeneously Catholic canton like Appenzell – but it is still a liberal society. Neither the popular assembly nor the government control the economy, as the Swiss seem to prefer a rather liberal market economy to some kind of socialism. This balanced system might prevent power abuse and oligarchisation, as Riklin and Möckli argue (1983: 55–56). And perhaps the most remarkable feat of the *Landsgemeinde* is its longevity and endurance: an institution that still inspires awe and enthusiasm in people after 600 years must have something going for it.

Town Meeting in New England

Assembly democracy may be practiced in city-states and small mountainous states, but it does not appear to be an attractive model for modern countries, which tend to be quite a bit larger than Appenzell or Athens. However, it has been applied to small towns in New England. These town meetings, as they are usually called, have almost equally solid roots in the past as the Swiss *Landsgemeinde* and its municipal counterparts, the *Gemeindeversammlung*. In the seventeenth century they were introduced by British colonists who were used to congregational meetings of their Puritan church and to parish meetings in rural

England (Daniels, 1993: 348; Johnson, 2002: 37–39). In the eighteenth century, town meetings not only discussed and decided local affairs, but also elected representatives and instructed them on how to vote at provincial assemblies (Zuckerman, 1970: 21–23). When towns grew into larger cities, they often discontinued the tradition. Sometimes the towns were divided into precincts, which would elect delegates to a 'limited town meeting' (Burns and Peltason, 1955: 874). In Massachusetts, where they were formalised in 1636, they have largely disappeared. Yet in Vermont they are still alive and kicking, as the case study of Jane Mansbridge and the extensive and thorough research of Frank Bryan show (Mansbridge, 1983: 37–135; Bryan, 2004).

Today, the autonomy of these towns is rather limited – which may explain the declining interest in town meetings (Bryan, 2004: 285). Yet town meetings can still levy taxes, appropriate public funds, construct and maintain roads, schools, parks, libraries and hospitals, pass by-laws and ordinances on public health, safety and morals, and administer poor relief (Zink *et al.*, 1958: 408–409; Gerstein, 1969: 310). They elect the 'selectmen' who carry out the town meeting's decisions, as well as other officials such as constables, road commissioners and school boards (Burns and Peltason, 1955: 874; Bryan, 2004: 233–253).

The selectmen prepare the meeting and set the agenda, published as a 'warning'. The meeting usually begins by electing a moderator who will chair it. Whereas in the seventeenth and eighteenth century access was restricted – at least officially – to 'freemen' or (male) property-owners, it is now open to all residents (Zuckerman, 1970: 190–191). Roughly twenty per cent of them actually show up, Bryan states, depending on the size of the town (2004: 57–81). Turnout tends to be significantly higher in smaller towns, except if they are inhabited mainly by commuters. It is also affected by the weather and by the agenda: 'conflict draws people to town meeting' (Bryan, 2004: 234). Gender, education and socio-economic class seem to be less relevant. Typical working-class towns do not differ from middle-class towns with respect to attendance (Bryan, 2004: 107–136). Only the down-and-out lower class and the upper class tend to stay away. Once they have arrived at the meeting, working-class people are not afraid to speak, whereas they generally tend to participate less in political activities than the middle class. As Bryan suggests, town meetings might help working class people to develop the civic skills they lack in other places (2004: 163–186). To a lesser extent this applies to women as well. Both the attendance and the active participation of women have grown steadily over the last decades. Now they equal men in small towns, but in the larger towns women are still less present, as well as less active than men.

At an average meeting, about one-third of the attendants will speak, usually only for a minute or two (Bryan, 2004: 139–160). Generally, many more people speak at a town meeting than at a Swiss *Landsgemeinde*.[7] Again, size may explain the difference. An average town meeting is attended by 137 people, as calculated by Bryan, which seems less inhibiting than the 3,000 to 5,000 people that often attend a *Landsgemeinde*. However, the New England towns hardly compare to a Greek *polis* in terms of autonomy and sovereignty. They do seem to share a democratic, egalitarian, and liberal culture, though pressure to avoid or cover up conflicts may cause conformism and occasionally fear, as Mansbridge noticed (1983: 59–76).

The 'Orçamento Participativo' in Porto Alegre

The participatory budget (*orçamento participativo*) of Porto Alegre is not exactly a town meeting. Porto Alegre is a coastal and industrial city of about 1.3 million inhabitants in Southern Brazil, and has little in common with the small towns in the mountains of Vermont or Switzerland. It cannot look back on several centuries of democratic experience and institutions. Brazil has often suffered authoritarian rulers: not only the Portuguese colonial regime and the Bragança emperors in the nineteenth century, but also quasi-fascist presidents and military dictators in the twentieth century. Even today, clientelism and patronage may hamper the development of effective (let alone democratic) government (Roett, 1997). Nevertheless, the constitution adopted in 1988, following the collapse of the dictatorship, granted substantial formal autonomy to local government (Nickson, 1995: 119). Municipal or city councils may still be weak, in many cases, but the mayor or prefect (*prefeito*) is elected by the people and can exercise considerable influence (Nickson, 1995: 120–121). He may use his influence to foster clientelism, or alternatively to empower grass-roots organisations.

In Porto Alegre, and several other municipalities, the mayors mainly seem to have followed the latter option. This chimes with the ideology of the Workers' Party (*Partido do Trabalhadores*, PT) to which they belong (Bruce, 2004a; Pont, 2004). From 1988 to 2005 Porto Alegre was governed by this party and its allies (Sintomer, *et al.*, 2012: 4–6; see also Porto Alegre, 2012). Yet the participatory budget was to some extent also an improvised reaction to peculiar circumstances. When elected, the PT government in Porto Alegre inherited a dire financial situation from its predecessor, while it was pressed by local community movements to invest in basic infrastructure, and so Olivio Dutra, the new mayor, decided to open up the budget to public scrutiny (Bruce, 2004b: 40). Gradually, public involvement increased, as did revenues (the two trends may have reinforced each other). The experiment was taken up by other Brazilian cities, and even by a state (Rio Grande do Sul) after Olivio Dutra had won the governorship in 1998 (De Souza, 2004). It was sufficiently institutionalised to survive the electoral defeat of the PT in Porto Alegre (Sintomer, *et al.*, 2012: 5; Porto Alegre, 2012).

In recent years, the participatory budget process has become fairly complicated. One could distinguish five stages (Passos Cordeiro, 2004; see also Baiocchi, 2001: 45–49 and Porto Alegre, 2008). During the first stage, in March and April of each year, informal preparatory meetings are held, often at the level of a neighbourhood, to discuss last year's achievements and goals for the future. During the second stage, in April and May, open public assemblies are convened in each of the city's sixteen districts (*Assembléias Regionais*), as well as six city-wide thematic assemblies (*Assembléias Temáticas*), dealing with transport; health and social services; economic development and taxation; culture; urban development; education, sports and leisure. The attending citizens vote for priorities for next year's budget (from a list of fourteen headings: water supply, paving, education, etc.), which will be elaborated at thematic and regional forums consisting of delegates elected by neighbourhoods and thematic assemblies. The district and thematic assemblies in April or May also elect the members of the Participatory Budget Council (*Conselho do Orçamento Participativo*) – two for each district and two for each thematic area. The council, which also includes one delegate from the Union of Neighbourhood Associations and one from the Municipal Workers' Trade Union, is sworn in at a massive but mainly ceremonial municipal meeting in July – the third stage of the process. In the fourth stage, in August and September, the council discusses and finalises the budget proposal, which is drafted by city hall and may be amended by the thematic and regional forums. Finally, the city council has to approve the budget, but this seems mostly to be a formality (Passos Cordeiro, 2004: 68–73).

In a strict sense, assembly democracy functions only at the second stage, when all citizens may attend assemblies which elect delegates and vote on a list of budget priorities in their district or thematic area. All other decisions are taken by delegates of some sort. They may be delegates with revocable mandates, but they are delegates nevertheless (Passos Cordeiro, 2004: 64). The open assemblies attract growing numbers of participants: in 1990 hardly 1,000 across the city, by 2,000 more than 15,000 and a few years later probably about 30,000 (Passos Cordeiro, 2004: 65; Bruce, 2004b: 45). These are impressive numbers, but they should be put into context: in a city of 1.3 million people, no more than 2 per cent of the population will attend this kind of meeting.

Research by the American sociologist Gianpaolo Baiocchi suggests, however, that participants at the assemblies, and to a lesser extent even the elected delegates and councillors, are representative of the total population in terms of education level, gender, income level and race (2001: 49–52). The collective learning process and possibly the more urgent needs of lower income groups – often living in slums without sewage or paved roads – must have compensated for their lack of education and political experience (Baiocchi, 2001: 53–61; see also Abers, 2003). As in Vermont town meetings, the participatory budget process in Porto Alegre might help working class people to develop the civic skills they lacked before.

After the former mayor of Porto Alegre had won the gubernatorial election in Rio Grande do Sul in 1998, he introduced the participatory budget in this state of about ten million inhabitants. In open regional and municipal assemblies the citizens could vote on priorities for public works and services at the level of the state (De Souza, 2004: 102–103). Based on these priorities, a budget is drawn up by a Council of the Participatory Budget, elected by delegates who are in turn elected by the municipal assemblies. Some members of the PT argue that the same principle could (and should) be applied at the federal level, but so far this has not been tried.

The idea has travelled widely in recent years, first of all in Latin America (for a survey see Sintomer, *et al.*, 2012). Porto Alegre inspired cantonal assemblies in Ecuador and Bolivia, analysed in depth by Donna Lee Van Cott (2008: 142). In Venezuela communal councils (*consejos comunales*) have been in operation since 2005, in which all members of the community (consisting of at most 400 families) aged fifteen years or older can participate (Motta, 2011: 36–37). Since 2000 around 200 cities in Europe, about 100 in Asia and more than 500 in Latin America have tried some form of participatory budgeting, even if often considerably diluted (Sintomer *et al.*, 2012: 3; see also Talpin, 2012: 185–187). Often they involve only a fraction of the municipal budget.

An example of a watered down version may be 'the forges of Hoogeveen' (*smederijen van* Hoogeveen), introduced in 2007 (Hoogeveen, 2008). Hoogeveen is a municipality in the North-East of the Netherlands, with about 54,000 inhabitants, divided into 25 more or less urban areas and 10 villages or rural areas. Local 'initiative groups' could take stock of the ideas and needs of the inhabitants. Together with their area director (*gebiedsregisseur*), an agent of the municipal government, the initiative group could organise an open public meeting where the inhabitants of the area discuss and vote on the various projects proposed by the initiative group and other local groups. The project that won approval in the meeting – in fact an assembly – was subsidised by the municipal government as well as the housing corporations. Turnout at the meetings varied from 300 to 600 – roughly a quarter of the inhabitants.[8] The area director co-operated with housing corporations, welfare agencies and the local police. In 2008 eighteen areas voted on projects that were awarded (collectively) about €750,000 – less than 1 per cent of all municipal expenditure (Buddingh', 2008). The other areas were also mobilised in subsequent years by initiative groups and area directors, but the total budget did not increase. The municipal council had to formalise the projects. The municipal budget as such is not a subject of deliberation in the area assemblies, however. It is still a long way from Hoogeveen to Athens.

Assembly democracy in political movements

Assembly democracy has not only been practiced by governments, but also by political movements that opposed (or ignored) the government at the local or national level. Particular movements with anarchist or libertarian-socialist sympathies often tried to anticipate their ideal in their own organisation ('privileging prefigurative methods', in the terms of Franks (2012: 216); see also Zúquete, 2011: 10). Reliable data are scarce, however, given the often subversive, informal and incompletely institutionalised character of most of these movements. Here, a few examples will be discussed very briefly.

In the 1970s an anarchistic movement developed in the Netherlands, called the Gnome (or Elf) Movement (*Kabouterbeweging*). The *Kabouters* tried to build an alternative anti-authoritarian state in Amsterdam and other cities from below, while boycotting or ignoring the existing institutions of the municipal and national government (De Jong, 1972: 206–208). In their 'Orange Free State' People's Departments would co-ordinate the many counter-cultural activities and 'alternative projects' that sprang up in the city, like health food and clothing co-operatives, squatting in empty houses, drug counselling, and meals for old-age people (Tasman, 1996: 216–289). Decisions would be taken by the people's assembly (*volksvergadering*), which took place every Thursday evening in different locations in Amsterdam. Anybody could attend, speak and vote. Attendance increased steadily from 150 to 500 between February and June 1970, but declined after that. The last assembly took place in March 1971 (Tasman, 1996: 83–84). Internal conflicts between anarchist hard-liners and reformists may have contributed to the declining turnout, directly as well as indirectly, by spoiling the ambience at the meetings and by diverting attention from the more constructive projects which had initially mobilised a lot of support for the movement (Tasman, 1996: 298, 308, 362–363). Even though the *Kabouters* had won five seats in the municipal council of Amsterdam (and seven more in other municipalities), they failed to control a 'real' government – unlike the anarchists in Marinaleda.

In the South of Spain, the small municipality of Marinaleda introduced a proletarian town meeting in 1979. No doubt it was inspired by anarchist traditions that originated in the nineteenth century and flourished during the Spanish civil war (Adolf, 2007; see also Leval, 1974). All important decisions are taken by the general assembly (*asamblea general*), which is convened 25 to 30 times a year (Marinaleda, 2007). According to the municipal government, the meetings are usually attended by 400–600 residents, out of a population of about 2,700 (Hamilton, 2010). Critics claim, however, that the mayor and his political movement, linked to a local trade union and an agricultural co-operative, control the town in an almost totalitarian manner (Adolf, 2007). Nonetheless, the movement, which is affiliated with the party *Izquierda Unida* (United Left), has continued to win absolute majorities at the municipal elections.[9]

In the South of Mexico, Zapatistas started a guerilla movement in 1994, though with minimal violence (Davies, 2007; Khasnabish, 2010: 1–61). In the roughly one thousand villages they now claim to control, decisions are taken by a community assembly where all inhabitants older than twelve or fifteen are supposed to participate and to strive for consensus (Khasnabish, 2010: 62–95; Starr, *et al.*, 2011: 104–105). According to Alex Khasnabish, a rather sympathetic observer, this 'assembly-based form of direct democracy would become one of the hallmarks of Zapatismo' (2010: 68). The communal assemblies elect representatives to municipal and regional assemblies.

The Global Justice Movement emerged in the late 1980s in protest against neo-liberal capitalist globalisation as promoted by the World Trade Organisation, the World Bank and the International Monetary Fund. It has been described as a 'movement of movements', as it consisted of a rather loose network of national and local organisations. Since 2001 members have met at the annual World Social Forum. The German sociologist Dieter Rucht and his team observed meetings of local movements in six countries in order to find out how decisions were taken. In accordance with the ideology of the movement, majority votes were rare, while most decisions resulted from tacit or explicit agreement after considerable deliberation (Rucht, 2012: 121–128). In a few cases, however, bargaining, pressure or 'agitatory persuasion' replaced deliberation (Rucht, 2012: 126).

In 2011 diffuse protest movements calling for more democracy emerged in cities such as Kairo and Tunis – 'the Arab Spring' – but later also in Athens, Barcelona, Madrid, New York, and all over the world: *aganaktismenoi, indignados* and 'Occupy Wall Street' (Van Versendaal, 2011; OccupyWallStreet, 2012). In Egypt and Tunisia the protest was directed primarily against the authoritarian state; in Greece, Spain and the US, more against the banks and multinational corporations, the financial crisis and growing unemployment. The movement would occupy a central square, often for days and weeks, articulating demands, discussing proposals, making music and sharing food. Decisions would be taken by the people assembled, preferably by consensus after discussing various options (OccupyWallStreet, 2012). Some disintegrated and disappeared when the square was evicted by the police or the military, others continued in a more fragmented form. The impact of the movements varied. In Egypt and Tunisia they triggered a shift from a more or less autocratic regime into a more pluralistic (though also a little chaotic) mixed regime, one might argue, whereas they did not achieve any visible change in Europe and the US – at least not by 2011 or 2012. It is too early, however, to reach any firm conclusions here.

The only conclusion we can safely draw is that assembly democracy was and still is on the agenda of several political movements across the world.

EVALUATION

At the end of this chapter, it is time to evaluate assembly democracy in terms of the criteria listed in Chapter 1. Is Neathena more than a utopian dream (or nightmare), as elitists would argue? Is it a feasible and sustainable project? And would it be a desirable state to live in for (classical) democrats? The answer could be summed up in 'Yes, but ...'

Yes, assembly democracy has been proven to be possible, no matter what Riker and other public choice theorists may say. It worked for 180 years in ancient Athens, and for more than 500 years in Appenzell and Glarus; it has worked in Vermont and Porto Alegre, in Hoogeveen and Marinaleda and probably in many other communities, too. And the evidence suggests it has worked fairly well.

Participation in assemblies has been massive, even if limited. No wonder, as it requires a physical presence that may be difficult or even impossible for citizens who are disabled, deaf or seriously ill, who suffer from agoraphobia, or who live in remote places, or who have to work even on holidays, like policemen, doctors and nurses. And even citizens who are able to attend the assembly may feel participation will cost too much time and energy. Evidence suggests that attendance at assemblies in Appenzell and Glarus, as well as at most town meetings in Vermont and possibly also in ancient Athens, has always been limited to roughly twenty per cent of the citizenry. However, it need not be the same twenty per cent all the time. As Albert Hirschman has argued, public involvement may be a substantive goal for large numbers of people for a limited period; then 'the pleasure segment penetrates the cost segment' and transaction costs become transaction benefits (1982: 88, 80). After a while most of them shift back to private concerns, however – which may explain why attendance at assemblies remains modest on average. Yet in spite of the limited access, assembly democracy offers a citizen more opportunities to take part in political processes and to exercise influence than any other regime we know. It has mobilised day labourers in Athens, industrial workers in Glarus and Vermont and unemployed men and women in Porto Alegre: categories that are rarely actively engaged in parliamentary politics. Political participation tends to be limited in any society, apart from totalitarian states where abstention is punished directly or indirectly. The number of citizens attending an assembly may be modest, but they are representative of different social categories, classes and sexes, as has been observed in town meetings and in the participatory budget meetings in Porto Alegre. As Bryan remarked, only the very well-to-do and the down-and-out underclass stay away systematically from town meetings.

The assemblies have not only elected and recalled public officials, they have also deliberated and decided on policies, declared war or peace, approved of budgets and passed decrees and laws. The quality of assembly decisions seems to have been quite reasonable, according to our historical sources. It has been restricted, however, by the time limits of the meeting – which rarely lasted more than half a day – and the number of participants. Manipulation by officials and logocrats – eloquent and well-trained speakers – has no doubt occurred, but on several occasions an assembly has voted against the advice of respected leaders and informal elites. Cyclical voting and deadlock have been observed very rarely in practice, and for good reasons (see Kurrild-Klitgaard, 2001). As Radcliff and Wingenbach argue, participatory institutions tend to encourage sophisticated and value-restricted preference formation, which renders cycles improbable or even impossible (2000: 993). Moreover, organisational structures might have eliminated or at least confined cycles – as happens in parliaments and parliamentary committees as well (Radcliff and Wingenbach, 2000: 986). Legislation is often prepared by an executive committee, a council, or legislators like the Athenian *nomothetai* – though today they would be slightly more professional. Even so, these bodies would be accountable to the assembly. Bills could also be proposed by private citizens, but even then they would be redrafted – as in Glarus and Appenzell, where all proposals are (re)drafted by the cantonal parliament. Decisions taken by an assembly have usually been implemented, as far as we know.

Inclusiveness in assembly democracies has varied considerably. In Athens it was limited to free adult males born from Athenian parents – a relatively small minority of the population. In Appenzell and Glarus it was much wider, but women were included only in recent times. In Porto Alegre hardly anyone seems excluded. Generally one could expect that assembly democracy might discourage participation by outsiders such as recent immigrants and visible minorities, if not formally then informally: if they feel at ease at all in the crowd, they might not speak much because they are not yet familiar with the language (or the dialect) and the local political issues and facts.[10]

Participation in assemblies also seems to have positive side-effects in terms of democratic values. It probably contributes to a stronger sense of efficacy and self-confidence among citizens. Because of the small scale of the polity, the consequences of political decisions become almost immediately visible, which may give participants a sense of responsibility. Participation in face-to-face meetings may also enhance mutual trust, a sense of belonging, and loyalty to the system. This has already been suggested by the mass surveys held by Gabriel Almond and Sidney Verba in 1958–1960 in five Western countries (Almond and Verba, 1963: 253–257), and has been confirmed more recently by observations and interviews in Ecuador and Bolivia by Donna Lee Van Cott (2008: 223).[11] Historically, the fear of liberals that assembly democracy leads to tyranny of the majority seems exaggerated, if not ill-founded. In the examples studied here, freedom of speech and freedom of organisation flourished, at least as much as in rival regimes under comparable economic and cultural circumstances.

Therefore, assembly democracy seems a feasible and desirable project, one might conclude. Yet, inevitably, there is a 'but'. The most successful and sustainable experiences we have looked at were far from pure. Even in Athens the power of the assembly was restrained, first by the *dikastèria*, and later also by the *nomothetai*. The *Landsgemeinde* had to share power with the cantonal parliament, the government and the court, too. The power of New England town meetings and the *assembléias* in Porto Alegre is even more limited. In the eyes of classical democrats, they are really mixed regimes, though with a few stronger democratic elements than in other countries. Anarchists and other democratic extremists such as Bookchin would object to their elitism. However, Bookchin's libertarian municipalism does not seem a very convincing model, given its theoretical weaknesses, as well as practical experiences in Athens and other historical examples. Even an assembly democracy seems unable to survive for any length of time without some kind of informal elite, whether it is in ancient Greece or in the Swiss mountains.

Libertarian municipalism requires a universe of politically and economically independent small states, which seems an unrealistic condition in a modern world with mega-cities and a globalised economy. Even large countries, let alone small ones, depend on export markets, foreign investment, migrant labour or mass tourism from abroad. It might not even work in the few remaining states with populations below 150,000 – presumably the size of classical Athens – that have survived until now. Most of them are island states, such as Antigua and Barbuda, Grenada, the Marshall Islands, Micronesia, or the Seychelles; or mountain states such as Andorra, Liechtenstein, San Marino and, in a way, also Monaco.[12] The latter have maintained their independence for several centuries, usually benefitting from a balance of power between large and powerful neighbour states. The former have acquired or regained independence from colonial powers in the twentieth century. In either case, the small state often enjoyed some kind of protection from large and powerful allies. Antigua and Barbuda,

St. Kitts and Nevits and Tuvalu maintain close ties with Britain, Palau and the Marshall Islands receive protection from the United States, Nauru from Australia, Monaco from France, and San Marino from Italy (The World Guide, 2007: 80, 460, 542, 417, 355, 387, 370, 465). Dominica, Grenada, St Lucia and St Vincent set up a confederation with a central bank in 1990 (The World Guide, 2007: 201). The small states could delegate powers in the realm of defence, trade and currency to a confederal agent who might escape from their control. As far as I know none of the small states has developed a direct assembly democracy.

Autarchy may not be a necessary condition for assembly democracy, but some measure of local independence or sovereignty may be a necessary condition for assemblies to function. New England town meetings decline when towns lose control over their affairs (Bryan, 2004: 285). We may not (yet) be able to define a minimum amount of independence required for a meaningful assembly democracy, but we can safely conclude that there is a correlation between local independence and effective assembly democracy.

Even if large states would be willing to be carved up into small independent units, or at least to decentralise power in a radical way, their citizens might not opt for assembly democracy but prefer to leave decision-making in the hands of professional politicians, parliamentarians, mayors and governors. And even if they chose to try assembly democracy, they might change their minds after a while. Factionalism or massive manipulation by pressure groups might destroy mutual trust and lead to a longing for authoritarian leadership or rule by a technocratic elite. Several Swiss cantons have replaced their *Landsgemeinde* with a parliamentary system, while town meetings have been abolished in Massachusetts, Connecticut and Rhode Island (Möckli, 1987: 50–55; Bryan, 2004: 31–32).

So, Bookchin's ambition to present libertarian municipalism as a universal model seems exaggerated, to say the least. His democratic extremism may appeal only to minorities, and only under certain conditions. Yet assembly democracy might be a desirable and feasible goal for classical democrats who accept a mixed regime.

Notes

1 Godwin, who like most of his contemporaries did not use the term 'anarchism', still used 'anarchy' in a negative sense (e.g. [1798] 1971: 262–267); it was the French printer and self-taught philosopher Pierre-Joseph Proudhon (1809–1865) who referred to himself with pride as an anarchist (Woodcock, 1962: 9–10 and 98–133; see also Gurvitch, 1965: 1–14).
2 Dahl's Anarchist rejects any coercion, presumably including that of an autonomous local community or workers' collective; the only historical example he gives are Inuit communities in arctic Canada, where social bonds and sanctions (usually) prevented coercion and violence (1989: 46). By narrowing anarchism in this way, Dahl can plausibly conclude it is irrelevant to modern societies.
3 Yet the Latin *municipium* enjoyed only limited autonomy as administrative unit within the Roman state; the word is probably derived from *municeps*, meaning one

who undertakes obligations (like military service or payment of taxes) to the Roman republic (Bispham, 2007: 11, 16).
4 Bookchin's followers might argue that the abundance of wealth in 'post-scarcity' society will solve all these problems; but this optimism seems naive, given the limited quantity of most material resources, as well as their unequal distribution in the world. As Marshall points out, the present (relative) material abundance of the USA has been achieved at the expense of other parts of the world (1992: 620).
5 In 2007 an extra-ordinary *Landsgemeinde* was held in Glarus to discuss municipal reforms.
6 Five municipalities elect their representatives in an open assembly; the sixth one does so at the polls.
7 Personal observation: in 2008 seven people spoke at the *Landsgemeinde* in Appenzell (apart from the retired and elected president) and almost 30 in Glarus.
8 Interview with area director Jan Bouwmeester, project manager Gea Lunsing, and alderman Klaas Smid, 30 May 2011, at Hoogeveen; see also Hofmans and Kalk, 2007: 29–56.
9 In 2011 it won 73 per cent and nine out of eleven seats, whereas the Socialist Party obtained the other two seats with 21 per cent of the vote and the conservative People's Party received 4 per cent and no seats; about 12 per cent of the population abstained or delivered an invalid ballot, which does not suggest a strong passive protest; so one must assume the mayor and his *Colectivo de Unidad de los Trabajadores/Bloque Andaluz de Izquierdas* (Workers Unity Collective/Andalusian Left Bloc) has not lost the support of the majority of the people (results from *El Pais* online: http://resultados.elpais.com/elecciones/2011/municipales/01/41/61.html, accessed 27 August 2011).
10 Personal observation: even foreigners with a fairly good knowledge of German may fail to understand the regional dialect of Glarus and Appenzell (especially the latter, in my experience).
11 My interviews in Appenzell Innerrhoden and Glarus in 2008 confirmed this, but were very limited in number and intensity.
12 Around 2004, Antigua and Barbuda had an estimated population of 85,514; Domenica 80,389; Grenada 105,391; the Marshall Islands 66,223; Micronesia 112,000; Nauru 14,028; Palau 20,174; the Seychelles 82,087; St. Kitts and Nevis 43,654; Tonga 103,000; Tuvalu 10,530; Andorra 67,450; Liechtenstein 35,125; San Marino 28,562; and Monaco 36,070 (*The World Guide 11th Edition*, Oxford: New International Publications, 2007).

4 Jacobinland
Bounded-delegate democracy

'Hi Dan.'

'Hi Roy. Glad that you're back. Why did you slam the door and throw your papers on the floor? Was the meeting that bad?'

'Yes, disgusting. What a waste of time!'

'Poor Roy. Let me pour you a whisky. Were your voters nasty to you?'

'Thanks Dan. Well, some were nasty. Others were just stupid, asking the same kind of questions. Why did I vote for amending the new health care law? Why did I not support Jim Warton's private bill? Stuff like that. Obviously they don't follow my blog or my weekly letters. I've explained everything dozens of times!'

'Sure. But perhaps some old people don't use the Internet?'

'Maybe some ninety-year olds, sure. But a couple of fifty-year-old women kept nagging me about the tax reform bill and health care insurance and so on.'

'And did your answers satisfy them?'

'No! The bitches said they want to recall me. They're going to circulate a petition. They feel that I am responsible for the tax hike. Well, good luck to them! You know, I wouldn't mind any more if they succeeded. I am beginning to hate this People's Delegate's job.'

'Are you serious? Last year you were really happy to get elected! Shaping the future, making a better world.'

'Please, Dan, cut the bullshit! Okay, I was naïve. I did not realise Delegates don't have any power any more; we are just secretaries writing the legislation that the voters dictate to us. And it is getting worse! Last year we had fifty referendums, this year we have already had forty and we are only halfway! We should really raise the threshold, you know. It is insane! We are working our asses off to work out the health care law that was passed by referendum two weeks ago, and already we have the results of the referendum on youth detention on our desk and people keep harassing us about that.'

'But couldn't you delegate that kind of work to your civil servants? You must have lawyers who can do all that?'

'Not really, Dan. It is not just legal technicalities we are working on. We have to take decisions about which services are covered by health insurance and which aren't. If we cover abortion in certain cases, or alternative cancer treatment, or diets for obese heart patients and so on. And remember the Industrial Democracy Act that I amended? Those are political decisions!'

'Sure, I remember. When you visited that pulp and paper mill up North, the workers cheered and applauded you because of that Industrial Democracy amendment, they were really happy. Thanks to you they could attend meetings of the factory council and follow courses and so on. So you are a bit more than a secretary working out what the voters dictated!'

'Shit, Dan, don't catch me with my own words.'

'Sorry, Roy – but at least it makes you smile.'

'Fair enough. Is dinner ready?'

Jacobinland has never existed, though it may remind some readers of Switzerland (and others of California, perhaps). The name is inspired by the Jacobins, who played a leading role in the French Revolution and spread their ideas to other parts of Europe in the 1790s. They realised that France was too big for an assembly democracy and that the people had to elect delegates to make the decisions they could not take themselves. Yet they were concerned that the delegates would develop into a new aristocracy that would ignore the needs and demands of the people. To prevent this, they discussed several options: binding mandates, a popular veto or referendum, and recall of disobedient delegates. The French constitution that was approved in 1793 not only granted practically all adult male citizens the right to attend primary assemblies to elect deputies (indirectly) to a national parliament, but also gave them the power to veto or initiate legislation.

Due to the civil war, the constitution of 1793 was never implemented, and the Jacobins soon betrayed their democratic ideals in a bloody terror against all opposition, including dissidents in their own ranks. By the end of the decade, power was concentrated in the hands of one man – a former Jacobin named Napoleon Bonaparte. Yet Jacobin ideals survived Napoleon's Empire as well as the restoration of the monarchy in 1813. They inspired not only French and Swiss Radicals in the nineteenth century, but also – indirectly, via the Paris Commune – Socialists and Communists of the twentieth century. Between 1917 and 1919 Jacobin principles were applied, in a new garb, to the revolutionary workers' councils that tried to capture power in Russia, Germany and Hungary. The workers could give a binding mandate to their delegate and recall him if he failed to follow their instructions. The council-democracy did not last very long, but theorists such as Anton Pannekoek and Otto Rühle continued to develop the theory of 'council-communism' or council-democracy, and may have inspired New Left movements in Western Europe and Latin America.

Today, Jacobinism and council-communism are no longer in fashion, yet the ambition to 'bind delegates' through imperative mandates, referendums and recall has not died. On the contrary, one could argue that it is becoming stronger again, in various movements and parties that are loosely classified as 'populist'. The bounded-delegate model has been advocated under very different historical circumstances, in different institutional contexts. It has not been theorised by one man, like Bookchin's libertarian municipalism, but its ideas have evolved out of political practice and have inspired other practices in turn (a dialectical process, Marxists would say). Therefore this chapter cannot be neatly divided into a theoretical and a practical section, as was the preceding one. Theories and practices are presented in their historical context, in (roughly) chronological order: first Rousseau, the Jacobins and other French revolutionaries; then the Paris Commune, Marx, Lenin and Pannekoek, and the New Left. At the end a short trip to Venezuela, Switzerland and California will illustrate how elements of a bounded-delegate model could function in the contemporary world. If American readers feel that their country, with its long and venerable tradition of democratic radicalism and populism, is treated in a cavalier way, they are right –but they might feel compensated by the fact that both Chapter 3 and Chapter 5 deal extensively with American theorists and practices.

THEORY

Jacobins and sans-culottes: disciples of Rousseau?

When the French king Louis XVI convened the three estates of his kingdom – clergy, nobility and commoners – at Versailles in May 1789, the delegates of the third estate from Brittany began to meet regularly in a local café (Maintenant, 1984: 9–10). It was soon called the *Club Breton*, even though delegates from other provinces were welcome to join. Under pressure from the third estate, the Estates General merged into one National Assembly. When the revolutionary masses forced the king to move from Versailles to Paris, the Assembly followed him, as did the *Club Breton*. It pursued its meetings in the library of the monastery of the Jacobins or Dominicans at the Rue St Honoré, not far from the royal palace. Its official name was now *Société des Amis de la Constitution* (Society of Friends of the Constitution). Its main goals were to contribute to a new constitution, to discuss other issues to be decided in the National Assembly and to maintain contact with like-minded clubs elsewhere in the country (Maintenant, 1984: 13). It opened its doors not only to members of the National Assembly but also to other citizens, provided they were good patriots and loved freedom and equality (Maintenant, 1984: 14). Their nickname became 'Jacobins' – initially against their will, but in 1792 they incorporated this into the new name of the club: '*Société des Amis de la Liberté et de l'Égalité, séante aux ci-devant Jacobins Saint-Honoré à Paris*' (Society of Friends of Liberty and Equality, residing at the former Jacobins St Honoré in Paris) (Maintenant, 1984: 59–60).

The new name may have reflected the growing self-confidence and political power of the Jacobins. Until 1792 their influence in the Assembly had been modest. When a group of constitutional monarchists left the Jacobins and founded the club of the Feuillants, most Jacobins in the Assembly joined the new club. The number of Jacobin assemblymen increased after new elections in August 1791, but they remained a fairly weak minority (Maintenant, 1984: 39; Higonnet, 1998: 32). However, in the summer of 1792 the Assembly was dissolved again and replaced by a National Convention, elected by universal suffrage, wherein the Jacobins obtained a clear majority. The primary purpose of the Convention was to produce a new constitution.

Conditions changed dramatically in 1792. The royal palace had been stormed by a revolutionary mob, the king had been deposed and arrested, the Feuillant club closed and several royalists had been imprisoned or executed. War had broken out with Austria and would be aggravated by a civil war (or rather a series of civil wars) in several parts of France. In order to save the revolution and its achievements, the Jacobins took more and more authoritarian measures, renouncing their liberal principles. By late 1793 'authoritarian universalism crowded out liberal-minded individualism', in the words of the historian Patrice Higonnet (1998: 16). The revolutionary women's movement was broken, while nationalism prevailed over internationalism, terrorist intolerance over political liberty, the use of the French language over dialects. The Convention adopted a highly democratic constitution in June 1793, but immediately suspended it because of the war. Diversity was no longer tolerated, either inside or outside the Jacobin club. Factions were regarded as 'traitors' that should be eliminated.

After the royalists had been dealt with, the republicans started quarrelling among themselves. Some Jacobins wanted to restore order, while others tolerated or even supported the disorderly behaviour of the *sans-culottes* – people wearing long trousers because they were too poor to buy the silk stockings and knee-breeches (*culottes*) worn by noblemen and the wealthy bourgeois (Palmer, 1964: 31; Soboul, 1968: 22). The former Jacobins were called *Girondins*, as many came from the Gironde valley in the South-West of France, or *brissotins*, after their leader Jacques Pierre Brissot de Warville, a journalist and a 'pure and natural radical', in the words of Palmer (1964: 50; 1959: 261–262; see also Maintenant, 1984: 45–46). The latter Jacobins were led by the lawyer Maximilien Robespierre (1758–1794), but were usually named *Montagnards* rather than 'robespierristes', because their representatives occupied the 'Mountain', i.e. upper aisles in the Assembly and the Convention (Rudé, 1975: 32). Their differences concerned strategy rather than ideology. Even so, the disagreement led to the expulsion of the Girondins from the Jacobin club and subsequently (in many cases) to their arrest and execution. By 1794, the once quite tolerant and heterogeneous Jacobin club had turned into an almost monolithic machine (Higonnet, 1998: 35–60). The 'mother society' in Paris controlled (by force, if necessary) more than 1,200 local clubs all over the country (Higonnet, 1998: 49). With the help of the guillotine, Robespierre and his political friends ruled France as a single-party state, through the Committee for Public Safety (*Comité de salut public*), the Committee of General Security and the revolutionary tribunals.

The Montagnard Jacobins did not completely control the Convention, however. Even after the elimination of the Girondins, many members lent support to Robespierre somewhat reluctantly – out of personal fear, concern about disunity in a time of war, or for other pragmatic or opportunistic reasons. In July 1794 ('Thermidor' in the revolutionary calendar) an anti-Robespierre coalition was forged in secret, which even included a few Jacobins. When Robespierre realised he had lost the support of the Convention, he abandoned the podium and refused to fight – whether he committed suicide or was killed or lynched is not quite clear (Higonnet, 1998: 59–60; cf. Maintenant, 1984: 116–117; Rudé, 1975: 52; Bouloiseau and Soboul, 1967: 588, 596, 602).

Five months later, in November 1794, the Jacobin club in Paris was closed down, and in 1795 the other clubs suffered the same fate. Some of the conspirators against Robespierre may have hoped to restore democracy without terror, but they lost out against more conservative forces. Famine and apathy had destroyed the revolutionary fervour of the *sans-culottes*, nostalgia for the monarchy spread among some of the poor, whereas the middle-classes longed for law and order. A rather elitist body, the Directory, tried – fairly successfully – to restore law and order rather than freedom and equality, even if it at least paid lip service to the revolutionary ideals. In 1799 a military coup ushered in an even more authoritarian regime. Ironically, its leader, General Napoléon Bonaparte, had also been an active member of a Jacobin club (Higonnet, 1998: 68). Jacobinism did not disappear entirely, however, even under the Empire of Bonaparte and the subsequent restoration of the Bourbon monarchy in 1813 (Maintenant, 1984: 124–125; Furet, 1988): more about that later.

It may not be easy to define the core of Jacobinism, as the Jacobins expressed different ideas at different times. Moreover, they often did not practice what they preached. The following summary does not pretend to give a complete picture, only a rough sketch. It is based mainly on the work of Higonnet. As children of the Enlightenment, Jacobins tended towards an optimistic and moralistic view of human nature. Man deserved to be free, to enjoy basic rights and to fulfil his duties towards his brothers (*fraternité*) and his country (*la patrie*). With regard to women, the Jacobins seemed more ambiguous. A few, such as Condorcet, and of course Jacobin women such as Olympe de Gouges and Etta Palm (a Dutch widow residing in Paris), argued for equal rights for both sexes, but failed to persuade the majority of the club (Higonnet, 1998: 91–96). In their most radical moments, however, Jacobins were less complacent and wanted to 'reconstitute human nature' (Higonnet, 1998: 137, quoting Henri-Baptiste Grégoire, a former priest). They were individualists and, in a sense, liberal. They defended private property and economic freedom, while opposing guilds and corporations but also criticising banks and the concentration of wealth (Higonnet, 1998: 82–87). Their ideal was a harmonious society of small-holders. No wonder, Marxist historians have pointed out: most Jacobins were petty-bourgeois or middle-class merchants, lawyers and other professionals, as well as clergymen, officers and artisans (Maintenant, 1984: 68). Yet in their most radical period (1793–1794), when the number of artisans and peasants had increased, they resembled social democrats (*avant la lettre*) in their support for maximum prices and minimum income security, basic education for all (boys and girls) and possibly even progressive taxation and a (rather vaguely defined) 'equality of enjoyments' (*l'égalité des jouissances*) (Higonnet, 1998: 121–123, 207; Maintenant, 1984: 99, 110–113, 122–123). The Jacobins were also nationalists – 'patriots' was the term at that time – as well as anti-clerical and anti-aristocratic democrats who cherished popular sovereignty. However, they were not very clear and consistent about the way popular sovereignty should be institutionalised. According to the French philosopher and historian Pierre Rosanvallon, their ambiguity can be attributed to a substantial extent to the 'dominant shadow' of Rousseau (Rosanvallon, 2000: 15, 41–91).

Jean-Jacques Rousseau was born in 1712 in Geneva, at the time an independent city-state. He spent most of his life in France, writing controversial philosophical, political, pedagogical and literary works, until his death in 1778 at Ermenonville, in the country house of a noble friend. With regard to his influence on the Jacobins and their allies, most historians seem to be in agreement (some with considerable qualifications, however: see MacDonald, 1965: 43–65). Higonnet concludes that the life and works of this strange hermit 'were to be a model for Jacobin revolutionaries, great and small, male or female' (1998: 319). According to Palmer, Rousseau's *Du contrat social* was 'the one book in which the revolutionary aspirations of the period from 1760 to 1800 were most compactly embodied', and 'the great book of the political revolution' (1959: 119). Though few revolutionaries might have read the book itself, its contents were probably known even among the less educated revolutionaries through secondary sources, popular almanacs, songs, newspapers and speeches, as Soboul tries to demonstrate (1966: 203–222). Moreover, Rousseau expressed similar ideas in his more widely read treatise on education, *Émile ou De l'éducation* ([1762] 1971: 313–317). A short and simplified summary of these ideas should suffice here.

'Man is born free, and everywhere he is in chains' (*L'homme est né libre, et partout il est dans les fers*): with this ringing sentence Rousseau opens *Du contrat social* ([1762] 2001: 46). Some men may feel they are masters over others, but they are not really free either. How could this happen? Rousseau does not give a complete historical explanation of the emergence of slavery and domination in this book; his main purpose is to suggest how this situation could be changed. After all, a society based on domination is unjust. Every society is constituted by a social contract, agreed on by all human beings involved. At that point, all are still free and equal. The contract constitutes the society as a moral and political community. It is the expression of the general will of all participants. The social contract may entail a delegation of power to a single individual or a small group of strong and able men, or it may allocate power to the people as a whole. These are the three classical forms of government: monarchy, aristocracy and democracy. Yet in all three forms of legitimate government, sovereignty remains in the hands of the people. This is a crucial point by Rousseau, and one which may distinguish him from most other political theorists. Sovereignty cannot be transferred like power; it is indivisible and inalienable (Rousseau, [1762] 2001: 65–66). If the people would agree to transfer sovereignty to a king or a group of noblemen, it would in fact mean the cancellation of the social contract and the dissolution of the people as a collective. The sovereign king or aristocracy could not express the general will any more, but will articulate a particular will and serve particular interests. This will eventually lead to anarchy or despotism – and neither can be considered a legitimate form of government. A despot treats his subjects as slaves serving his own particular or private interests, while in anarchy all individuals pursue private interests.

So, even in a (legitimate) monarchy and aristocracy the people continue to exercise sovereignty, according to Rousseau. This means that all laws should be approved by the people, somehow, or at least by a majority: '*la puissance legislative appartient au peuple, et ne peut appartenir qu'à lui*' ('legislative power belongs to the people, and cannot belong to anyone else') (Rousseau, [1762] 2001: 96; see also 148). Legislative power cannot be delegated to a minority, even if it is elected by the people. The English people may believe they are free, Rousseau asserts, but they are only free on election day; the rest of the time they are the slaves of Parliament ([1762] 2001: 134).

The execution and implementation of laws, however, can be delegated to a government, of whatever form. In a small state the people might exercise both legislative and executive power and divide all offices among themselves – preferably by sortition and rotation – to maintain perfect equality. However, this would place heavy burdens on all citizens. Therefore, Rousseau concludes that real democracy would only suit gods, not normal human beings ([1762] 2001: 107). Practically all (legitimate) governments are mixed, i.e. combine democratic, aristocratic and monarchic elements. Hence, all suffer the risk that monarchs or aristocrats will usurp power and oppress the people. The risk may be smaller if the government is elected rather than hereditary, although these elections do not guarantee freedom.

Rousseau did not end his political treatise with clear practical recommendations. This is not because he was incapable of drafting practical proposals: he did offer his thoughts on a new constitution for Poland and one for Corsica, when the island had seceded from the republic of Genoa (Rousseau, 1971a; 1971b). In both cases, he suggested modest reforms rather than revolutionary change. In his opinion, Poland should remain an elective monarchy, even if election had to be combined with sortition to prevent factions and intrigues (Rousseau, 1971a: 562). Ultimately, serfs should become free farmers and citizens with a voice in the expression of the general will, too, but this was a long-term goal and not something to be realised in one step. Corsica, being poorer and less dominated by aristocrats, could incorporate more democratic elements into its constitution (Rousseau, 1971b: 496). So Rousseau did not preach revolution. Even when the bourgeois middle class confronted the patrician aristocracy in his native Geneva and asked him for advice, Rousseau held himself apart (Palmer, 1959: 127–133). It seems doubtful, therefore, that the anxious and cautious philosopher would have welcomed the French Revolution with great enthusiasm, certainly in its radical stage. It seems rather unfair to blame Jacobin terror and dictatorship on Rousseau. Even so, it is hard to deny that Jacobins and *sans-culottes* were inspired by the philosopher from Geneva.

The Jacobins as well as the *sans-culottes* struggled with the question of how the people could exercise sovereignty without leaving legislative power in the hands of representatives, but also without allowing complete anarchy. Obviously, France was too big to be ruled by a popular assembly. Transformation of the centralised monarchy into a loose confederation of small autonomous republics might have solved the problem in the spirit of Rousseau, but went too much against the grain of French political culture – whether Jacobin or monarchist – and was not seriously considered by his disciples (Urbinati, 2008: 65; MacDonald, 1965). They feared that even a small step in this direction would undermine the unity and cohesion of the republic. The constitution drafted in 1792 by the (former) Marquis de Condorcet implied a modest decentralisation – by expanding the communes or municipalities – rather than a federalist system (Urbinati, 2008: 209). By imputing a federalist tendency to this project, the *Montagnards* obviously tried to discredit it (Badinter and Badinter, 1988: 543). More important to them may have been the fact that Condorcet was close to the Girondins – also suspected of federalism – even though he refused to take sides in the struggle between the factions.

Born in 1743, into a noble family of ancient lineage but modest fortune, Marie Jean Antoine-Nicolas Caritat de Condorcet had devoted most of his life to mathematics and the sciences, including the 'moral sciences' that we would now refer to as the social sciences (Badinter and Badinter, 1988: 180). During the 1770s he had already combated feudalism, capital punishment, slavery of and discrimination against Protestants and Jews, and defended equal rights for men and women. He was one of the first members of the Jacobin Club in Paris, yet soon criticised their 'sectarian spirit' (Badinter and Badinter, 1988: 285, 287). In 1791 he was elected to the Legislative Assembly; a year later he won a seat in the National Convention. In 1793 he was purged and condemned to death while in hiding; in March 1794 he was caught and died in a prison cell, possibly caused by poison but more likely by a stroke (Badinter and Badinter, 1988: 581–618).

The Convention had been elected in order to adopt a new constitution and Condorcet was appointed to the committee in charge of drafting it. In December 1792 the committee presented its draft. It mainly reflected the ideas of Condorcet and, to a lesser extent, those of Emanuel Joseph Sieyès and Thomas Paine – the Englishman who had inspired the American Revolution but who became an (honorary) French citizen in 1792, and who had also been elected to the Convention (Palmer, 1964: 54–55; Higonnet, 1998: 253; Badinter and Badinter, 1988: 534–535).

How did Condorcet and his committee try to solve Rousseau's problem – the institutionalisation of popular sovereignty – without federalism? It was a compromise between direct and indirect or representative democracy. Laws would be made by a national assembly or legislative body, elected by the people. The legislature would be elected (each year) by primary assemblies, to which practically all adult males in a district would belong – and hopefully, in the near future, women also (Badinter and Badinter, 1988: 537; Urbinati, 2008: 207–216). Yet the role of the primary assemblies was not restricted to annual election of legislators and other public officials; it was also expected to discuss legislation passed by the national assembly. If the primary assemblies in two departments objected to a law, it would be submitted to a referendum. If a majority of all primary assemblies voted against the law, it would be withdrawn. Moreover, they could enforce new elections of the legislature. According to Elisabeth and Robert Badinter, the biographers of Condorcet, his complicated project would transform public life into permanent deliberation and politics into continuous elections: '*le recours constant aux assemblées primaires transformait la vie publique en délibération permanente et la vie politique en élection continue*' ('the constant appeal to primary assemblies would transform public life into permanent deliberation and political life into continuing elections') (1988: 539). Urbinati, however, points out that Condorcet presented a 'third-way solution' to the dilemma that has faced democracy since the eighteenth century: 'the mystique of sovereignty as immediate and existential presence and the allegedly objective realism of electoral democracy as the death of sovereignty' (2008: 180). On the one hand, he offered citizens the possibility of deliberating and voting on all legislation, fulfilling Rousseau's criterion of popular sovereignty. On the other hand, he also allowed representation of the people by an elected assembly. One might expect that the representatives would anticipate the reaction of the primary assemblies, avoiding a clash in most cases, either by accommodating their constituents or by convincing them that the law passed by the national assembly served the common interest. Nonetheless, the representatives had to deliberate and make decisions themselves; they were not bound by an imperative mandate.

In spite of her admiration for Condorcet, Urbinati admits that his proposal was 'imperfect, complicated, and impractical' (2008: 221). Perhaps it was also too radical, even for the *Montagnards* in the National Convention, who distrusted Condorcet anyway. So they had sufficient reasons to reject his draft, even besides its supposedly federalist tendencies. The proposal was shelved without much discussion. Yet the alternative proposal that was drafted rather hastily by the *Montagnard* Marie Jean Hérault de Séchelles, and which was approved with a few amendments in June 1793, bore a striking resemblance to Condorcet's project (Badinter and Badinter, 1988: 260, 571; Jardin, 1985: 131–132; Urbinati, 2008: 178). Popular sovereignty would be exercised by the primary assemblies, consisting of all citizens of 21 years or older living (for at least six months) in the canton, according to Article 2 and Article 11: '*Le peuple français est distribué pour l'exercice de sa souveraineté en assemblées primaires de cantons*' ('for the exercise of its sovereignty the French people is divided into primary assemblies at the cantonal level') (Constitution de la République Française 1793 Juin 24, 1964: 378, 380). The number of citizens in a primary assembly could vary between 200 and 600 (Article 12). They would elect (directly or indirectly) the members of the legislative body (*corps législatif*), judges and administrators, but they would also deliberate about the laws proposed by the legislative body, as Articles 7, 8, 9 and 10 stipulated: '*Le peuple souverain ... délibère sur les lois*' ('The sovereign people ... deliberates about the laws') (Constitution de la République Française 1793 Juin 24, 1964: 380). The proposal would become law only if more than half of the primary assemblies did not object to it within 40 days (Article 59, Constitution de la République Française 1793 Juin 24, 1964: 386). An assembly could be convened at the request of one-fifth of the citizens.

The constitution was ratified in a referendum by 1,801,918 citizens – only 11,610 voted against it, but more than five million citizens did not vote at all (Palmer, 1964: 110).

The constitution also bore the stamp of Robespierre, the Jacobin leader at the time, though he did not agree with every detail (Rudé, 1975: 108–109). It was less complicated – but in some ways less radical – than the draft of Condorcet and his friends, in particular with respect to the direct election of public officials. Even if Robespierre often referred to 'Jean-Jacques' in his speeches and must have read *Du contrat social*, he did not reject representation altogether (Rudé, 1975: 96–100; Soboul, 1966: 240, 267). The definition of democracy which he gave in the speech quoted already in Chapter 1 reflects his ambiguity:

> La démocratie n'est pas un état où le peuple, continuellement assemblé, règle par lui- même toutes les affaires publiques. [...] La démocratie est un état où le peuple souverain, guidé par des lois qui sont son ouvrage, fait par lui-même tout ce qu'il peut bien faire, et par des délégués tout ce qu'il ne peut faire lui-même.
>
> (Democracy is not a state in which the people in a permanent assembly deals with all public affairs directly. [...] Democracy is a state in which the people, as sovereign, guided by laws of its own making, does directly all that it can do well, and by its delegates what it cannot.)
> (Robespierre, 1967: 352–353)

When Robespierre and his *Montagnard* friends consolidated their power through the Committee for Public Safety and the National Convention, from which they had purged their main rivals by early 1794, they felt that they could take most decisions themselves without consulting the people. They broke the alliance with the *sans-culottes*, who had supported and encouraged them in their struggle against the Girondins, but had become increasingly unruly and critical of Robespierre's leadership.

The *sans-culottes* advocated more extreme ideas about democracy than either Condorcet or Robespierre. They did not articulate their ideas in a draft constitution, but practiced them in a rough sort of way. They met frequently, often daily, in their urban district or *section* to discuss and decide local issues as well as national questions. Paris had been divided into sixty and later forty-eight districts, which enjoyed a certain autonomy and raised their own National Guard battalions (Soboul, 1968: 121–129, 159–166; Palmer, 1964: 39). Many *sans-culottes* attended the meetings of the National Convention in the public gallery, and they tried to influence its decisions by loudly expressing approval or disapproval, shouting threats against enemies and brandishing pikes or other arms. Sometimes the Convention gave in. Quite a few enemies of the *sans-culottes* were declared '*hors la loi*' – which meant that they could be arrested and executed without trial. In line with Rousseau, the *sans-culottes* regarded the members of the Convention as mere delegates or *mandataires du peuple*, commissioned by the people to serve the public interest and express the general will; the people, therefore, had the right to censure, control and recall them (Soboul, 1968: 111–120). When electing delegates, the people should also give them a binding mandate (*mandat impératif*).[1] In some districts, the *sans-culottes* succeeded in imposing binding mandates and recalling delegates (Tønneson, 1988). Checks and balances, independent judges and courts of appeal were rejected as they would only obstruct the will of the people. The *sans-culottes* regretted that the constitution of 1793 did not allow binding mandates or recall of delegates, yet they regretted even more that the constitution was not implemented at all. However, suggestions to this effect met with fierce sanctions: many leaders of the *sans-culottes* were arrested and executed in 1794 – just like their enemies, the Girondins (Soboul, 1966: 240–256). Even after the fall of Robespierre, in the midst of a recession and famine, the surviving *sans-culottes* called for 'bread and the Constitution of '93' (*Du pain et la Constitution de '93*) (Furet and Richler, 1973: 299). Again it was in vain, as the wind was now blowing in a different direction.

Neo-Jacobins and other democratic radicals in the nineteenth century

Yet Rousseauism and Jacobinism did not die with Condorcet, Robespierre and the *sans-culottes*. Though repressed by Napoleon's Empire and by the Bourbon monarchy that was restored in 1813, the ideas were kept alive and transmitted to new generations via secret conspiratorial societies, Masonic lodges and informal networks (Jardin, 1985: 343–344). In 1830 radical democratic ideas surfaced again, in the revolution that broke out in Paris. Radicals played a leading role on the barricades, but lacked the military and political strength to establish a republican regime (Jardin, 1985: 284–293; Nordmann, 1974: 25–41). Yet the liberal monarchy of Louis Philippe de Bourbon – the son of a member of the royal family who had sided with the Jacobins – would allow them more freedom to spread their ideas. In February 1848 another revolution swept away the liberal monarchy. A provisional government was established which consisted of moderate as well as radical republicans and a few socialists.

The radical republicans were inspired by Rousseau and cherished the Jacobin ideas of liberty, equality and fraternity. In the Constitutional Assembly, elected by universal suffrage in April 1848, they were called *Montagnards*, like the Jacobins in the National Convention of 1792 (Jardin, 1985: 355). They were defined as 'radicals' or even 'ultra-radicals' by their leader, the lawyer Alexandre-Auguste Ledru-Rollin: '*Nous sommes des ultra-radicaux, si vous entendez par ce mot le Parti qui veut entrer dans la réalité de la vie le grand symbole de la liberté, de l'égalité et de la fraternité*' ('We are ultra-radicals, if you mean by that term the party that wants to realise the great symbols liberty, equality and fraternity') (Nicolet, 1961: 17). Yet Ledru-Rollin (1807–1874) was no Robespierre, even if he imitated him in the way he dressed (Aminzade, 1993: 50). He lacked the wherewithal, but also the will, to exterminate his rivals and install a terrorist dictatorship. As Minister of the Interior in the Provisional Government of 1848, he organised free and fair elections which resulted in a minority for his political friends. Less than 100 out of 900 seats were won by radical republicans and their socialist allies, whereas moderate and conservative republicans obtained more than 500 seats, and monarchists most of the remaining 300 (Jardin, 1985: 354–355; Rosenberg, 1938: 89–90).

As is to be expected, the constitution that this assembly would adopt a few months later did not meet the demands of radical democrats. Though favourable towards popular sovereignty, the assembly voted for a mixed system, balancing a legislative assembly and a strong executive, while both the legislature and the president would be elected directly by the people (Jardin, 1985: 357–359). In the spirit of Rousseau, Ledru-Rollin objected to granting all legislative power to elected representatives. According to him, the people should exercise all sovereignty directly. In primary or electoral assemblies, the citizens would not only elect delegates, but would also initiate and approve of laws. Thus, all legislative power would rest with the people, while an annually elected parliament would take care of the details (Calman, 1921: 85).[2]

Louis Blanc, one of the first (and few) Socialists elected to the Constitutional Assembly, wanted to grant citizens the right to give binding mandates to their representatives and recall them if the mandate was not fulfilled (Golliet, 1903: 81–82; Humilière, 1982: 88, 94). The Social Democrats or Democratic Socialists led by Blanc distinguished themselves from the Radicals of Ledru-Rollin mainly in the socio-economic realm: the latter defended private property and the market economy, whereas the former favoured a co-operative economy with substantial state support. Socialism was a new term, and a new idea. Or rather, it was a rather diverse family of ideas, often quite idiosyncratic and utopian. Followers of Saint-Simon, Fourier, Proudhon, Cabet and Buchez disagreed about the final goal as well as the way to get there (Bruhat, 1972). Most of them stayed away from electoral politics, but the leading disciple of Fourier, Victor Considérant (1808–1893), was a successful candidate at the elections of the Constitutional Assembly and joined the *Montagnard* group (Collard, 1910: 113). Though initially critical of universal franchise and leaning towards a kind of socialist corporatism, he later argued for 'direct government by the people' (Collard, 1910: 210–211, 273). In local or primary assemblies citizens should draft proposals that would be aggregated and integrated by an elected '*Commission de l'assemblée générale du peuple*' (Rosanvallon, 2000: 173). Considérant realised that this procedure would make legislation a slow and complicated process, but may not have seen this as a disadvantage: the fewer laws, the better. As with Fourier, his ideas bordered on anarchism, though he did not want to do away with central government altogether. Similar ideas were voiced by the young philosopher Charles Renouvier and by the German journalist Maurice Rittinghausen, who was a member of the parliament that met in Frankfurt in 1848, went to France in exile, and would later be elected to the German *Reichstag* as a Social Democrat (Curti, 1882: 198–207; Rosanvallon, 2000: 155–170).

In March 1848 a revolution broke out in many parts of Germany. Delegates from the German states met in Frankfurt to draft a constitution for the German Empire – even though there was no agreement about its boundaries. The delegates started meeting in coffee houses to discuss their ideas. The most extreme leftwing group, called the 'radical-democratic party' (*'radikal-demokratische Partei'*), met in Café Donnersberg. In a manifesto, it called for a federal and parliamentary republic, wherein the people would govern themselves through primary assemblies as well as delegates (*'unumschränkte Selbstregierung durch seine Urversammlungen und durch seine Abgeordneten'*; unlimited self-government [of the people] through its primary assemblies and through its delegates') (Hildebrandt, 1975: 249). Of course, parliament would be elected by universal suffrage. But equally important was the participation of citizens in primary assemblies (*Urversammlungen*). In the primary assembly, all citizens or voters would be able to veto laws passed by parliament and to recall members of parliament (Hildebrandt, 1975: 70, 187). Rittinghausen wanted to divide the population into units of 1,000 citizens that would deliberate and vote about legislation proposed by (elected) ministers (Rosanvallon, 2000: 165–166). As in France, in Germany there were Socialists and Social Democrats who wanted to add social equality to political equality and who criticised the petty-bourgeois faith in private property of the radical democrats. They constituted a marginal minority without much support. Among them, however, were Karl Marx and Friedrich Engels. Together with Rittinghausen they had founded the *Neue Rheinische Zeitung*. After the repression of the revolution in Germany, they would leave Germany for England (Rosanvallon, 2000: 159–160).

In Britain the democratic movement of the 1830s and 1840s was also divided into a working-class movement (the Chartists) and a middle-class party (the Radicals), even though some people belonged to both. In England the term 'radical' was introduced earlier than in France: probably around 1770, to refer to the Society of the Supporters of the Bill of Rights and similar groups who proposed to have parliament elected by all citizens each year (Royle and Walvin, 1982: 14–31). These Radicals could build on the tradition of the Commonwealthmen and the Levellers in the seventeenth century, who had also called for universal (male) suffrage and a parliament that would act as a delegate of the people rather than a sovereign power. The example of the American and the French Revolutions and the popular writings of Thomas Paine had increased the radical audience in the 1790s, but the movement was repressed swiftly and effectively within a few years (Royle and Walvin, 1982: 48–79; Palmer, 1964: 459–505).

After 1800 a Radical party (in an informal sense) emerged to the Left of the Whigs in parliament. Their members of parliament regarded themselves as delegates bound by 'pledges' made to their constituents, rather than representatives with a free mandate (Thomas, 1979: 87–88). The Radical politicians maintained close ties with the Philosophic Radicals and often shared their utilitarian principles. Jeremy Bentham, the *spiritus rector* of the Philosophic Radicals, came to favour the Radical programme, in its essence: 'annual parliaments and universal suffrage' (Thomas, 1979: 28, 64). Yet other Philosophic Radicals, such as James Mill and his son John Stuart Mill, were much more critical (Thomas, 1979: 196; Thompson, 1976: 112–118). John Stuart Mill in particular seemed rather ambivalent about any form of direct democracy and tempted by the idea of an intellectual aristocracy. On the one hand, he argued that every citizen ought to 'take an actual part in the government, by the personal discharge of some public function, local or general'; on the other hand he worried that in a democracy the 'instincts of the majority' would prevail over the minority of 'instructed minds' (Mill, [1861] 1948: 141, 198–199). Moreover, he disapproved of annual parliaments and of pledges: 'the delegation theory of representation seems to me false' (Mill, [1861] 1948: 255). Thus, John Stuart Mill may be regarded as a social liberal, but not as a democratic radical. In fact, many Radical politicians would also end up in the Liberal party – which, in a way, resulted from a merger of Whigs and Radicals – as 'advanced Liberals': 'the Radicals had begun to lose their edge' (Bentley, 1987: 58).

Radical ideas were voiced not only by Radical members of parliament, but also by the Chartist movement, which emerged in the 1830s. The movement, which was mainly of working-class origin, gathered signatures for a People's Charter, a new constitution which would grant universal suffrage, equal electoral districts, a secret ballot, and, again, annual general elections (Royle and Walvin, 1982: 160–180). If implemented, this would usher in 'a Parliament regularly and frequently responsible to the whole people': not quite what Rousseau and Considérant had in mind, but still radical in a way (Thompson, 1984: 335). Like Paine and his friends, the Chartists failed to achieve their purpose, even though (apart from annual elections) most of their proposals were later realised.

In practically every part of Europe the radical democrats or democratic radicals were defeated and often repressed after 1848. In France, a nephew of Napoleon was elected president in December 1848 and gradually reduced parliament to impotence; four years later he had himself crowned Emperor Napoleon III. After a half-hearted attempt at insurrection in 1849, Ledru-Rollin and other Radicals fled to England, and Considérant to Belgium (Collard, 1910: 134). In Britain, as in most of Northern and Western Europe, the Radicals were too weak to start a revolution. Switzerland proved to be the exception. In Rousseau's native land, democratic radicals won power through elections and maintained it throughout most of the nineteenth century.[3] While more pragmatic and moderate than Ledru-Rollin, Rittinghausen and Considérant – yet partly inspired by them – the Swiss Radicals managed to introduce the constitutional referendum in 1848, and the legislative referendum and people's initiative in 1874 (Dürrenmatt, 1976: 730–738; Curti, 1882: 158–207, 238–294; Gerstein, 1969: 22) Having realised most of its programme, the *Parti Radical Démocrate* (as it is still called in the French-speaking part of the Swiss republic) evolved into a fairly conservative Liberal party in the twentieth century (Kriesi, 1995: 134–141). More about Switzerland in the second part of this chapter.

The Paris Commune and Karl Marx

In a way, democratic radicalism resembles a phoenix: the bird that burned itself to death yet would rise again from its own ashes. This seems particularly true in France, where it rose and died in the 1790s, revived in 1848 and died again in 1849, yet came back to life around 1870. In all events, internecine struggles added to repression by the forces of order.

In 1870, Emperor Napoleon III had waged war against Prussia and lost, rather badly. When he and a large part of the French army was made prisoner by the Prussians, a provisional government of national defence was formed which tried to continue the war with fresh recruits (Jardin, 1985: 402–403; Rosenberg, 1938: 174–176). Yet the latter proved no match against the well-trained and well-armed Prussian soldiers. By January 1871 the Prussian army had occupied a third of France and besieged Paris. An armistice was declared. Prussia wanted to negotiate peace with a legitimate French government, so the provisional government rather rapidly organised general elections. The National Assembly (elected by universal suffrage) agreed to a peace treaty with the victorious enemy. It was dominated by monarchists of different persuasions – some favouring an absolute monarchy, others a more liberal regime (Jardin, 1985: 403–404). Paris, which had largely become a working-class city, felt betrayed. Large numbers of workers and craftsmen had joined the National Guard and were prepared to defend their city against the Prussians, confident that they would repeat the military success of 1792 against the enemies of the First Republic. They refused to disarm, and in March 1871 prevented the regular forces from removing the cannons meant for the defence of the city. After a short skirmish, the army retreated – for the time being. These skirmishes escalated into civil war, almost by accident. The National Guard took control of the city, somewhat reluctantly; however, it did not want to govern the capital, and so a civilian government was elected, which proclaimed the Commune of Paris on March 28 (Edwards, 1971: 115–186).

The Commune was primarily a municipal government, combining executive and legislative functions. Yet it was also more than that. It claimed substantial autonomy, if not sovereignty. Other municipalities should follow suit, transforming France into a federation of autonomous communes (Edwards, 1971: 156). At the same time, the Parisians were tempted to act as revolutionary government for the whole of France – as they had done in 1792. In May the Commune decided – against strong opposition from a minority – to set up a Committee for Public Safety in true Jacobin style (Edwards, 1971: 247). Historians have interpreted the Commune as the last, apocalyptic burst of Jacobinism and sans-culottism, but also as the birth-pangs of revolutionary socialism (Rosenberg, 1938: 176–196; Rose, 1972; Rihs, 1973: 185–191, 266). Most scholars seem to agree that it was a bit of both. Quite a few *Communards* referred to the Commune of 1792, the Constitution of 1793 and the spirit of the *sans-culottes*, the revolutionary calendar, and the political clubs of the 1790s (Edwards, 1971: 277–312). Participants such as Jean Allemane and Paul Martine also later acknowledged this. The former did so reluctantly: 'la Commune, dit-il, plus jacobine que socialiste' ('the Commune, he said, [was] more jacobin than socialist') (Winock, 1973: 376). Martine wrote: 'nous étions bien les fils des hommes de 93, les héritiers directs des Jacobins les plus résolus' ('we were indeed the sons of the men of (17)93, the direct heirs of the most determined Jacobins') (Rougerie, 1973: 79). The continuity seems most obvious in their ideas about popular sovereignty and, to a lesser extent, in the patriotism or nationalism that went with this. Elected representatives were expected to act as 'mandatories, referring matters back to the local population in their clubs and National Guard battalions' (Edwards, 1971: 359; see also Rihs, 1973: 185–91). They could be recalled by the voters (Rubel, 1972: 39). They would act according to binding mandates – even if, at the time, there was no consensus regarding exactly what this meant (Aminzade, 1993: 52; Rosanvallon, 2000: 256). Sovereignty was indivisible; the Commune combined executive and legislative powers. All public officials should be elected, including police officers and military officers, and be paid a worker's wage – the National Guard practiced this already (Rihs, 1973: 265–267).

Yet the Commune of 1871 differed from the Commune of 1792 in many other aspects. Its federalism and libertarianism contrasted with the centralisation and authoritarianism of the Jacobins in the 1790s. The guillotine stood idle. Violence was not avoided completely – some officials of the old regime were lynched, and in the end hostages were killed – yet the number of victims that died at the hands of the *Communards* was very small compared to the number of *Communards* killed by their enemies. The historian Edwards estimated that about 25,000 Parisians were shot by the invading troops, either in battle or afterwards, while quite a few died a slow death in a penal colony to which they were deported (1971: 346–348). Ideologically, the Commune of 1871 was much more diverse than its predecessor: neo-Jacobins mingled with followers of Blanqui, Proudhon, Bakunin and other socialists (Edwards, 1971: 210–216; Rihs, 1973: 63–74, 177–217). Some of the latter belonged to the International Workingmen's Association (later called the First International) founded in 1864, in which Marx and Engels played an important role. The socialists were in a minority and exercised only a modest influence on the decisions of the Commune. Some abandoned workshops and small factories were taken over by the workers, night shifts in bakeries were abolished, factory discipline was relaxed a little and payment of housing rents was suspended (Edwards, 1971: 249–276).

When Karl Marx wrote a report on the Commune for the International Workingmen's Association, he may have exaggerated the socialist elements in the Commune (see Rosenberg, 1938: 193). He described it as a 'essentially a working-class government, the produce of the struggle of the producing against the appropriating class, the political form at last discovered under which to work out the economic emancipation of labour'. (Marx, [1871] 2001: 83). The Commune was to transform the means of production, capital and land from means of repression and exploitation into 'instruments of free and associated labour' and regulate national production according to a plan – 'in other words: communism!' (Marx, [1871] 2001: 76–77). The defining characteristics of its political form, according to Marx, were the replacement of a standing army by 'the people in arms'; the direct election and possible recall of the members of the Commune as well as its civil servants, judges and police officers, who would be paid a worker's wage; and the combination of executive and legislative functions. The Commune was to be 'not a parliamentary but a working body' ([1871] 2001: 70).

One might be tempted to interpret Marx's enthusiastic and unqualified defence of the Commune as a tactical move to claim its political legacy, or as a defiant provocation of the reactionary forces that had smothered it in blood. To some extent, this may be true (see Lichtheim, 1967: 112–121). However, Marx did not retract or correct his report later. The text was republished several times, and in several languages. In 1891, eight years after Marx's death, his friend Engels added a few critical comments on the Commune in his introduction, yet concluded emphatically: 'Look at the Paris Commune. That was the dictatorship of the proletariat' (Engels, [1891] 2001: 21). With 'dictatorship', he obviously did not mean an authoritarian regime – the Commune was anything but authoritarian, which Blanqui and his followers regretted – but the domination of one class by another. As Marx and Engels had already argued in the Communist Manifesto published in 1848, practically all societies in history were dominated by a particular class: the Roman Empire by slave-owners, feudal societies by landowners, and modern industrial societies by the bourgeoisie or the capitalist class (Marx and Engels, [1848] 1995). The dominant class owned the means of production – slaves, land, factories and other forms of capital – and appropriated or extracted the social surplus produced by its slaves, serfs or workers, leaving the latter with only the basic necessities in life, such as food, shelter and clothing. Yet the dominant class also controlled (directly or indirectly) the political system. The material mode of production and the relations between producers and owners determined the social, political and cultural life of a society. This insight into the intimate connection between economic and political power constituted the core of Marx's theory, as he defined it himself ([1859] 1971: 15). In a feudal society it seemed to be self-evident, as the landlords exercised political power directly, waging war, levying taxes and appointing judges, bailiffs and other officials. In a bourgeois society, it was more complicated: the capitalist class had delegated this direct power to the bourgeois state and its apparatus – army, police, judiciary, legislature, civil service – which it controlled only indirectly. How it managed to do so was a topic Marx did not dwell on extensively – unlike some of his later disciples (see, for example, Miliband, 1969; Therborn, 1980).

At any rate, it seemed obvious to Marx that if the working class could win political power, it could also change the economic order, and vice versa. In England, where the working class constituted the majority of the population in the nineteenth century – unlike in France or Germany – universal suffrage would bring about a political as well as a social revolution, he wrote in 1852 (Marx, [1852] 1973: 264). In the end, the precise political form of the 'dictatorship of the proletariat' may not have mattered all that much to Marx, so long as the working class managed to overthrow the power of the capitalist class and gain control of the means of production – the factories, capital and land. Engels seemed to agree; in the same year that he identified the dictatorship of the proletariat with the Paris Commune, he also described it as a 'democratic republic', wherein power would be concentrated in the hands of parliament, limited only by the referendum and popular initiative (Engels, [1891] 1972: 89, 92). By the way, many Socialists attached importance to referendum and initiative at the end of the nineteenth century, in France as well as in Germany (Rosanvallon, 2000: 289–292). In 1891 the German SPD demanded 'direct legislation by the people through the right to propose and reject' (*Direkte Gesetzgebung durch das Volk vermittels des Vorschlags- und Verwerfungsrechts*) (Sozialdemokratische Partei Deutschlands, [1891] 1960: 351). At any rate, in spite of the confusing use of the term 'dictatorship of the proletariat' by Marx and Engels, it seems clear that they approved of a Jacobin-style bounded-delegate model, as embodied by the Commune, and integrated it into their political-economic theory of socialism. Some of their followers would ignore or reject this and replace the Jacobin ideas with liberal or parliamentary democracy, but others would continue to be guided by the polar star of the Commune in their journey to socialism.

Soviet democracy and Lenin

Russian Marxists such as Lenin looked at the Paris Commune as a political model for a socialist Russia. The lawyer Vladimir Ilich Ulyanov, known from 1901 by the pseudonym Lenin (1870–1924), was one of the founders of the Russian Social Democratic Workers' Party in 1903 and the leader of the left-wing faction which was called Bolsheviks – 'majority men' – because it counted more delegates at the founding congress (Carr, 1966: I, 42–44). In 1912 the two factions split and Lenin became leader of the Bolshevik party. The Bolsheviks quarrelled with the Mensheviks (minority men), mainly over organisational and strategic issues: Lenin rejected the democratic mass party model favoured by the Mensheviks as well as most European Socialists and strove for a small, centralised and hierarchical party.

The Bolshevik party remained illegal until the revolution of February 1917, when the tsar was forced to abdicate and a provisional government took power and tried to establish a liberal bourgeois democracy in Russia, while continuing the war with Germany. In April, Lenin returned to Russia from his exile in Switzerland. He immediately began to advocate a 'republic of Soviets of Workers', Poor Peasants' and Peasants' Deputies' (Carr, 1966: I, 91). The bourgeois revolution should be followed by a second, socialist revolution. It took him a few days to convince the other party leaders, and subsequently the party rank-and-file, who were inclined to accept the 'bourgeois character' of the revolution. The party conference followed Lenin. In August 1917, he presented his views on the future in a short book, *State and Revolution*, and devoted one chapter to the Commune. Extensively quoting Marx, he argued that the Commune was the first attempt by a working class to smash the bourgeois state and replace it with 'proletarian democracy' (Lenin, [1917] 1964: 418–437).

Proletarian democracy differed from bourgeois democracy in four aspects, as Lenin had learned from Marx: replacement of the standing army by the people-in-arms; direct election and revocability of all public officials; payment of a worker's wage to those officials; and replacement of the powerless bourgeois parliament by a 'working body' that performs legislative as well as executive functions. Having briefly described the Commune in the context of Marxist ideas about the state and the proletarian revolution, in 1917 Lenin applied these ideas to the Russian situation. His aim was to mobilise the proletariat in the fight 'to overthrow the bourgeoisie, to destroy bourgeois parliamentarism, for a democratic republic after the type of the Commune, or a republic of Soviets of Workers' and Soldiers' Deputies, for the revolutionary dictatorship of the proletariat' (Lenin, [1917] 1964: 495). This would be merely a transition towards socialism, when

> the mass of the population will rise to taking an independent part, not only in voting and elections, but also in the everyday administration of the state. Under socialism, all will govern in turn and will soon become accustomed to no one governing.
>
> (Lenin, [1917] 1964: 492–493)

Clearly, this smacks of democratic extremism. Yet Lenin added a subtle elitist element, too, when he defined the dictatorship of the proletariat as 'the organisation of the vanguard of the oppressed as the ruling class for the purpose of suppressing the oppressors' ([1917] 1964: 466).

In 1917, Lenin seemed to regard the Paris Commune and the Soviets of Workers' and Soldiers' Deputies as one of a kind. Was this more than rhetoric? The Soviets of Workers' Deputies (*sovety rabotsjich deputatov*) had sprung up spontaneously, first in 1905 and then again in 1917, when the First World War brought military as well as economic disaster to Russia. Initially they co-ordinated strikes in areas where trade unions were weak or absent (Anweiler, 1958: 45–61). Workers would meet in their factory to elect delegates and give them a binding mandate to negotiate with the management, but also with local political authorities. Delegates could be recalled by their electors at any time (Sirianni, 1982: 29–30, 69). The delegates constituted factory committees (*fab-zavkomy*) at the plant level and Soviets at the local level, but their functions were not clearly distinguished and the same workers might sit on both bodies; occasionally the two bodies merged (Anweiler, 1958: 155; Sirianni, 1982: 17, 68; see also Mandel, 2011).

At first, both the factory committees and the Soviets acted as critical opposition to the management and the local government, monitoring and checking rather than intervening directly (Anweiler, 1958: 130). Yet in the course of 1917 the workers became more militant, while some managers deserted their factory or tried to close them down. In those cases, the factory might be taken over and managed by the factory committee or the Soviets. In some areas local government had broken down and was taken over by the workers' councils, sometimes acting together with councils of peasants and soldiers. In turn, the councils would elect deputies directly to regional and indirectly to national (All-Russian) congresses of workers', peasants' and soldiers' deputies. In the eyes of more and more workers, the Soviets enjoyed greater legitimacy than the provisional government of (bourgeois) Liberals and (Menshevik) Social Democrats. The government had failed to resolve the main problems facing Russia at the time: the war and the economic crisis which had resulted in shortages of food and fuel. The army began to disintegrate, and soldiers deserted or obeyed the orders of their elected Soviets rather than their officers. In the cities, workers began to arm themselves and formed Red Guards to maintain order and security in their factories and neighbourhoods (Sirianni, 1982: 85). Through recall and new elections, the Soviets radicalised rapidly (Anweiler, 1958: 139). In September 1917 the Bolsheviks won a majority in the Soviets of the two most important cities, Moscow and Petrograd (Sirianni, 1982: 72). Anarchists and Bolsheviks demanded 'all power to the soviets!'. The first All-Russian congress of Soviets (in June) had rejected this idea, but the second congress, held in October, proclaimed the transfer of all power to the Soviets. The previous day, armed workers led by the Bolsheviks had occupied key points in Petrograd and arrested the members of the Provisional Government who failed to escape (Carr, 1966: I, 109). In January 1918 Bolshevik guards dissolved the Constituent Assembly that had just been elected – where Bolsheviks held only a quarter of the seats (Carr, 1966: I, 120–129).

So, Soviet power seemed to have won the competition with 'bourgeois democracy'. Yet its victory proved to be a bitter and short-lived one. As the sociologist Carmen Sirianni observed in his study of the Soviet experience, 'effective power gravitated to executive committees and their even smaller bureaux' at every level of the Soviet system (1982: 70). Plenary sessions became increasingly symbolic, except in periods of intensive popular debate, such as during the negotations of the Brest-Litovsk peace treaty with Germany (Sirianni, 1982: 203). The executive committees and presidia of the Soviets were increasingly controlled and manned by Bolsheviks, who were keen on monopolising power. This process of oligarchisation had already begun before the October revolution, and was encouraged by Lenin and his political friends. Economic hardship, famine and civil war contributed to the process. Within a few years the Bolsheviks disempowered the councils (Soviets as well as factory committees) and established a party dictatorship instead of a dictatorship of the proletariat – against resistance from leftwing dissidents in their own ranks as well as Anarchists, Mensheviks and other parties (Sirianni, 1982: 95–158, 198–239; Carr, 1966: I, 191–219).

In 1920, Lenin summed it up quite clearly:

> the dictatorship is exercised by the proletariat organised in the Soviets; the proletariat is guided by the Communist Party of the Bolsheviks.... No important political or organisational question is decided by any state institution in our republic without the guidance of the party's Central Committee.
>
> ([1920] 1970: 40–41)

The party had been fairly centralised and hierarchical from the start, but had tolerated some diversity and even competing factions until the tenth party congress held in March 1921 (Carr, 1966: I, 205–211). Now it was evolving into an increasingly monolithic machine, devoid of internal democracy, dominating a growing and increasingly repressive bureaucratic state apparatus. In fact, it had more in common with aristocracy than with democracy, as argued in Chapter 2. Nevertheless, the party continued to refer to the Soviet system as an ideological shibboleth in order to legitimate its dictatorship. The term was incorporated into the name of the state: Russian Socialist Federal Soviet Republic, and subsequently, Union of Socialist Soviet Republics (USSR) or 'Soviet Union' for short (Carr, 1966: I, 403–413). Yet by then the Soviets were mere territorial units, where the inhabitants could elect representatives – i.e. vote for the list of candidates nominated by the party or its auxiliary organisations (Carr, 1966: I, 136–138; Ulam, 1974: 97, 106).

Without any doubt, the Soviet of the 1920s had very little in common with the Paris Commune of 1871. On paper they at least shared the merger of executive and legislative powers and the direct election of officials, but the dominance of the Bolsheviks made the reality quite different. If we go back to 1917, the similarities may be more numerous: then, both the Soviets and the Commune represented different tendencies and parties, their members could and would be recalled, and they relied upon 'the people in arms'. Yet even then, we should not overlook an important difference. The Commune was a territorial unit, in principle representing all inhabitants of Paris – and not merely the members of one particular class or profession. True, workers were probably over-represented, and noblemen or members of the *haute bourgeoisie* practically absent, but that was a coincidence and not the consequence of conscious policy. The linkage between political and economic power propagated by Marx and practiced by Lenin would have seemed alien to the *Communards*. Yet in spite of its tenuous historical legitimation and perverse evolution from radical democracy to party aristocracy, the Soviet system excited and inspired many radical democrats all over the world, throughout the twentieth century.

Council-democracy and Pannekoek

The First World War caused a crisis not only in Russia, but also in Western and Central Europe. Workers went on strike, especially in the war industries. In Budapest, Berlin, Glasgow and Turin they occupied factories and began raising revolutionary demands (Gluckstein, 2011; Sirianni, 1980). When the Austrian Empire fell apart, Hungarian Communists and Socialists proclaimed a Soviet Republic in April 1919, inspired by the Russian example; it was more pluralist and democratic, however, and not dominated by one faction or party (Tökes, 1967: 137–140). Disunity may have contributed to military defeat in August 1919. Workers' councils also emerged in many German cities. In Kiel, sailors elected a soldiers' council and refused to fight a final naval battle against Britain in November 1918. Their revolt marked the end of the war, and the collapse of the German Empire. In Bremen the workers' councils proclaimed a Council Republic (*Räterepublik*) in January 1919, which was repressed within a few weeks (Kolb, 1978: 328–331, 339–347). In April of the same year a Bavarian Council Republic was initiated by Anarchists in Munich, taken over by Communists, and finally destroyed by rightwing militias in a bloodbath in May (Neubauer, 1966; Mitchell, 1967; Kolb, 1978: 332–339, 347–358). In other German cities, council republics were repressed even sooner.

All of the attempts to follow the Russian example had one thing in common: they lacked the cohesive force and ruthless determination of the Russian Bolsheviks. Unlike their exemplar, the German and Hungarian council republics shared the libertarian spirit of the Paris Commune – and its tragic and bloody end. Whereas Lenin and his comrades had spent years building a disciplined vanguard party, the German and Hungarian revolutionaries had only just broken away from the Socialist or Social Democratic parties of their countries and tried to build a revolutionary (Communist) party while leading a revolution and fighting a civil war at the same time – a mission impossible.

By 1920, the revolutionary hopes had been dashed all over Europe and workers' councils had disappeared or were disempowered (Rosenberg, 1938: 319–322). Reflecting upon the Soviet experience, workers and their representatives in the labour movement drew three different types of conclusions. In most countries, the majority rejected the Soviet model altogether and came to accept the 'bourgeois' liberal model of parliamentary democracy. It seemed superior to any 'dictatorship of the proletariat', as it guaranteed at least basic human rights, the freedom to organise unions and parties, and to negotiate with employers about wages and working conditions. Gradually, this majority relinquished any hope for a socialist revolution and paid only lip service to Marxism, if they did not dismiss it completely. They emphasised that they were Social Democrats, rather than Communists.

The name 'Communists' became a synonym for 'supporters of the Soviet Union'. The Communists drew a very different conclusion. In their eyes, Russia was a 'workers' paradise' and a paradigm of proletarian democracy. The council republics in Germany and Hungary had failed mainly because they lacked a disciplined and centralised Bolshevik vanguard party. Therefore, this kind of party had to be built everywhere, following the guidelines developed by Lenin. During the 1920s and 1930s, Communist parties all over the world tried to apply the Leninist or Bolshevik model, expelling all dissidents and critical members until only obedient 'yes-men' remained (Dermott and Agnew, 1996: 14–80; Shirinia, 1996).

Some of these dissidents had argued a third position, criticising both the Social Democratic acceptance of bourgeois democracy and the Leninist defence of the Russian party dictatorship. A similar position was defended by many anarchists. The Communist dissidents clung to the original Soviet or workers' council model and tried to theorise it, in the hope that it would be implemented under more favourable circumstances in the future. Initially they also claimed the name 'Communists', often enriched with the prefix 'Council-', but later some distanced themselves from the association with the Soviet Union and Leninism and preferred the label 'Council-democrats' (*Rätedemokraten*) or 'Council-Socialists'.

The theory of the workers' councils, sometimes called 'councilism', was mainly developed by the German school teacher Otto Rühle and the Dutch astronomer Anton Pannekoek. Yet many others contributed, too: the German shop stewards movement (especially Richard Müller and Ernst Däumig), and, at some stage, the Hungarian philosopher Györgi Lukàcs, his German colleague Karl Korsch and the Italian theorist Antonio Gramsci (Bonnet, 2011; Hoffrogge, 2011). Here I will focus on Pannekoek, because of his consistency and influence (on Lenin, among others), and refer only in passing to Rühle (see Sirianni, 1982: 266).

Antonie (usually called Anton) Pannekoek (1873–1960) joined the Social Democratic Workers' Party (*Sociaal-Democratische Arbeiderspartij*, SDAP) in the Netherlands probably in 1899, while preparing a PhD in astronomy. As a principled Marxist, he often clashed with the moderate leadership of the party. When a group of younger leftwingers broke with the SDAP in 1909 and founded the Social Democratic Party, Pannekoek joined them (Voerman, 2001: 25–31). At that time, the astronomer lived in Berlin and was involved in political education with the German Social Democratic party (SPD). In 1910 he moved to Bremen, where the local branch of the SPD was dominated by leftwing radicals. With leftwing leaders such as Rosa Luxemburg and Karl Liebknecht, Pannekoek often criticised the restrained reformist strategy of the party leadership and advocated a more offensive and revolutionary course, in particular supporting spontaneous mass strikes (Bock, 1976: 76–82). Lenin agreed with Pannekoek's critique, even if he regarded it as too abstract ([1917] 1964: 488–495). Because of the First World War, Pannekoek had to return to the Netherlands in 1914. When the leftwing Social Democratic Party transformed itself into the Communist Party of the Netherlands (CPN) in 1918, Pannekoek followed. Yet three years later he would leave the party that accepted all instructions from Moscow and began to 'bolshevise' itself. Unlike his friend, the poet Herman Gorter, Pannekoek did not join the Communist Workers' Party founded by other leftwing dissidents (Voerman, 2001: 112–116). The scientist began to concentrate more on his academic career, and obtained a chair in astronomy at the University of Amsterdam, yet he continued to elaborate and publish his ideas on communism and councilism under a pseudonym.

Pannekoek mainly blamed the failure of the workers' councils on the lagging class-consciousness and ideological weakness of the working class. The workers had not yet emancipated themselves completely from bourgeois and petty-bourgeois ideologies, such as belief in religion, nationalism, and parliamentarism (Pannekoek, [1946] 1971: 30–31). This emancipation would not be easy. After all, the bourgeoisie controlled the press, the radio and the cinema, as well as the banks and the civil service (Pannekoek, [1933] 1972: 66; [1946] 1971: 85–86). The workers had accepted the division of labour within the industrialised production process as well as the political divison of labour in society. They saw politics as the domain of professional politicians, party leaders, members of parliament and trade union officials. The workers cherished the illusion that their leaders would realise socialism and liberate them, the workers, through negotiations, elections and legislation rather than trying to liberate themselves through their own day-to-day struggle in the workplace. They passively and uncritically followed the leaders of Social Democratic parties and unions, even in revolutionary situations, though these organisations had evolved into instruments of the bourgeoisie and were led by professionals with quasi-bourgeois ideas (Pannekoek, [1946] 1971: 48–53). Otto Rühle (1874–1943) added a psychological dimension. Workers lived in a petty-bourgeois environment, were raised in petty-bourgeois families and were educated in bourgeois schools. No wonder that 'the worker treats his wife and children the way he is treated by his boss and expects submission, subservience and authority' (Rühle, [1924] 1972: 51).[4]

Thus, the German workers' councils were dominated by leading members of the SPD, whose main goal was to obtain powerful positions within the state apparatus without abolishing capitalism (Pannekoek, [1927] 1972: 23–4; [1932] 1972: 56; [1946]1971: 150–152). In Russia, still mainly an agrarian country, the working class was more radical than in Central and Western Europe, but was also a lot smaller. Yet the Russian bourgeoisie was not very strong either, and the state apparatus had outlived itself. So a well-organised and determined political party could capture power and establish a dictatorship. Subsequently the party evolved into a new ruling class, a new kind of bourgeoisie that abolished the remnants of feudalism, destroyed the church and modernised agriculture (Pannekoek, 1972 [1932]: 58–59). Capital would be in the hands of the state rather than the hands of private owners, but the directors and managers appointed by the state (or the party) oppressed and exploited the workers the same way as capitalists and their managers in the West – if not worse! (Pannekoek, [1946] 1971: 160). Communism had become a pernicious and perverse ideology in the hands of Lenin and his party (Pannekoek, [1946] 1971: 161). Furthermore, Pannekoek considered Lenin's philosophy a form of bourgeois materialism – a serious insult in Marxist circles (Pannekoek, [1936d] 1972: 132; [1938] 1973).

Not that Pannekoek frowned on materialism himself – quite the contrary! He wholeheartedly embraced Marx's historical materialism, believing that 'the human spirit is completely determined by the environment', and that thought and human consciousness do not shape, but reflect social reality (of the past as much as the present) (Pannekoek, [1919] 1972: 15; [1946] 1971: 99). The mode of production determines not only the legal system, but also ethical notions, religious beliefs, philosophy and political ideologies, even personal character and the way children are reared (Pannekoek, [1946] 1971: 8–12, 44–45, 95–119). The growth of production leads to growing tensions ('contradictions') within social reality and also to change at the ideological level. Eventually, the working class will emancipate itself from bourgeois ideologies, shake off its apathy and develop a revolutionary class-consciousness (Pannekoek, [1946] 1971: 88). Yet the astronomer realised this would take a long time, and would have ups and downs; revolutionary experiments would be followed by periods of repression and resignation.

In spite of all setbacks, Pannekoek maintained his belief in workers' councils as the 'embryo' of a new proletarian democracy as well as the only revolutionary form of workers' organisation. The councils usually emerge in a situation of intensified class conflict, wild cat strikes, and political strikes and allow the workers to educate and emancipate themselves. In the 1920s he had argued for a revolutionary vanguard party, albeit different from the hierarchical Bolshevik model. Yet in the 1930s he began to see all parties as conservative and elitist organisations that would block rather than foster revolution (Pannekoek, [1927] 1972: 37; [1936b] 1972: 111–117). Rühle had already argued in 1924 that political parties copied the authoritarian and centralistic structure of the bourgeois state and could never become revolutionary proletarian organisations ([1924] 1972: 32). The only type of party that found favour in Pannekoek's eyes was an informal study group or think tank ([1932] 1972: 60–62). Pannekoek's view of trade unions evolved along a similar line. He praised the courage of syndicalists such as the American Industrial Workers of the World (IWW) and followed with some sympathy the General Workers Union in Germany (*Allgemeine Arbeiter-Union Deutschlands*), though without illusions about their revolutionary potential (Pannekoek, [1932] 1972; [1936a] 1972: 107–108).

Why were workers' councils unique and superior to both the political party and trade unions or industrial unions? Pannekoek pointed to four characteristics of this type of organisation. First of all, the councils transcend the division between politics and economy, a fundamental feature of bourgeois society ([1946] 1971: 36–40). They are based on the basic economic units in society, the factories or workshops, while articulating economic as well as political demands. Thus they represent relatively homogeneous 'natural units' (*natuurlijke eenheden*) or 'natural groups', whereas a bourgeois parliament represents geographical constituencies which are heterogeneous and artificial units (Pannekoek, [1936c] 1972: 124). Representation is rather different in the two institutions. On the one hand, parliament is dominated by professional politicians and 'specialists' who tend to ignore the interests of the majority of the voters and serve the interests of the bourgeoisie – to which they very often belong themselves. On the other hand, the workers' councils consists of class-conscious workers; if the latter ignore the interests of their voters, they will be recalled very quickly (Pannekoek, [1933] 1972: 68–71; [1946] 1971: 37–38). The council members have to account for their action at the factory assembly. And, finally, the councils combine executive and legislative powers, whereas bourgeois parliaments can only legislate – and are increasingly losing even those powers, as Pannekoek observed, due to the growing influence of cabinet and civil service ([1933] 1972: 70, 74). His conclusion was obvious: only workers' councils can be truly democratic; parliamentary democracy is really a fraud.

Pannekoek's theory suffers from several weaknesses, according to even sympathetic observers. In the first place, he may be asking too much from the average worker. The worker would have to interrupt his or her manual labour to prepare for a factory assembly, and form an educated opinion about the management of the factory but also about local and national economic planning and various political questions. After all, the worker would have to give binding instructions to his delegates in the workers' council and indirectly to the delegates at the local council and the councils at higher levels, assess their activities and recall them if they neglect his interests. Perhaps the same worker has to take part in a workers' militia – to defend the revolution against its numerous enemies. No wonder most workers would attend the assemblies only in times of danger or crisis, or just vote for a colleague who appears to be a nice bloke. As Sirianni observed in revolutionary Russia, participation in workers' councils tends to decline fairly rapidly. As time went by, decisions were increasingly taken by executive committees and presidia, rather than by the Soviets, let alone the factory assemblies that elected the latter. Moreover, the influence of bureaucrats and experts increased as the Soviets had to deal with more economic and administrative problems. As the German political scientist Udo Bermbach argues, the coordination of a socialist economy would be difficult enough even without the involvement of the grass roots (1968: 24–29). Alienation between delegates and their constituents, the workers in the factories, might be practically inevitable.

The merging of executive and legislative functions would not alleviate this problem. It might even exacerbate it, as this institutional monism may hamper critical opposition and diversity of opinions in the councils. Council members who voice criticisms will be easily accused of disloyalty and sabotage – especially in times of crisis and external threats, which are to be expected in a revolutionary process. Thus workers on the factory floor may often perceive the council as a unified bloc which seems closed and insensitive to criticism. Though Pannekoek's rejection of vanguard parties seems reasonable, given the historical record of the Bolsheviks, his tendency to do away with parties altogether may not contribute to pluralism and liberty either. He may have underestimated the historical weight of parties and unions anyway, as Sirianni concluded (1982: 352). At the same time, the principles of binding mandates and recall do imply a certain homogeneity in the population. As Urbinati pointed out in her critical interpretation of Rousseau, 'imperative mandate could ... express the "general interest" *only if* the society was rigorously homogeneous, made up of individuals who shared identical economic interests, the same culture, religion, and ethical values' (2008: 68). Imagine an assembly giving two contradictory instructions to its delegates – it would disempower itself by this act, and lose all credibility if this were to happen often.

Finally, one could criticise Pannekoek's strategy – or the lack of it. In his eyes, revolution was a spontaneous process, caused by anonymous economic forces and the development of class-consciousness. Intellectuals could speed up the development by spreading the right ideas – as Pannekoek was doing most of his life – but should not intervene directly. The workers had to emancipate themselves, especially by organising strikes and setting up councils whenever the opportunity arose; meanwhile, there was not much to be done. Involvement in a trade union or a political party would hamper rather than help the process. Jaap Kloosterman, a Dutch scholar who edited Pannekoek's work in the 1970s, linked the strategic weakness and the underestimation of organisational problems in Pannekoek's work to his economic determinism or economism (1972: 229–231). With hindsight, one can also state that Pannekoek – like many other Marxists at the time – underestimated the capacity of capitalism to improve the conditions of the working class (Kloosterman, 1972: 231).

In spite of all these weaknesses, Pannekoek's ideas did not die with him. Council-democracy or 'councilism' experienced a revival in the late 1960s and 1970s and inspired in particular the most radical elements in the European New Left, as will be shown below.

The New Left, 'autogestion' and council-democracy

By 1940, council-communists and anarchists had been practically exterminated in Russia by the Stalinist regime, and in Germany, Italy and Spain by Fascists and National Socialists. Even the mixed regime of liberal democracy almost succumbed to the onslaught of these extremist forces in Europe in 1939–1941. Yet the alliance between Nazi Germany and the Soviet Union broke down in 1941; the latter joined the Allied forces and helped to defeat the other dictatorships. In 1945 democracy appeared to have triumphed, whether in its Western, liberal garb or in the Marxist–Leninist sense of the word. Economic growth, full employment and social security added to the popularity of both systems in their part of the world. The Cold War between them left very little space for any 'third position'. Yet a few marginal groups of (mainly) intellectuals kept the torches burning. Two of them seem particularly relevant here: first the French group *Socialisme ou Barbarie*, and then the Situationist International. Both could be seen as important sources of inspiration for the New Left that emerged in France, and to a lesser extent in other parts of Europe, in the 1960s (see Hecken and Grzenia, 2008; Gilcher-Holtey, 2008; Lucardie, 1980).

Socialisme ou Barbarie (Socialism or Barbarism) was founded in 1948 by Cornelius Castoriadis (1922–1997) and Claude Lefort (1924–2010). Castoriadis had joined the Communist youth organisation in Greece but was soon disappointed by its Stalinist policies. When he moved to France in 1946, he adhered to the French section of the Fourth International (Gombin, 1971: 39–40; Howard, 1977: 263). The Fourth International had been founded by Leon Trotsky in 1938, after he had been exiled from Russia, in an attempt to unite all Marxists striving for a global socialist revolution (Frank, 1973: 47–51). Trotsky felt Stalin had betrayed the cause of the world revolution by giving priority to socialism in one country. As a result, socialism was degenerating rapidly in Russia. Even so, Trotsky regarded the Soviet Union as a 'workers' state' which deserved (critical) support and strongly condemned the view that it was a case of 'state capitalism' ruled by a new kind of bourgeoisie. The latter idea, proposed by council-communists as well as anarchists, did appeal to some of his followers, however. It was discussed, and rejected, at the second congress of the Fourth International, held in 1948 – eight years after its founding father had been assassinated by a Stalinist agent (Frank, 1973: 58–60). Castoriadis and Lefort, who belonged to the dissident minority, left the organisation and founded *Socialisme ou Barbarie*. The group published a journal with the same name.

Socialisme ou Barbarie agreed not only with Pannekoek's critical analysis of the Soviet Union, but also with his alternative socialism based on workers' councils. Under the pseudonym 'Pierre Chaulieu', Castoriadis elaborated and to some extent radicalised Pannekoek's idea. In a socialist society, important decisions should be taken preferably by general assemblies of workers (in factories, workshops, etc.), which should meet one day a month (Chaulieu [Castoriadis], 1957). The workers' council elected by the assembly would implement the decisions of the latter. Municipal councils, based on geographical units, might survive in a transitional period, but should not overrule the workers' councils. The latter should co-ordinate their planning through federal assemblies. The councils should make sure that the content of work and the use of technology changed within the socialist society. This was a point neglected by Marx – and Pannekoek – in the eyes of Castoriadis. The Greek theorist also disagreed with Pannekoek about the strategic question of how to bring about the socialist society. Though critical of the Leninist party model, Castoriadis argued that a socialist revolution required a vanguard party of some kind. Once the revolution was over, the party should atrophy – so he hoped, perhaps rather naïvely.

Castoriadis did not convince the whole group. Lefort objected to any notion of a vanguard. Like Pannekoek, he believed that the revolution should result from spontaneous grass roots actions of workers, without guidance from a party. In 1958 Lefort broke with Castoriadis and set up a less ambitious group (and journal) called *Informations et Liaison Ouvrières* (Workers' Information and Liaison) and later renamed – even more modestly – *Informations et Correspondance Ouvrières* (Workers' Information and Correspondence) (Gombin, 1971: 145–151). The group would mainly exchange information about workers' struggles. As a philosopher, Lefort came to question not only the notion of a political vanguard organisation but also the pretension of a 'vanguard theory'. Society is not transparent enough to be explained and predicted by theorists, he would conclude (Howard, 1977: 222–228). In his later work, Lefort moved further away from Marxism and councilism – but that story does not belong in this chapter.

Castoriadis did not remain an orthodox Marxist either. In the last issues of *Socialisme ou Barbarie* he argued that Marxism could no longer serve as a revolutionary theory (Howard, 1977: 264). The group *Socialisme ou Barbarie* fell apart in 1965. Though it had never been a large organisation, its influence should not be underestimated. It inspired a wide variety of groups and individuals, from the anarchist student leader Daniel Cohn-Bendit to leftist Social Democrats, as well as Situationists (about Cohn-Bendit see Lemire, 1998: 22, 31, 72).

The Situationist International (*Internationale Situationniste*) was a small international organisation, founded in 1957 by painters, architects, filmmakers and other artists. They felt it was time to transcend art and 'create situations' that would do away with the separation between art, politics, work and leisure (Martos, 1989: 11–65). This separation had stifled creativity and turned every activity into an alienating spectacle and every participant into a passive

Jacobinland: bounded-delegate democracy 89

consumer (Debord, 1967). Initially, the best way to overcome alienation seemed to them to be 'unitary urbanism': integrating architecture, art and urban planning. At the individual level, the Situationists also proposed *la dérive*, wandering for a day or so at random through different parts of a city, open to any event and encounter: 'pour se laisser aller aux sollicitations du terrain et des rencontres qui y correspondent' (Debord 1958: 19). After 1960, however, the Situationists became more radical and more political. Contact with *Socialisme ou Barbarie* may have raised their interest in the theory of workers' councils (Martos, 1989: 140–144; Sanders, 1989: 132). Gradually, they came to see the councils as the only institution that might help to break out of the '*société du spectacle*' and end the alienation. A minority (mainly Scandinavian and Dutch members) questioned this old-leftist reliance on the working class as the revolutionary agent that would usher in a new society. They were soon expelled, if they did not leave voluntarily (Martos, 1989: 125–129).

The Situationists did not appropriate the councilist theory without adding their own touches. With Castoriadis, they agreed that the most important echelon should not be the council itself but the workers' assembly that elected it (Riesel, 1969: 65). The historical councils had generally neglected this level, thus creating the first separation between workers and delegates; no wonder they soon abandoned most power to executive committees and bureaus. Next to workers' councils, the Situationists also favoured neighbourhood councils – and not merely as transitional measure, as Castoriadis had argued. They did not specify how the two types of councils should co-ordinate policies; coherence would be guaranteed, as René Riesel wrote, by the fact that the councils eliminate any other power (1969: 71–72).[5] Unlike Pannekoek and Castoriadis, however, the Situationists regarded the council-system as the beginning rather than the end of the revolution – the latter remained indeterminate and open (Riesel, 1969: 73). Moreover, the revolutionaries would not only have to transform the relations of production and expropriate the capitalists, but also transform the production process itself, the environment, education, justice and so forth (Anonymous, 1966: 30–31). Castoriadis, Pannekoek and most other councilists had neglected this aspect, in the eyes of the Situationists, and tended to reproduce the separation between work, art and leisure of the *société du spectacle* (Sanders, 1989: 133, 167).

For the first ten years of its existence, the Situationist International remained a rather obscure sectarian movement. Yet in 1966 they began to exercise some influence on radical students, first in Strassbourg, then in Paris. When the student protest turned into a mass movement in May 1968, the Situationists provided it with images, slogans and graffiti. Their expressive and violent language captured the spirit of the movement, apparently. 'Vivre sans temps morts et jouir sans entraves' (To live without pause and enjoy without restraint), 'Ne travaillez jamais!' (Never work!) and 'L'humanité ne sera heureuse que le jour où le dernier bureaucrate aura été pendu avec les tripes du dernier capitaliste' (Mankind will not be happy until the last bureaucrat has been hanged with the guts of the last capitalist) covered many walls in France (Gombin, 1969: 27–42;

Le Goff, 1998: 38–42, 51–55). The Situationist language was more violent than their actions, but their militant student sympathisers, called *les enragés*, did disturb lectures and harass faculty members as well as administrators. They mobilised a widespread latent discontent. Students went on strike and occupied universities all over France. Barricades were erected in Paris. Police brutality led to public protest and a short solidarity strike organised by unions. When young workers occupied an airplane factory near Nantes, they triggered a chain reaction. Within a few days, almost nine million workers went on strike, without any call from union headquarters (Gilcher-Holtey, 2008: 116–117; Le Goff, 1998: 59–67, 85–101). Workers' councils emerged in a few cases, though they did not last very long. Situationists were engaged in a Council for the Maintenance of the Occupations. Even if they failed to stop the tapering off of the movement, in a way it was their finest hour. Though they could easily have recruited many new members after May 1968, the Situationists did not have the patience nor the will (nor possibly the organisational talents) to develop a real mass movement. Instead of expanding the movement they purged it and fell apart in bickering factions, until the International was finally dissolved in 1972 (Martos, 1989: 261–276).

May 1968 had a radicalising impact upon many leftwing organisations in France, and upon the Catholic trade union movement and the United Socialist Party in particular. The *Parti Socialiste Unifié* (PSU) was, as its American historiographer Charles Hauss characterised it, the party of the French New Left (1978). Its origins go back to 1954, when a motley crowd of progressive Catholic intellectuals, disillusioned Trotskyists, leftwing Socialists and former members of the (increasingly conservative) Radical Party set up the *Comité de liaison et d'initiative pour une nouvelle gauche* (CLING), the Liaison and Initiative Committee for a New Left (Levin, 1970: 176–180). Six years and two mergers later the PSU was founded, and was joined by dissidents from the Communist party and the Socialist Party (Nania, 1973: 61–64; Cayrol, 1969: 9–18). The PSU played an important role in the opposition to the war in Algeria, but remained quite small in terms of parliamentary seats and members.

In 1968, however, the PSU enjoyed a sudden boost: membership went up from 12,000 to 15,600 and its electorate almost doubled, from 2.3 to 3.9 per cent (Cayrol, 1969: 33, 41). At the party congress in 1969 the PSU opted for workers' self-management in industry: important decisions should be taken by workers' councils, which would elect and, if necessary, also recall the managers: *l'autogestion, c'est-à-dire la prise des décisions essentielles, le choix des directeurs et leur révocabilité par des conseils élus par les travailleurs de l'entreprise* ('self-management, i.e. taking essential decisions, choosing and recalling managers by councils elected by the workers of the company') (Parti Socialiste Unifié, 1969: 151). However, the party did not call for the abolition of the parliamentary system. In its 1972 Manifesto, it moved even closer to council-democracy. The workers' or producers' councils should deal not only with economic decisions in the strict sense, but also with (adult) education, environmental planning and leisure (Parti Socialiste Unifié, 1972: 112). They should co-ordinate this with local neighbourhood councils, which would be elected according to similar principles (direct participation, recall) (Parti Socialiste Unifié, 1972: 111, 113). How the coordination should take place, and what the role of parliament would be, the party did not specify; discussion in the theoretical party journal did not really clarify this either. Alain Guillerm suggested a central council elected by the workers' councils (1973: 85–86). Yet as Alain Richard pointed out, even in this fairly orthodox councilist proposal – Guillerm referred to both Chaulieu/Castoriadis and Pannekoek – it remained unclear how the interests of producers and consumers would be reconciled (1974). The PSU did not get a chance to realise its programme. Torn apart by factional struggles, it gradually dwindled into insignificance and disappeared in 1989 (Pina, 2005: 136–139).

The Catholic confederation of trade unions had changed its name to Democratic Confederation of Labour (*Confédération Française Démocratique du Travail*, CFDT) in 1964. In its constitution it mentioned the redistribution and democratic control (*une répartition et un contrôle démocratique*) of economic and political power as one of its goals (La CFDT, 1971: 61). Radicalised by the events of May 1968, it redefined this in 1970 as *autogestion*: 'management of the company by the workers, but also [management] of the economy and the city by the people' (La CFDT, 1971: 131).[6] In the end, the CFDT wanted to do away with all intermediaries between workers and economic power, as well as between citizens and political power (Maire and Julliard, 1975: 175). Self-management was to be generalised throughout society. The Russian and German workers' councils were explicitly mentioned as examples, though the union remained sceptical of specific blueprints and models (Maire and Julliard, 1975: 175).

The CFDT and to a lesser extent the PSU contributed to the transformation of the Socialist Party in the early 1970s. Until then, the party had retained the rather dated name given in 1905, 'French Section of the Workers' International' (*Section Française de l'Internationale Ouvrière*, SFIO) as well as the ideological rhetoric that belonged to that bygone era, whereas its policies had become more conservative and its organisation rather bureaucratic. Its membership and electorate had dwindled. In 1971 the old SFIO merged with several political clubs, becoming the new *Parti Socialiste* (PS). *Autogestion* became the symbol of its new identity. In 1975 the party approved a manifesto drafted by Gilles Martinet, a former member of the PSU, which called for socialisation of major industries under the management of workers' councils, with supervision by representatives of consumers and of the state (Parti Socialiste, 1975). The PS also adopted New Left slogans such as '*changer la vie*'. A large part of the PSU had joined the new party a year earlier. The political scientist Roland Cayrol concluded that the PS had been 'PSU-ised' (*PSU-isé*) (1975). The embrace of *autogestion* was not only the result of external influence, however, but also of internal pressure from the Centre for Socialist Study, Research and Education (*Centre d'études, de recherches et d'éducation socialiste*, CERES).

CERES had been founded in 1966 by Jean-Pierre Chévènement, Didier Motchane and other young graduates from the National School for Public

92   Jacobinland: bounded-delegate democracy

Administration (*École Nationale d'Administration*, ENA). Inspired by various Marxist theorists, including Castoriadis, they also advocated workers' self-management – to be achieved step by step, in combination with nationalisations and democratic planning of the economy (Charzat, Chévènement and Toutain, 1975: 179–189; 248). However, they wanted to apply the same principles of direct elections and recall of delegates to neighbourhood councils and local government. And unlike all of the other groups discussed here, they also favoured the referendum (Charzat, Chévènement and Toutain, 1975: 230–231). CERES did not only engage in theory, but also in practical politics; through clever tactics their faction exercised considerable influence on the PS in the 1970s (Hanley, 1988).

When the PS won a parliamentary majority in 1981, after its leader François Mitterrand had won the presidential elections, it took a few modest steps in the direction of workers' control – like giving workers more freedom on the shop floor (Ross, 1987; Portelli, 1992: 117). However, when its radical reformism met with resistance (inside and outside France) the party leadership soon abandoned it and switched to 'normal' social democratic policies. The slogan '*changer la vie*' was eventually replaced by '*la France unie!*' (Kergoat, 1997: 100). CERES fell apart. Chevènement and some of his friends left the PS in 1993 and founded the *Mouvement des citoyens* (Citizens' Movement; later called *Mouvement Républicain et Citoyen*, MRC), which advocated protectionism and national sovereignty – with vague references to 'real democracy' (*véritable démocratie*) but not to any kind of workers' self-management (Chabrun and Hériot, 1999: 85–86, 134–138).

New Left ideas about self-management did not disappear completely from French politics, however. Many *soixante-huitards*, including Cohn-Bendit, found a new political home in the ecological movement and the green parties that emerged from it and would eventually coalesce into *Les Verts* (after various mergers and splits) (Le Goff, 1998: 377–393; Sainteny, 1992: 11–25). The ecologists called for *la démocratie participative*, through popular initiative and referendum, but also industrial democracy: *la participation aux décisions ... dans l'entreprise* ('participation in the decision-making ... in the company'), though without any Marxist references to class struggle and workers' councils (Les Verts, 1999: 141–150).

In the twenty-first century, the only advocates of something like workers' councils in France may be found in the Trotskyist New Anti-capitalist Party (*Nouveau Parti Anticapitaliste*, NPA). This seems rather ironic given the fact that Trotsky did not hesitate to disempower the workers' councils in Russia after the revolution. The NPA called for 'workers' power at every level of political, economic and social life' (*le pouvoir des travailleurs et travailleuses dans toutes les domaines et à tous les échelons de la vie politique, économique et sociale*) and for the right to recall representatives (*révocabilité des élus*) (Nouveau Parti Anticapitaliste, 2009). Trotskyist parties elsewhere pursued similar policies. For example the (tiny) Socialist Party in the United Kingdom argued for committees at every level, in communities and workplaces, that would elect representatives to regional and national government that would be accountable and subject to instant recall (Socialist Party, no date). The Belgian economist Ernest Mandel, one of Trotsky's brightest disciples and a key figure in the Fourth International, remained a consistent advocate of workers' councils throughout his life that began in 1923 and ended in 1995 (Mandel, 1973: 113–156; Mandel, 1977: 97–98; see also Samary, 1999; and Blackburn, 1999).

New Left ideas travelled quite well in the 1960s and 1970s. A few examples will suffice here. In The Netherlands the Pacifist Socialist Party (*Pacifistisch Socialistische Partij*, PSP) followed almost the same trajectory as the PSU in France, at least until the 1980s. It was founded in 1957 by dissident Communists, leftwing Social Democrats and Christian pacifists who refused to join the Cold War and who were searching for something new: democratic and spiritual renewal (Pacifistisch Socialistische Partij, 1957: 4; see also Van der Land, 1962). Factional struggles halted its growth in the 1960s. In the 1970s, Trotskyists, reformists and Christian pacifists left the party, leaving it in the hands of libertarian socialists (see Lucardie, 1980: 94–123). In its 1977 platform, the PSP opted for a 'socialist council-republic' (*socialistische radenrepubliek*): 'direct democracy, consisting of popular assemblies of all concerned. They elect delegates to councils for central decisions. These delegates can be recalled immediately' (Pacifistisch Socialistische Partij, 1977: 9).[7] This principle would apply to neighbourhood councils as well as to councils in economic units. Democracy was incompatible with capitalism, in the eyes of the PSP: the means of production had to be socialised. The question of whether parliament would continue to exist next to the councils was left open. In the 1980s the PSP moderated its views. In 1989 it joined a Green Left coalition with Communists, Radicals and progressive Christians; two years later it dissolved its organisation. The Green Left also wanted to 'democratise' society; workers should be able to elect their managers (GroenLinks, 1994: 80). Gradually, however, the party dropped most of its radical-democratic demands (Lucardie and Pennings, 2010: 159–161).

In Germany the New Left was a more intellectual affair than in France or the Netherlands. Its core was constituted by the German Socialist Student League (*Sozialistischer Deutscher Studentenbund*, SDS) (Klimke, 2008: 98). Until 1961 it had been affiliated with the SPD, but while the latter shifted towards the right and purged its programme from Marxist elements, the SDS moved in the opposite direction (Fichter and Lönnendonker, 1977: 13–72). The students began to read Marx again, and rediscovered Lukàcs, Korsch and Pannekoek, as well as Wilhelm Reich, who had developed a peculiar synthesis of Freud and Marx in the 1920s: the sexpol movement. They were often also inspired by the Critical Theory of the Frankfurt School: Max Horkheimer, Theodor Adorno and Jürgen Habermas, as well as Herbert Marcuse, the German philosopher who had emigrated to the United States in 1934 (Bock, 1976: 194–205, 230–238). After 1965 the SDS tried to turn theory into practice and to mobilise mass protests against nuclear armament, the Vietnam War and the new emergency laws prepared by the German government, which students perceived as a step towards an authoritarian regime (Fichter and Lönnendonker, 1977: 81–105; Klimke, 2008: 103–104; see also Otto, 1977). Some attempts were moderately successful, especially in West Berlin.

To a considerable extent, the SDS owed its modest success to the eloquence and charm of its main spokesman, Rudi Dutschke. Alfred Willi Rudi Dutschke was born in Brandenburg in 1940 and came to West Berlin in 1960 – a year before the wall would make this type of migration rather difficult (Dutschke, 1996: 18–30). He studied sociology, and discovered Lukàcs, Marx, Marcuse and a few years later Pannekoek (Dutschke, 1996: 39–40, 113). In 1963 he joined a small 'cell' of Subversive Action (*Subversive Aktion*), a somewhat secretive network which had been set up by a German member of the Situationist International, Dieter Kunzelmann (Kraushaar, 1976). The group occasionally engaged in provocative actions, but spent most of the time discussing Marx, Freud and the revolution. The revolution had to be a cultural and psychological transformation as well as a socio-economic transformation. Dutschke and his friends expected more from the impoverished peasants and workers in the Third World than from the relatively affluent consumerist working class in Germany and other European countries (Dutschke, [1964] 1976). In 1964 the Subversive Action group joined the SDS and contributed to its radicalisation (Dutschke, 1996: 61–62; Fichter and Lönnendonker, 1977: 78–81). On several occasions Dutschke argued that a council-democracy should replace the parliamentary pseudo-democracy: 'a direct council democracy [*Rätedemokratie*], where free individuals would elect temporary and rotating leaders that can be recalled at any time, in industry as well as in university, schools, public service' (Dutschke, 1996: 142; see also 264, 418–419). He was not the only one; even academics such as Wilfried Gottschalch and trade union officials Dieter Schneider and Rudolf Kuda (both employed by the German metal-workers union IG Metall) showed sympathy for the idea in 1968 (Gottschalch, 1968; Schneider and Kuda, 1968: 42–62; see also Bock, 1976: 230–252). Leading marches and speaking at teach-ins in Berlin, Dutschke gained a fairly wide audience. He paid a heavy price for his popularity, however: in April 1968 he was shot on the Kurfürstendamm in Berlin by a man with confused rightwing ideas (Dutschke, 1996: 197–200). Dutschke survived with brain damage; he died eleven years later in his bathtub. Shortly before his death, he was involved in the preparations for the Green party and contributed to its programme (Dutschke, 1996: 446–450, 464, 470–473).

The German party The Greens (*Die Grünen*) was officially founded in 1980. The Greens were in many ways the 'true heirs' of the German (and international) New Left, as Andrea Levy has argued (2007: 31). In their first programme, they defined their identity in four terms: ecological, social, radical-democratic and non-violent (*ökologisch, sozial, basisdemokratisch, gewaltfrei*). To them, radical democracy meant

> realisation of decentral, direct democracy ... the core idea is the control of all public officials and representatives and institutions by the grass-roots, as

well as their revocability, in order to make organisation and politics transparent and to prevent that people are cut loose from the grass roots.

(Die Grünen, 1980)[8]

More specifically, they advocated the referendum and people's initiative, while practising rotation, recall and binding mandates within their own party organisation – at least initially (Demirovic, 1998). Though the party has moved away from grass roots democracy in recent years, it has never renounced direct democracy altogether. Even in the party programme of 2002, *Die Grünen*, wanted to 'supplement parliamentary democracy with direct democracy' and to 'democratise society', though they did not specify how (Bündnis 90/Die Grünen, 2002: 129, 130).

Time to sum up this long section. The New Left expressed a double refusal: of Western capitalism and its political system of parliamentary representation as well as of Soviet communism and its one-party system. Consequently, many New Leftists were delighted to discover predecessors of this position, in particular council-democrats such as Anton Pannekoek and Otto Rühle. The Situationists, the group *Socialisme ou Barbarie*, the PSU in France, the PSP in the Netherlands and the SDS in Germany all embraced a form of council-democracy. Yet they differed from Pannekoek and his generation in two respects. They seemed reluctant to grant the workers' councils an absolute monopoly of power and to exclude housewives, pensioners, shopkeepers and the unemployed from the decision-making process. These people should have the opportunity to take part in neighbourhood councils. How the latter had to be co-ordinated with the workers' councils was usually left open. By broadening the council principle, New Leftists also tended to dilute it and relax (if not relinquish) the unity of economic and political power so dear to Marx, Lenin and Pannekoek. In line with this, the New Left also abandoned the economic determinism and the 'productivism' of the orthodox Marxists in favour of a voluntarist belief in 'action' and 'cultural revolution'. The Greens continued on this road and moved even further away from Marxism, abandoning the belief in the working class as a privileged agent of social and political change. Initially they favoured the bounded-delegate model, at least as an abstract principle, but gradually most Green parties came to accept the parliamentary system – supplemented, perhaps, with referendums and popular initiatives.

Populist democracy: Torbjörn Tännsjö and Heinz Dieterich

Yet even in recent decades, advocates of a kind of council-democracy can be found – though sometimes in unlikely places. Two of them will be discussed briefly in this section, the Swedish philosopher Torbjörn Tännsjö and the German-born sociologist Heinz Dieterich. The former calls himself a populist, while the latter defended a regime that has been qualified as populist by most observers.

Populism is a rather controversial and confusing term. Originally, it denoted the ideology of the People's Party in the US, which was founded in 1892 and disappeared about fifteen years later (Taggart, 2000: 27–37; see also The Shorter Oxford English Dictionary on Historical Principles, 1980: II, 1630).[9] The party's primary aim was 'to restore the government of the Republic to the hands of "the plain people", with whose class it originated', and the main instruments to achieve this seemed to be the initiative and referendum as well as the direct election of public officials (People's Party, [1892] 1961: 441, 444). Direct legislation by the people became 'almost an obsession with the Populists', according to their historian John Hicks ([1931] 1961: 408). However, in the course of the twentieth century the term 'populism' was used much more loosely, referring to any political movement that mobilised 'ordinary people' or 'marginalized social sectors' against any elite, without necessarily calling for referendum or initiative (Jansen, 2011: 82; Kazin, 1995: 1). The concept was applied to agrarian Socialists in Tsarist Russia and Communists in China, military dictators in Latin America and the independence movement in Tanzania, the New Left in the US and even presidents such as Richard Nixon and Ronald Reagan (MacRae, 1969; Worsley, 1969; Kazin, 1995: 195–218, 248–266). At the beginning of the twenty-first century, most (but not all) experts seem to agree on at least the following constituent components of populism: a positive valorisation of 'the people' and denigration of 'the elite', both of which are seen as relatively homogeneous and antagonistic units, and the belief in popular sovereignty (Decker, 2006: 12; Houwen, 2013: 61; Mudde, 2004: 543; Surel, 2004: 97–98; Stanley, 2008: 102).

The belief in popular sovereignty need not imply direct legislation by the people, however. Populist leaders might claim to know and represent – even incarnate – the will of the people without a popular vote. Some experts regard populism as at least potentially, if not actually, anti-democratic (Abts and Rummens, 2007; Pasquino, 2008). Even if populist leaders submit questions to the people, they seek acclamation rather than popular participation. It is a top-down process, plebiscitary rather than participatory, to use the terms of Robert Barr (2009). Other scholars see populism as essentially ambivalent, both 'threat' and 'corrective' to democracy (Decker, 2006; Rovira Kaltwasser, 2012; Mény and Surel, 2002). If party democracy declines due to professionalisation and loss of ideological identities, populist democracy might be the only (democratic) alternative, Peter Mair argued (2002). Ernesto Laclau goes even further, suggesting that 'populism is the democratic element in contemporary representative systems', while it is necessarily fluid and empty of meaning (2005: 176, 191).

The confusing variety of scholarly opinions about the relationship between populism and democracy may be caused (at least partly) by the fact that few political parties and leaders refer to themselves as 'populist'.[10] There is no Populist International, no European Populist Federation, and no agreement on classical populist thinkers. One of the few philosophers who published an explicit defence of populism may be Torbjörn Tännsjö, born in 1946 and Professor at the University of Stockholm. However, his conception of populism hardly fits with the literature discussed so far. The populist democracy Tännsjö defends is 'systematic collective decision-making in accordance with the majoritarian principle or the principle of unanimity' (1992: 3). In other words, it is the classical notion of democracy as introduced in Chapter 1. In fact, Tännsjö himself also uses the term 'classical' democracy, while contrasting it with the 'realistic' notion of Schumpeter and Riker (Tännsjö , 1992: 1–10). The Swedish philosopher does not refer to 'the people' as a homogeneous and virtuous unity, nor does he depict the elite as evil or corrupt. His 'communalist utopia' (terms he uses himself) resembles the council-democracy advocated by Castoriadis and Dutschke: 'all citizens take direct part in democratic decisions concerning matters they know something about and feel are of deep concern to them' (Tännsjö, 1992: 93). Other decisions are left to elected and revocable delegates, both at the workplace and at the local or regional level. Ideally, workers should own or at least control their factories and workshops. In the long run, the same principles should be applied at every level, local, regional, national and even global: a World Parliament should elect a World Government (Tännsjö, 1992: 106–122). Yet Tännsjö is pragmatic enough to also accept a representative or parliamentary system, depending on the circumstances. If direct participation in decision-making (in the workplace or at a neighbourhood assembly) sinks below a minimal level and full-time activists begin to dominate the process, it should automatically make way for a representative (election-based) system as the default option (Tännsjö, 1992: 100–101).

The 'socialism of the twenty-first century' advocated by Heinz Dieterich does not differ much from Tännsjö's communalist utopia, but is embedded in a more orthodox Marxist theory. Dieterich, born in 1943, studied sociology in Bremen and in Frankfurt, where he followed the lectures of Adorno and Habermas (Tieleman, 2012). Since 1977 he has taught at the Autonomous Metropolitan University in Mexico City. With Marx, he believes capitalism will create the objective conditions for socialism, but the subjective conditions depend on 'political praxis' and revolutionary theory. The state socialism of the Soviet Union and China came too early, in his opinion: the objective conditions were not yet fulfilled. These countries lacked the advanced technology to develop production; hence, they could only foster economic growth by intensifying the exploitation of the working class (Dieterich, 2005: 232–233). The Russian and Chinese workers could not control production. Moreover, the Soviet Union (and later China) had to adapt to the world market and calculate the prices of products and services in market terms, whereas in a socialist economy they should be calculated in terms of labour time invested in those products and services. This calculation was technically impossible at the time of the Russian and Chinese revolutions: it requires a sophisticated use of computers that did not exist then. At last, in the twenty-first century, it has become possible to plan the economy in line with the principle of equivalence of time inputs rather than supply and demand in the global market (Dieterich, 2005: 109–130, 157–161).

Planning the economy should be a democratic process. At the national (and possibly global) level, investment plans should be submitted to the people in a referendum (Dieterich, 2005: 150). At the local level, workers should decide the quantity they want to produce, and consequently the income that they will earn

(Dieterich, 2005: 179–180). Factories and companies should be managed by councils of workers and consumers (*consejos de consumidores y productores (trabajadores)*) (Dieterich, 2005: 235). Participatory democracy (*democracia participativa*) should be introduced in every sector of society, not only in industry, but also in university, mass media and so on. Dieterich's definition seems similar to the one offered by Tännsjö: 'the real capacity of the majority of citizens to decide about the main public issues of the nation' (2005: 134).[11] The sociologist does not specify any details, such as how potential conflicts are to be resolved between consumers and producers or what should be done with a factory that wants to produce more (or less) than is required by the national plan. He referred to Marx, Engels and Lenin, but not to Pannekoek or other councilists.

Participatory democracy is contrasted with formal 'bourgeois democracy', which according to Dieterich is in fact manipulated by a global 'plutocratic oligarchy'. An elite of roughly 10,000 wealthy businessmen, politicians and military leaders controls not only the banks and industries, but also the mass media and the established political parties (Dieterich, 2005: 62–68, 135, 138). Elections serve only to redistribute power within the ruling class. If the people really voted for change, a military coup would probably rob it of all power and restore the oligarchy – as happened in Chile in 1973. Yet the situation does not seem entirely hopeless; the power of the elite cannot be absolute. At least in parts of Latin America, Dieterich observes the potential for change in the direction of socialism and participatory democracy. Under the leadership of President Hugo Chávez, Venezuela might become the centre of a regional power bloc against the global elite. The admiration between Chávez and Dieterich was mutual, it seemed, at least in 2005 (Tieleman, 2012; Dieterich, 2011; see also Priester, 2012: 121–122; Werz, 2007: 15).

Unlike Marx and the most orthodox Marxists, but in common with many New Leftists, Dieterich is not convinced that the working class will be a hegemonic force in the transition to socialism. He regards it as an important part of a revolutionary alliance with indigenous people, women, *precarios* (people employed temporarily or part-time or working in the informal economy) and other oppressed groups all over the world (2005: 146–157). Occasionally he refers to the alliance as 'the people', in opposition to 'the elite' (Dieterich, 2005: 62). This would make him a populist, in the eyes of most political scientists – more so than Tännsjö, in fact – even if Dieterich does not use the term himself. His hero Chávez is also considered as 'the most quintessentially populist figure Latin America has seen since Juan Perón, the legendary Argentine leader who was virtually synonymous with populism in the region', as Kenneth Roberts points out (2012: 136). According to Kirk Hawkins, who has (with his assistants) analysed speeches from forty political leaders, past and present, across the world, Chávez scored higher on populism than anyone else, including Perón (2009: 1053). Yet a caveat is called for. Since 2005 Dieterich has gradually lost his faith in Chávez. The president seemed unable to prevent the rise of a new ruling class in Venezuela, pursuing its own interests rather than building a participatory democracy. Human rights have been neglected, committed socialists have been assassinated, and the economy is not becoming socialist but is, at best, a social market economy like Germany in the post-war period (Dieterich, 2009; 2011; Tieleman, 2012). In the next section, Dieterich's claims will be evaluated in a brief analysis of populist democracy in Venezuela.

PRACTICE

Populist democracy in Venezuela?

Between 1958 and 1998, Venezuela was considered to be one of the most stable liberal democracies in Latin America, even if the presidency enjoyed primacy over other branches of government (Trinkunas, 2010; Hawkins, 2010: 86–94). Christian Democrats and Social Democrats alternated in power. Yet in the 1980s and 1990s corruption and discontent increased to an alarming degree, while the two parties began to pursue neo-liberal policies. Junior military officers started plotting against the government. One of them was Hugo Rafael Chávez Frías (1954–2013). Born in a provincial town, of mixed descent (American Indian, African and European), Chávez had opted for a military career but was gradually politicised by leftist friends and relatives (Marcano and Tyszka, [2004] 2006: 8–37). He has been described as bold and charismatic, with a messianic streak, witty, direct and honest, but also erratic and unpredictable (Gott, 2000: 9, 33, 228; Marcano and Tyszka, [2004] 2006). In the 1980s he founded a small conspiratorial 'Bolivarian Revolutionary Army' – inspired by the man who had led the liberation of Venezuela from Spanish colonial rule in the nineteenth century, Simón Bolívar (Marcano and Tyszka, [2004] 2006: 49). In 1992 he and his co-conspirators attempted a coup, but failed to mobilise enough support. Chávez was imprisoned, but pardoned and released in 1994. His action made him a popular hero, especially among the poorer classes of society. In 1998 he was elected president with a substantial majority (56 per cent of the popular vote), against the candidates of the discredited established parties and with the support of a heterogeneous coalition of (mainly) leftist groups and parties.

As president, Chávez realised the constitutional changes he had promised. A Constitutional Assembly was elected which elaborated a new constitution, approved in 1999 by a large majority (71 per cent) in a referendum (Gott, 2000: 153–159). The constitution has been modified since then, but the principles remain the same (Roberts, 2012: 148–150; Hawkins, 2010: 16–25). In the first two articles, Venezuela was declared a 'Bolivarian Republic', 'irrevocably free and independent', and a 'Democratic and Social State of Law and Justice' (*un Estado democrático y social de Derecho y de Justicia*) (Gobierno Bolivariano de Venezuela, [1999] 2006: 9; Asamblea Nacional Constituyente, 1999). Sovereignty resides 'untransferable in the people' [sic], who exercise it both directly and indirectly according to Article 5 (Gobierno Bolivariano de Venezuela, [1999] 2006: 10). The government should be 'democratic, participatory, elective, decentralized, alternative, responsible and pluralist, with revocable mandates' (Gobierno Bolivariano de Venezuela, [1999] 2006: 10). Participation of the people in the exercise of their sovereignty could take various forms: voting for public officials as well as referendum and initiative or revocation of elected officials (Article 70) (Gobierno Bolivariano de Venezuela, [1999] 2006: 31). Statutes and presidential decrees have to be submitted to the people upon the request of 10 per cent and 5 per cent (respectively) of all registered voters (Article 74) (Gobierno Bolivariano de Venezuela, [1999] 2006: 33–34). At least 40 per cent of the voters have to participate in a referendum, otherwise it would be invalid. The conditions for recall of elected officials are more restrictive: half of their term has to be completed, at least 20 per cent of the voters in their constituency have to sign a petition for recall and the number of voters for recall has to be equal to or larger than the number of voters who had elected him (or her) in the first place (Article 72) (Gobierno Bolivariano de Venezuela, [1999] 2006: 32–33). Elected officials are not subject to mandates or instructions (Article 201) (Gobierno Bolivariano de Venezuela, [1999] 2006: 87). Article 184 suggests participation in local government through creation of new 'decentralized organs at the parish, community, ward and neighborhood levels' and in the management of public enterprises, but does not elaborate upon this (Gobierno Bolivariano de Venezuela, [1999] 2006: 78–79). At the same time, the constitution granted extended powers to the President, specifically in Article 236. He would direct the government and the armed forces, sign international treaties, issue decrees or executive orders with the force of law, administer the Public Treasury and appoint various officials (Gobierno Bolivariano de Venezuela, [1999] 2006: 96–98).

The constitution looks quite radical on paper, but it is questionable to what extent it has been implemented. Academic observers disagree in their assessment, partly depending upon their political opinions, yet they seem to agree on a few points. On the one hand, hardly anyone denies that Chávez used his presidential powers extensively (Roberts, 2012: 137, 154–155; Hawkins, 2010: 18; Werz, 2007: 17–18). He might have done so more easily as neither the National Assembly nor the judiciary seemed willing or able to resist him. The coalition that supported him in the Assembly remained rather heterogeneous, even after the creation of a large government party – eventually named the United Socialist Party of Venezuela (*Partido Socialista Unido de Venezuela*, PSUV) (Ellner, 2005; Spanakos, 2011: 22; Priester, 2012: 158). Opposition parties and critical media are tolerated, but also discouraged and harassed in various ways – by tax inspection, or threats and occasionally violent action by militant *Chávistas* (Corrales, 2010: 33–34; Roberts, 2012: 157). On the other hand, most scholars seem to agree that popular participation has increased, particularly at the local level. The number of referendums has been modest. A campaign to recall the President himself failed in 2004. Yet millions of Venezuelans who used to be marginal and alienated outsiders in the system have joined communal councils, Bolivarian circles, missions and other new institutions (Ellner and Hellinger, 2003: 223; Hawkins, 2010: 100, 166–230; Motta, 2011: 36–37; Roberts, 2012: 152–153; Azzellini, 2012).

Since 2004, when Chávez began to pursue more radical and explicitly socialist policies, several nationalised industries have experimented with workers' control or co-management. The experiments were promoted by a government agency, but were sometimes obstructed by other parts of the government or by the trade unions, as Dario Azzellini reports (2012: 387–388). He describes in some detail the case of Inveval, a factory producing valves for the oil industry, where most decisions were taken by a monthly factory assembly and a factory council elected by the workers. The latter could also recall the council members (Azzellini, 2012: 393–395). There seems to be a growing movement for this kind of workers' control, supported by Chávez but initiated bottom-up, by workers in factories, by a leftwing faction in the unions and by a loose network of Socialist Workers' Councils (*Consejos Socialistas de Trabajadores*). The network seems to be inspired by Marx, Gramsci, Trotsky and Pannekoek (Azzellini, 2012: 396). Yet Pannekoek would probably object that while the factory councils may exercise economic power, they have hardly any political power. Thus, the New Left ideal of workers' self-management may have been realised in Venezuela, albeit on a modest scale, but it is not (yet) council-democracy or council-communism.

Facts can be interpreted differently, of course, depending on one's theoretical framework and political preferences. The most critical experts emphasise the authoritarian tendencies of Chávez and his militant supporters, whereas sympathetic observers stress the participatory aspects. Whilst Javier Corrales characterises the regime as 'competitive autocracy' and Kirk Hawkins views it as 'semi-democratic', Sara Motta regards it as 'popular democracy' and Steve Ellner and Daniel Hellinger see it as participatory democracy with paternalistic and clientelistic elements (Corrales, 2010: 56; Hawkins, 2010: 16; Motta, 2011; Ellner and Hellinger, 2003: 219). The German sociologist Karin Priester interprets even the workers' councils as repressive institutions, aimed at breaking the power of the unions which still criticise the regime (2012: 147–148). As an outsider, one cannot help but conclude that the regime must be a hybrid with radical democratic as well as autocratic and aristocratic elements. It seems quite likely that this rather incoherent mixture will change – if not explode – following the death of the regime's lynch-pin in 2013. One could expect a power struggle between radical leftists and more conservative factions within the *Chávista* movement as well as between the movement and the liberal/conservative opposition. The outcome seems impossible to predict at this point, however, and depends also on the stability of the oil-based economy and the influence of external forces.

Plebiscitary democracy in Switzerland and the United States

In the previous pages, we have followed the development of democratic radicalism, and specifically the bounded-delegate model, through (more or less) Marxist ideas and experiments with workers' councils and other forms of council-democracy. This is only one branch of the lineage of democratic radicalism, which bifurcated, one might say, after the Paris Commune of 1871. While the

Marxists tried to merge economic and political democracy, other radicals ignored the former and concentrated on the latter. Adapting the Jacobin and Rousseauian heritage to modern mass society, they began advocating forms of plebiscitary democracy. The term 'plebiscitary democracy' has negative connotations and associations with authoritarian regimes, but denotes here any regime where referendum, initiative and/or recall play an essential or pivotal part in the political decision-making process. So, here the Second Empire of Napoleon III and Hitler's Third Reich are not considered to be 'plebiscitary democracies' as they used plebiscites only to seek legitimation for decisions already taken by the autocratic rulers (see also Gerstein, 1969: 327–331).

Practical examples of plebiscitary democracy may be found at all levels of government in Switzerland, and in the United States in states such as California, North Dakota and Oregon. Rather than analysing these political systems in depth, I will only peruse the literature to find out the extent to which they are indeed plebiscitary and whether they satisfy the criteria introduced in Chapter 1 to evaluate classical forms of democracy.

Switzerland has been described as a direct democracy, or at least a semi-direct democracy, in view of the frequency and importance of its plebiscites (Gerstein, 1969: 1; Kriesi, 1995: 80; Fossedal, 2002). It is the only nation in the world 'where political life truly revolves around the referendum', in the words of Kris Kobach (1994: 98). In 1848 the Swiss introduced the obligatory constitutional referendum. Later, in 1874, they added the optional legislative referendum, which was subsequently extended to international treaties and collective security issues. In 1891 came the popular initiative for partial or total revision of the constitution (Curti, 1882: 158–198, 238–294; Kriesi, 1995: 81–84). During the nineteenth century, while referendums were very rare in the world, and popular initiatives practically non-existent, the Swiss organised fifty-eight of them (Schweizerische Bundeskanzlei, 2010). In the twentieth century, Swiss citizens could vote 429 times for (or against) constitutional amendments, treaties or laws – probably more than all other countries put together (Butler and Ranney, 1994: 5; Leduc, 2003: 20–22). The first decade of the twenty-first century has already seen seventy-eight plebiscites held in the alpine state (Schweizerische Bundeskanzlei, 2010).

The frequency of the Swiss referendums and initiatives should be put in perspective, however. The Swiss political scientist Hanspeter Kriesi points out that only 12 of the 198 initiatives that citizens proposed between 1891 and 1993 were accepted by the electorate, while 82 of them did not even qualify for a vote because of insufficient support. Until 1977 50,000 signatures were required; since then, 100,000 (Kriesi, 1995: 82, 107; see also Bundesverfassung der Schweizerischen Eidgenossenschaft, [1999] 2005: Articles 138 and 139). Of the 192 propositions for constitutional change submitted to the people between 1848 and 1994, 139 were accepted and 53 rejected (Kriesi, 1995: 98–99). Between 1874 and 1994, 1761 laws and treaties could have been submitted to the people, but only in 122 cases was an optional referendum held, and no more than 61 (3 per cent) of the 1761 laws and treaties were eventually rejected (Kriesi, 1995:

98–99). An optional referendum requires support from 50,000 voters or from eight cantons, according to Article 141 of the Swiss Constitution (Bundesverfassung der Schweizerischen Eidgenossenschaft, [1999] 2005). So, the overwhelming majority of the laws, treaties and constitutional revisions decided upon by the Swiss political elite has been accepted either tacitly or explicitly (in a plebiscite) by the Swiss people.

Nevertheless, as Swiss political scientists argue, the optional as well as the obligatory referendum hang as a sword of Damocles above the heads of the elite – it will not kill them personally, of course, but it might kill their proposals (Kriesi, 1995: 88–89; see also Kriesi, 2012: 42). Therefore, the Swiss parliamentarians and party leaders will anticipate the preferences and objections of the voters, negotiate with pressure groups and try to build a broad consensus before passing potentially controversial laws. The consensual or consociational tradition has perhaps been reinforced by the federal system and by the religious segmentation of the population – which required a certain tolerance. In recent years, the rise of new and radical parties may have led to increased polarisation and reduced the consensus, but even in the twenty-first century Switzerland can be regarded as a consociational system, as Adrian Vatter has shown (2008).

The increasing frequency of the plebiscites, as well as the growing complexity of (some of) the issues may have led to diminishing participation. Average turnout has declined from 60 per cent around 1950 to 40 per cent around 1975 (Kriesi, 1995: 114). Since then it has fluctuated strongly, depending on the importance, controversial nature and complexity of the issue at hand and the intensity of the campaign, to between 28 per cent and 78 per cent (Kriesi, 1995: 115; see also Budge, 1996: 95–100). Some voters will always turn up and others will never go to the polls, but the largest category consists of selective participants who will vote when they understand the issue and consider it important enough (Kriesi, 1995: 114–115). Surveys suggest that most voters are aware of the issues at stake (Kriesi, 2012: 47–50). They base their vote either on substantive arguments or on cues provided by opinion leaders. The influence of money seems quite limited, according to Kriesi, but may help to defeat the government's proposal in an optional referendum. However, if the 'bourgeois parties' – i.e. the Christian Democrats, Liberals and Conservatives – put up a united front, leftwing parties and movements are rarely able to defeat them (Kriesi, 2012: 46–47).[12] The turnout does not affect the validity of the outcome in Switzerland, as it does in Venezuela.

According to Kriesi, plebiscitary institutions have a positive impact upon political culture and political interest among citizens, but also upon the quality of public services, tax morale, the level of public expenditure and public debt, and general satisfaction with life (2012: 50–52). These conclusions are based on a comparative study in the twenty-six Swiss cantons, which differ in terms of the weight they attach to plebiscitary democracy. German-speaking cantons tend to prescribe lower thresholds for a plebiscite. Some cantons allow a referendum or an initiative on administrative and financial questions, whereas others restrict these to legislative and constitutional issues (Kriesi, 1995: 84–85). Similar differences exist at the local and municipal levels.

Switzerland may be the fatherland of the referendum, but the United States has developed and practiced a wider variety of plebiscitary institutions: not only the referendum and the initiative, but also recall and direct primaries and, in earlier days, even the binding mandate (Cronin, 1989: 24–26). Plebiscitary democracy of sorts has been advocated by Populists and Progressives throughout the nineteenth and twentieth century. Occasionally, they have referred to the Swiss example (Gerstein, 1969: 279–286; Cronin, 1989: 48–51).

Direct primaries were introduced in several states between 1900 and 1915, mainly to restrict the power of party bosses and grant all citizens a degree of influence upon the selection of representatives (Lawrence et al., 2011: 4–7, 11, 15). However, I would consider them to be a very weak element of plebiscitary democracy as they do not grant the voters any power over the representatives once they have been elected.

Referendum, initiative and recall give more power to citizens. They put 'a bit between the teeth' of the representatives and provide voters with a 'gun behind the door' of the legislature – to use the vivid imagery of American culture (Bowler and Donovan, 2006: 649; see also Cronin, 1989: 38–59). Between 1898 and 1912 seventeen states introduced these measures, often owing to Populist pressure. In states such as California, Oregon and North Dakota, several hundred plebiscites have been held since the beginning of the twentieth century.

California deserves special attention here, as it has become a controversial case in recent decades: a shining example for some and a dire warning for others. In a way, it has acted as a laboratory for plebiscitary experiences. As political scientists Shaun Bowler and Todd Donovan remarked, California 'is engaged in the modern world's most ambitious experience of direct democracy', at least outside Switzerland (2000: 644). According to the Californian political scientist Jack Citrin, the Golden State 'moved from representative to plebiscitary government': since 1978 'all major policy decisions in California have been settled by a popular vote or a threat of such a vote' (2009: 7). In 1978 Howard Jarvis, leader of a taxpayers' organisation, initiated Proposition 13 in order to prevent the state government from raising property taxes or imposing any new tax or tax increase without a two-thirds majority (Citrin, 2009: 3–5; see also Clark, 1998: 467–469). He enjoyed the support of local homeowners' associations and some developers, but fought a powerful alliance of Democratic and Republican politicians, trade unions and large corporations who were concerned about a decline in public services, rising unemployment and public debt. Yet the initiative won the approval of 65 per cent of the voters. It had a profound impact upon Californian politics, leading to a shift from property taxes to income and sales tax, a rather incoherent and inflexible budgeting system, and a shift of influence from elected politicians to campaign consultants and lobbyists – at least in the eyes of Citrin (2009: 8). He seems more sceptical about the influence of ordinary citizens than some of his colleagues, such as Bowler and Donovan (2000) or the British scholar Ian Budge (2012: 33), but his scepticism may be shared by another expert, David Magleby (1994).

The Constitution of California sounds promising enough. 'All political power is inherent in the people', according to Article 2, and the people have 'the right to alter or reform government when the public good may require' (Government of California, no date, Article 2, Section 1). More specifically, citizens have the right to take part in primary elections (to select candidates for the Presidency as well as for Congress and state offices), to elect legislators as well as judges (of the Supreme Court of the state) and other officials, to propose and vote for initiatives, to approve or reject statutes (passed by the legislature) and to recall elected state officers (Government of California, no date, Article 2, Sections 5–13). In order to qualify for the ballot, an initiative needs the signatures of 5 per cent (in the case of a statute) or 8 per cent (if an amendment to the Constitution) of the voters for all candidates for Governor at the last gubernatorial election. A referendum to repeal a statute also requires a petition, signed by 5 per cent of the gubernatorial electorate, which has to be delivered within ninety days following the enactment of the statute. By the end of the twentieth century, this requirement meant almost 500,000 signatures (Bowler and Donovan, 2000: 645). To recall a state officer, citizens have to deliver (within 160 days) a petition signed by 12 or 20 per cent of the last vote for the office, distributed across the state in a certain way.[13] Since 1913, five officers have been recalled – two State Senators, two State Assemblymen and one Governor – while four attempts failed at the polls and 146 attempts failed at an earlier stage, usually because the organisers did not gather sufficient signatures within the required time (Government of California, 2013). Initiatives tend to be more successful, on the whole: between 1911 and 1998 almost 35 per cent of the initiatives that qualified for ballot were approved by the electorate; however, less than 30 per cent of the initiatives filed satisfied the conditions for a vote, so one could also say that only 10 per cent were successful in the end (Bowler and Donovan, 2000: 647). In other American states the success rate seems similar (Magleby, 1994: 251). Participation in plebiscites tends to fluctuate with the issue and the circumstances; in California they are usually combined with regular elections.

In recent years, the collection of signatures for recall, referendum or initiative has been professionalised and commercialised in California. Professionals accost people in shopping malls and other public places and are paid one or two dollars for each signature (Bowler and Donovan, 2000: 646). This is one reason why scholars such as Citrin worry that lobbyists and consultants benefit more from California's plebiscitary system than ordinary citizens or grass roots movements without much money to spend on petitions and campaigning. Their concern could be alleviated by stricter regulation of campaign spending, but so far California has been reluctant to introduce this (Cronin, 1989: 90–124; Budge, 2012: 36). However, even under the present circumstances, research suggests that the influence of money should not be overestimated (Bowler and Donovan, 2000: 654; see also Lupia and Matsusaka, 2004: 470–472). Popular initiatives in favour of taxes on tobacco products, regulation of toxic chemicals and a higher minimum wage have been successful in spite of opposition from moneyed interests (Bowler and Donovan, 2000: 644). Arthur Lupia and John Matsusaka have shown that 'money matters, but in a nuanced way' (2004: 472). By heavily funding a campaign against a proposed initiative, business groups are often able to prevent change; yet 'without pre-existing public support, the financial resources of business groups are ineffective in changing the status quo, and the financial resources of most citizen groups are too scarce to bring about much change' (Lupia and Matsusaka, 2004: 472). This conclusion applies not only to California, but also to many other American states that have introduced initiatives or referendums.

Lupia and Matsusaka as well as Bowler and Donovan also assessed other pros and cons of plebiscitary democracy on the basis of empirical evidence. A common objection to referendum and initiative is that the average citizen lacks the competence to understand complicated political issues and to develop an opinion grounded in facts and rational argument (Cronin, 1989: 180–194; Budge, 1996: 59–83). Kriesi countered this criticism in the Swiss context, as we have seen earlier. His American colleagues reach similar conclusions. Bowler and Donovan report that Californian voters 'appear able to figure out how to vote in ways which accord with their interests or ideology', often by following cues provided by elites, which are presented in a (non-partisan) ballot leaflet delivered to each voter (2000: 650). In other states, voters seem equally competent, as Lupia and Matsusaka show. While well-informed voters base their decision on arguments, their fellow citizens with less knowledge use short-cuts. Usually, if they are really confused by the issue, they do not vote at all (Lupia and Matsusaka, 2004: 467–470).

This does raise the question of whether plebiscites are easily manipulated by political elites. If that were to happen often, it might placate concerns about voter incompetence but frustrate the expectations of radical democrats. The Danish political scientist Mads Qvortrup, who analysed 128 referendums in twelve different countries, found that most of them were not controlled by the government and that a (narrow) majority led to 'anti-hegemonic' outcomes, i.e. going against the recommendations of the government (2000). Lupia and Matsusaka also point out, as Kriesi had done before, that elites often anticipate the policy decisions of the people (2004: 472). The threat of an initiative may prompt legislative action. On the whole, citizens seem to be quite satisfied with plebiscitary institutions and their outcomes (Lupia and Matsusaka, 2004: 476–479). The results are often a little more conservative than political elites may wish, particularly regarding government expenditures, taxes, and moral issues such as women's emancipation or abortion, but they do reflect the opinion of the majority of the population at the time (Lupia and Matsusaka, 2004: 476–479).

Critics of plebiscites also express fear that ethnic, cultural, sexual or political minorities will be the victims of prejudiced majorities. Californian citizens did repeal affirmative and bilingual education programmes and declared English to be the state's official language, against the interests of a large Spanish-speaking minority (Bowler and Donovan, 2000: 654). However, this outcome could also be interpreted as evidence that 'special interests' have limited influence in a plebiscitary democracy. As Thomas Cronin pointed out some years ago, few plebiscites have really damaged minority rights, and some have clearly strengthened them (1989: 210–222).

The research surveyed by Bowler, Donovan, Lupia and Matsusaka does not address all of the arguments against plebiscites, however. It does not really answer the critique of Sherman Clark, law professor at the University of Michigan, who argues that through plebiscites 'we may learn what the most people want, but we do not learn what the people want most' (1998: 482). Plebiscites measure single-issue majority preferences, but cannot reflect voter priorities. In other words, a referendum can 'obscure the voice of the people by precluding them from trading outcome A in return for higher priority outcomes' (Clark, 1998: 451). Therefore, Clark argues, citizens need representatives to do this trading and logrolling for them, in election campaigns and in the legislature. Elections, in his eyes, are 'multi-issue referenda', as candidates will search for a set of positions that will garner the most votes (Clark, 1998: 463–467). However, if voters do not show a clear preference on an issue, the candidates will follow their own judgment, once they are elected. This does not worry Clark, even if he defines himself (perhaps provocatively) as a populist: 'independent judgment, ideals, and principles are some of the things people might want' when they elect representatives (1998: 476). So, Clark concludes that 'representation checks majority power without limiting popular voice' (1998: 478).

The experience of California seems to provide some empirical support for Clark's critique of plebiscitary democracy. Bowler and Donovan, though generally more sympathetic towards the Californian system, admit that it is rather rigid. Mistakes, ambiguities or inconsistencies in initiatives that have been approved are difficult to correct (Bowler and Donovan, 2000: 652). Even so, Clark seems to exaggerate the weaknesses of the plebiscitary democracy while idealising the role of representatives (see also Budge, 1996: 133–171). His critique does not seem very relevant to representative systems where plebiscites serve as a safety valve or emergency brake. Even in California, and certainly in Switzerland, political parties and politicians still perform a mediating and integrating function in the political system. Clark's critique should be of concern to the citizens of Jacobinland, however, where representatives enjoy very limited powers.

Ian Budge, who sketched a system quite similar to Jacobinland two years before Clark's article appeared, seemed to anticipate the problem, to some extent (1996: 181–188). In his utopia, a government – elected directly by the people or by parliament – will present a more or less coherent programme to the people. Parliament will investigate and debate the programme and advise the people. Through interactive electronic networks – rather embryonic when Budge wrote his book – citizens will discuss the programme, as well as possible amendments. Citizens might get a 'civic leave' to study and discuss the measures. The programme might be approved for a year, through an electronic referendum whereby people can vote at home. Budge does not seem quite sure if the programme should be amendable after it has been approved. He does suggest a high frequency of plebiscites, like fifty a year. Though this model sounds quite radical, it is not extremist. Budge rejects 'unmediated direct democracy' or 'Rousseauesque democracy' and presents his model as a synthesis between representative and direct democracy – as in his more recent publications too (see Budge, 2012: 33–37). Mediation should also prevent voting cycles – the problem raised by Riker in particular, which was discussed briefly in Chapter 3 (Budge, 2012: 30–31).

Budge also reminds us that plebiscites or 'direct policy voting' (the term he prefers) continue to increase, no matter what the critics say (2012: 35–36). Neither his utopia nor Jacobinland have been realised yet, but in a not too distant future they might become reality, given the increasing demand for plebiscites across the world (see also Leduc, 2003: 185–191).

EVALUATION

The bounded-delegate model does not exist, except as an ahistorical abstraction. The historical survey in this chapter showed that we should really distinguish two bounded-delegate models (sub-models, if you prefer): Jacobin or populist plebiscitary democracy and Marxist council-democracy.

The two share a fundamental distrust of trustees or representatives who may be elected but cannot be recalled or instructed by the people. In Europe this distrust no doubt goes back to Rousseau, while the American tradition has different roots which have not been investigated in this chapter. Legislative power cannot be delegated to a minority, the philosopher from Geneva asserted, even if it is elected by the people. In a legitimate regime, the people have to approve (or veto) all legislation. The Jacobins and their extremist allies, the *sans-culottes*, tried to apply the teachings of their spiritual master and experimented with binding mandates, recall and a referendum. The French Constitution of 1793 granted all citizens the right to deliberate and vote on legislation in primary assemblies. It was never implemented, however. At the height of the revolutionary fever, the *sans-culottes* practiced a rather rough and violent version of bounded-delegate democracy, imposing their will upon their delegates in the national parliament by shouting threats and swinging pikes. Thermidor and Napoleon made an end to all this. However, the Jacobin idea did not die, but was reborn in the French (and to some extent European) revolution of 1848 and in the Paris Commune of 1871.

The experience of the Commune led to a bifurcation of the Rousseauian tradition of bounded-delegate democracy. On the one hand, Marx and his disciples interpreted the Commune as the first experiment with working-class rule – the 'dictatorship of the proletariat' – which would merge economic and political power. The Soviets or workers' councils that sprang up in Russia, Germany and Hungary in 1917 and 1919 were seen as a more mature application of the same principle. Marxists took a leading part in most of those councils and encouraged them to capture power and disregard the 'bourgeois' parliaments that had just been elected. Power should be based on economic rather than geographical units, factories rather than local districts. The success of the Soviets or council republics proved short-lived, however. In the Soviet Union the Soviets continued to exist but under the control of a new party aristocracy, while the councils were brutally repressed by reactionary forces in Germany and Hungary. Yet their defeat marked not the end, but rather the beginning of the development of council-democracy as a theory. Elaborated by Pannekoek and Rühle in the 1920s and 1930s, the theory inspired several theorists, radical activists and a few political parties in the 1960s and 1970s. Indirectly, it might even have contributed a little to experiments with workers' councils in Venezuela in the twenty-first century.

On the other hand, the Paris Commune meant the end of a revolutionary Jacobin tradition, but also the beginning of a more moderate democratic radicalism or populism which aimed at institutional reforms, specifically the introduction of referendum, popular initiative and (sometimes) recall of elected delegates. The reformists did not develop grand theories like the councilists, but were more successful in practice. In Switzerland they introduced the (obligatory) constitutional referendum and the (optional) legislative referendum as well as the constitutional initiative. In California and quite a few other American states they brought the legislative initiative, referendum and recall.

These historical facts already tell us a great deal about the feasibility of the two bounded-delegate models. Obviously, council-democracy has a rather weak record. Council republics have existed only briefly during revolutionary upheavals and collapsed under external pressure, but internal strife, declining participation and oligarchisation must have contributed to their downfall as well. Experiments in later periods – not discussed in this book – seem to have followed a similar path – in Portugal in 1974–1975, for instance (Robinson, 2011). Whether the recently established workers' councils in Venezuela will blaze a different trail remains to be seen. One reason why council-democracy succumbed under external pressure may have to do with its revolutionary character. It requires a total change of society – not only the political system, but also the economy. Workers' councils take power away from the capitalist managers and owners of the companies they work in. Without the expropriation of private capital or the socialisation of the means of production (to use the Marxist terms), workers' councils would remain powerless or exercise advisory powers at best. Moreover, most theorists agree that an effective council-democracy requires not only a socio-economic and political revolution, but also a cultural revolution. Bourgeois individualism and egoism should give way to proletarian collectivism, class solidarity and egalitarianism. No wonder experiments with council-democracy rouse fear and hostility not only among the bourgeoisie, but also the petty-bourgeoisie of independent producers, farmers, small businessmen and professionals who worry about their freedom and independence. In fact, quite a few workers appear less than keen on this kind of revolution too. The conclusion seems clear: council-democracy is not a very realistic model as far as the historical evidence goes.

Plebiscitary democracy seems to do a lot better, at least in its moderate forms. Though the initial, rather incoherent Jacobin experiments did not survive the first French Revolution, later attempts in Switzerland and the US have turned out quite successful in terms of stability and duration – enduring for more than a hundred years, in most cases. In both countries, however, plebiscitary democracy has been combined and integrated with a representative parliamentary or presidential system. Political elites, i.e. party politicians elected by the people, prepare and take many (if not most) decisions. And even when they have to submit their bills and other projects to a referendum, they often succeed in persuading the voters to approve their plans. Even so, they may anticipate the wishes and needs of the people to a much larger extent than elected politicians in regimes without plebiscites. The political agenda in California and Switzerland is set not only by the elites, but also by activists who prepare or threaten to prepare a legislative or constitutional initiative. Given their frequency, the initiative and referendum seem more than just a safety valve or emergency brake in these parts of the world.

Possibly, the realisation of Jacobinland, being a more radical version of plebiscitary democracy, might pose more practical problems, at least in the long run. It is not too difficult to imagine Switzerland or California evolving in this direction, given the increasing frequency of initiatives and referendums. However, as the story that opened this chapter suggests, in the long run competent politicians may experience increasing frustration due to their limited powers. They might cede their seats to less competent candidates who care more for the pecuniary awards and perks of the job than for their constituents. The problem may be solved, at least to some extent, by raising the requirements as well as the rewards for competent delegates.

When applying the criteria for desirability, introduced in Chapter 1, we again notice substantial differences between the two bounded-delegate models. Both offer citizens numerous opportunities for participation in effective decision-making, but in differing contexts. In theory, council-democracy seems superior to plebiscitary democracy. Plenary factory assemblies should be held frequently – once a month, Castoriadis suggested – so that workers could discuss and vote on policies and recall their council delegates quite easily, if they wished. The workers' councils themselves might meet once a week or so. Moreover, the merger of economic and political power offers the councils more clout to change society. Plebiscites are usually only held on request, and require more activity from citizens: they have to draft a proposal, gather signatures and mobilise support in the streets and in the media. The costs may be considerable, as the example of California shows – though in Jacobinland, the costs will probably be more modest.

In practice, however, participation in workers' councils has been high only during revolutionary moments. In Russia attendance at plenary sessions declined rapidly within a few months, while most substantial decisions were taken by executive committees and presidia which were increasingly dominated by the Bolshevik party. This oligarchisation process may be explained in part by the impoverished conditions of the Russian working class, but also by the institutional arrangement of the councils itself. Councilism may demand too much from the average worker, even under more prosperous and peaceful circumstances. Workers would have to interrupt their labour to prepare for a factory assembly, where they would not only have to form an educated opinion about the management of the factory, but also about local and national economic planning and various political questions. They would also have to monitor their delegates at various levels and recall them if they neglected their duties or the interests of their rank-and-file. Coordination problems of the various factory councils and (possibly) neighbourhood councils would probably add to the oligarchisation.

These problems may also arise in plebiscitary democracy, as Clark argued, but at a higher level. Modern plebiscitary democracy lacks the intermediate levels that characterise both council-democracy and the Jacobin system of primary assemblies, which was tried out briefly in the 1790s. Citizens across the country vote on the same day, on the same issue. If they vote against a law passed by the legislation, it will be repealed at once. If they vote in favour of an initiative, it has to be translated into law – though here political elites could sabotage or defer the process. Participation in plebiscites tends to vary with the nature of the issue at stake and the resources mobilised by advocates and opponents. On the whole, it seems likely that plebiscitary democracy offers citizens more realistic opportunities to take part in the political decision-making process than council-democracy.

The quality of decision-making may be higher in council-democracy, however. At least workers' councils are designed as deliberative bodies, and factory assemblies should offer opportunities for deliberation as well. Whether the workers will use these opportunities does not depend only on space and time, but also on their competence and commitment. Training and facilitation may help to develop these qualities. Deliberation is usually considered a weak point in plebiscitary democracy – unless the Jacobin primary assemblies would be resurrected in a modern garb. Ideally, plebiscites should be preceded by public debates about the pros and cons of the propositions, but the discussion may be dominated and manipulated by moneyed interests, professional consultants, spin doctors and partisan propagandists, or – at best – experts and intellectuals. The average citizen may occasionally watch a debate on television, if the issue interests him, and perhaps ask a relative or a colleague about her opinion. Ian Budge may be a little too optimistic when he expects large groups of citizens to take part in serious debates on the Internet. Matthew Hindman, a political scientist at Arizona State University, showed that the Internet is not as egalitarian and open as many advocates have argued (2009). The link structure of web sites has created new hierarchies and new elites – which appear very similar in terms of social background to the old elites, in fact. The most widely visited web sites and blogs in the US have been produced by 'a de facto aristocracy dominated by those skilled in the high deliberative arts', i.e. professional journalists, lawyers and academics who graduated from elite universities and are mainly white and male (Hindman, 2009: 139, 102–128). Hence, deliberation remains a rather elitist process in plebiscitary democracy.

Plebiscitary democracy scores better with respect to inclusiveness. Practically all citizens can take part in a referendum, recall or initiative – in theory, at least. The act of voting does not cost much time or energy, even in a polling booth, let alone via the electronic voting system at home, as anticipated by Budge and as practiced in Jacobinland. However, in practice the self-selection of the usual suspects – the well-informed, well-educated citizens – might create a legitimation problem. If less educated voters stay home, the results may go against their interests. In a council-democracy, the problem is almost reversed. Intellectuals, independent professionals and businessmen (as far as they still exist in a socialist or communist economy) do not work in factories and will not be able to participate in factory assemblies or vote for workers' councils. In modern, New Left versions, however, they would be allowed to take part in neighbourhood councils. Given their verbal competence, they will probably do so quite effectively.

The indirect impact of the two (sub-)models on society also differs considerably. As mentioned above, council-democracy requires and reinforces a total revolution of the social, economic and cultural system of society. As the history of the Soviet Union taught us, this kind of revolution might produce a totalitarian and rather repressive society. In fact, it has done so, not only in Russia, but also in all regimes that followed the Soviet example (with or without Soviets or workers' councils), from Cuba to Cambodia. Plebiscitary democracy has a more humane historical record, at least if we exclude the Second Empire in France and other authoritarian regimes that sought legitimation through occasional plebiscites, usually manipulated by the government and its agents. Yet Marxists will argue that even a perfect plebiscitary democracy will be manipulated by capitalist interests. Capitalists dominate the mass media, pay the signature collectors and could even blackmail governments, political parties and public opinion by threatening to withdraw capital, reduce investments and create massive unemployment if the outcomes of certain popular initiatives would harm their interests. The Marxists may have a point, even if empirical research suggests that plebiscites do not always spare capitalist interests. One does not have to accept council-democracy or council-communism in its extreme form, however, in order to address this problem. A more moderate version of democratic socialism (or social democracy), with measures such as restrictions on campaign expenditures, transparency of political donations, public financial support for non-conformist media and some industrial democracy might also help to reduce the influence of capitalists on plebiscites. Jacobinland seems to do so, even with reluctant delegates such as Roy in the story that opened this chapter.

Notes

1 The binding mandate was not a new invention, but a traditional feature of the representation of estates and cities that went back to medieval times in France, but also in Spain, the Low Countries, Poland and other countries, as Keane shows (2009: 173–263).
2 In French: 'Le peuple exerçant sa souveraineté sans entraves dans les Assemblées électorales, ... ayant l'initiative de toute loi qu'il juge utile, votant expressément les lois ... Une Assemblée de délégués ou commissaires, nommés annuellement, préparant les lois, et pourvoyant par les décrets aux choses secondaires et de grande administration' (Calman, 1921: 85).

3 Rousseau was born in Geneva, which was not part of the Swiss Confederation in 1712 but would join it in 1815.
4 In German: 'Der Arbeiter ... behandelt Frau und Kinder so, wie er von seinem Chef behandelt wird, verlangt Unterwerfung, Bedienung, Autorität'.
5 In French: 'La cohérence des Conseils, elle, est garantie par le seul fait qu'ils sont le pouvoir; qu' ils éliminent tout autre pouvoir et décident de tout' (Riesel, 1969: 71–72).
6 In French: 'L'autogestion, c'est la gestion des entreprises par les travailleurs mais aussi de l'ensemble de l'économie et de la cité par le peuple' (La CFDT, 1971: 131). Presumably, 'city' refers not only to urban areas, but also to any community, or to the state as a whole.
7 In Dutch: 'een direkte demokratie, die is samengesteld uit volksvergaderingen van alle betrokkenen. Zij kiezen afgevaardigden naar raden voor centrale beslissingen. Deze afgevaardigden zijn direkt terugroepbaar' (Pacifistisch Socialistische Partij, 1977: 9).
8 In German: 'Verwirklichung dezentraler, direkter Demokratie ... Kerngedanke ist die Kontrolle aller Amts- und Mandatsträger und Institutionen durch die Basis sowie die jederzeitige Ablösbarkeit, um Organisation und Politik für alle durchschaubar zu machen und der Loslösung einzelner von ihrer Basis entgegenzuwirken' (Die Grünen, 1980: 212).
9 See *The Shorter Oxford English Dictionary on Historical Principles*, Oxford: Clarendon Press, Third Edition with Corrections, 1980, II, 1630.
10 The Irish Sinn Féin seems the exception that proves the rule:

> Sinn Féin's political project is truly populist but a populism that is democratic, egalitarian and progressive ... we seek to mobilise in support of a New Republic in which popular sovereignty is restored and political and economic power returned to where it rightly belongs, in the hands of the people.
>
> (Ó Broin, 2013)

However, the political reforms it proposes are very moderate: a 'more democratic' electoral system, an end to political appointments to state boards, abolition of the Senate (Sinn Féin, no date).
11 In Spanish: '"democracia participativa" se refiere a la capacidad real de la mayoriá cuidadana de decidir sobre los principales asuntos públicos de la nación' (Dieterich, 2005: 134).
12 A recent example may have been the plebiscite against excessive rewards for corporate officials, the initiative "gegen die Abzockerei"; against the advice of the federal government, on 3 March 2013 68 per cent of the electorate voted in favour of restrictions and for more powers for stockholders (Schweizerische Bundeskanzlei, 2013).
13 In five counties at least 1 per cent of the electorate has to sign the petition (California Constitution, no date: Article 2, Section 14.b).

5 Aleatoria
Sortitionist democracy

Today is my last day as People's Representative. I was sworn in one year ago, after I had passed the Entrance Examination. That was really a formality. As far as I know, nobody in my sample failed. I had to confirm the information they had already gathered about me: my parents, my assets and so on. Pretty soon, I realised I would have little privacy as a People's Rep! Yet I felt excited and happy. Three months of preparation had gone by rapidly.

It all started 18 months ago, when the red Selection Letter was delivered to our door in Elmsville. When I opened it, I could not believe my eyes: me, selected by lot to represent my people for a year? I was all excited and immediately phoned Ted, my husband, at the garage where he works. He did not react very positively. I could not blame him: he would not see me very much over the next year. Elmsville is not very close to the capital: it takes at least ten hours to get there by car or train. However, I soon found out that I could use Government planes that would take me to the capital in an hour and a half, so I could be home before the children's bedtime. Occasionally I had to stay the night in the capital. Even so, the children would miss me when they came home from school. And I would miss them! Ted complained about having to do the household chores all by himself, despite the fact that the Government would pay for a household assistant. Actually, she turned out to be a problem, as I felt she flirted with my husband too much. Anyway, I almost sent a letter of refusal to the Government, claiming that I was indispensable to my family. Just as I was about to take the letter to the post office, Ted grabbed my arm and said, 'No, Dora, forget the refusal. I was wrong, you have to go; it is your duty as a citizen!' So I signed the Selection Letter and agreed to the conditions.

I attended all of the preparation seminars. Most of them were quite interesting. First we visited the House of People's Representatives and watched the debates. Then we listened to serious lectures about our political history, the Sortitionist Revolution and so on. We should have learned all that in school, of course, but I never paid much attention to civics and history – in fact, I was not very interested in school at all, and got a job as soon as I had passed the high school exam. No university for me! Yet now I paid more attention to the professors that taught us history, constitutional law, economic policy and all that. They did it well, trying to keep us awake and actively involved, showing a lot of *pictures, films and cartoons. Other seminars familiarised us with debating techniques and parliamentary procedures. We also went to visit the headquarters of various pressure groups, in order to prepare us for their attempts to influence us, and to important departments, where we were introduced to senior civil servants that would later provide us with important information and assist us with our legislative work. I was quite impressed, and also a bit intimidated by all these people in suits – mainly men in their forties and fifties – with university degrees and very serious demeanours.*

We, the 450 People's Reps, also started socialising among ourselves. Actually, we were not quite 450. Some Reps never showed up, for various reasons. Apparently that always happens when they take a random sample from the adult population. In spite of all the Government help you get, you can't expect a mentally disabled person or an ailing ninety-year-old to leave her home in the South to take part in meetings in the capital. Others attended only the first few meetings and then disappeared – disillusioned, bored, whatever – foregoing their generous government allowance. Still, the remaining Reps looked like a real cross-section of our population. There were dairy farmers and farmer's wives, teachers, car mechanics, lawyers, controllers, social workers, policewomen, salesmen and -women, secretaries, shop owners, waitresses, nurses, quite a few housewives and old-age pensioners. All came from different places, of course – the sample is taken region by region. And different age groups, different religious denominations – most were Christians, but three were Muslims. One woman was wearing a long veil. She seemed very shy and withdrawn at first but gradually opened up. And we all had different political ideas, of course.

We did not notice this straight away, when we started our deliberations. First we had to elect the Executive Committee – the ministers that would lead the Government in fact. Not surprising, we elected the better-educated amongst our sample: the lawyer, the engineer, the university teacher, the vet, the journalist. Some turned out to be not very competent and were later replaced. Then we divided ourselves up into standing committees. Most Reps opted for a committee in the line of their work. In my case, as a shop assistant I did not feel competent or interested enough to join the committee on commerce and trade. I had been involved in the local Parents–Teacher Association, so I opted for the education committee. Over the next few weeks we had to finalise decisions prepared already by the preceding House: bills that had been sent back by the Constitutional Court, e.g. because they were inconsistent or incompatible with the Constitution. Only after a month or so did we begin to discuss new bills, drafted by the Executive Committee or by other members of the House.

Some divisions emerged, especially on moral issues like sexual education in school or adoption by homosexual couples, but also on new tax laws. Most of us held strong opinions on these issues. However, I often felt uncertain and full of doubts. Sometimes I consulted the minister of our local church, but he would only remind me of the moral principles of the church rather than give me specific advice. Quite a wise person! Often I consulted Ted, but we did not always agree. He tends to be more conservative on many issues. Of course, I talked a lot with my parliamentary assistants, Jane and Edgar, both university-educated and quite knowledgeable. Usually they would patiently explain the pros and cons of different views, the constitutional constraints and consequences, rather than tell me what to do. That was their duty, of course. I could also consult the dozen think tanks in the capital, but was a bit reluctant to do so, as I knew they defended rather dogmatic positions: the Family Council would favour stricter moral laws and oppose homosexual families, while the Gay Movement would do the opposite. The Free Enterprise Institute would always argue for lower taxes and less government intervention, the Institute of Policy Studies would do the opposite. And so on. Often, they would phone or mail me, rather than the other way around. I would listen patiently, ask a few questions, and tell them I would think about it. Some pressure groups were more subtle. Once or twice, they tried to bribe me. One organisation – no, I won't tell you the name – sent me a voucher for a free family getaway to Disneyland. Just like that! Well, when I phoned to find out what they expected in return, they were very cautious: oh, nothing, just perhaps a chance to talk to me for an hour about general questions… No thank you, I said! My kids would have yelled at me for turning this offer down, but I wanted to be completely clean before the Exit Exam, which will be tomorrow. Two of my colleagues were caught by Government agents while enjoying their weekend in Disneyland and could not prove they had paid for it themselves. Instead of passing the Exit Exam, they're going to pay a very heavy fine, I'm afraid. In fact, I consulted my colleagues more than anyone else. And gradually a group of more or less like-minded Reps emerged. We were called the Waffle, because we rarely held very strong opinions and often waffled. Yet we were not like the political parties that existed before the Sortitionist Revolution: there was no party whip, no discipline, no formal chairman – even if Jack, the dentist, would often lead the meetings in a rather informal way. We often had lunch together, and occasionally a quick dinner, when a meeting had to continue in the evening.

For me, a woman of forty without college education and limited work experience – first a cashier in a supermarket, then an assistant in a department store – it has been an extremely instructive and exciting year. Whether I have been a faithful representative of the people, I don't know – some journalists said so, others were more critical. Tomorrow I will appear before the Exit Examination Committee, which consists of a constitutional lawyer, a judge and an intelligence officer. If they are satisfied, I will return to Elmsville as a simple citizen, yet with a People's Medal as a valuable memento – it allows you a few privileges, like free use of the public library. Yet I wonder, will my life ever be the same again?

Like Neathena, Aleatoria is an imaginary state. The imagination on display is only partly mine. The original idea and the name were invented by the British philosopher Barbara Goodwin. She described it – rather briefly – in the preamble to her philosophical treatise on 'justice by lottery' as an alternative to 'market justice', probably to tickle the imagination of the reader (Goodwin, 1992:

3–23,142; see also Cochran, 1994: 849). It seems a good start for a theoretical exploration of sortitionism. I will first discuss the stronger forms of this relatively unknown, new and incomplete ideology, starting with Goodwin and then moving on to John Burnheim's 'demarchy', Simon Threlkeld's citizen juries, and the citizens' assembly of the Spanish Chance Party. Subsequently weaker or hybrid forms of sortitionism will be analysed, as presented by Ernest Callenbach and Michael Phillips, Keith Sutherland, Lex Zakaras, Ethan Leib and Kevin O'Leary. They advocate randomly selected bodies which supplement rather than replace elected legislatures. Having discussed the theories, we will look at the way sortition has been practiced in ancient as well as contemporary political systems: the Athenian Council of 500, the criminal jury, and recent experiments with citizen juries, citizen assemblies and deliberative opinion polling.

THEORY

Barbara Goodwin's House of Lots

In Goodwin's utopia, sortition is used not only to select political representatives, but also to allocate practically all scarce goods and values, including jobs. The social system is not based on competition in a market but on a Total Social Lottery. Some political decisions are even taken by throwing dice. This might make democratic extremists very suspicious – and quite likely other democrats as well. Not all political decisions in Aleatoria are taken by the people. In a strict sense, the people are not involved in the decision-making process at all, only a randomly selected fragment of the people. Every year, a random sample is drawn from the population to fill one-fifth of the seats in the House of Lots, as parliament is called in Aleatoria. The Lotreps, as the members of this House are called, serve for five years – ensuring some continuity in parliament – before being assigned another job by lot. They cannot be reselected. Every two years, a number of them are selected by lot to form an executive committee or government.

Goodwin does not tell us how big the House of Lot is in proportion to the total population of the country. We may assume it to be modest, in order to allow 'genuine debate'. According to the British philosopher, genuine debate would flourish better in a sortitionist parliament than in an elected legislature with political parties controlling and curtailing debates (Goodwin, 1992: 5). Let us suppose that fifty Lotreps are selected each year, from a population of ten million adults (though Goodwin does not specify this either, I assume only adults can be selected). Even if Aleatorians lead long and healthy lives, the average citizen would have a chance of less than 1 per cent of joining the House of Lots once in her life. The only reason why Aleatoria can still be considered as a democratic polity has to do with the faithful statistical representation of the population by the House of Lots. Assuming the selection process to be fair and transparent, all interests and shades of opinion in the population will be represented. Of course, the Total Social Lottery requires a perfect registration system: every Aleatorian will have a unique citizen number, so that random selection is a simple computer process. Presumably, the outcome of the lottery is accepted universally – extreme circumstances excepted perhaps, such as a deaf and dumb person being selected to direct an orchestra. Yet that same person might well serve as a Lotrep, assuming the availability of sophisticated communication tools. So, hardly any citizen selected for the House of Lots will be allowed to refuse this position. The IQ of a Lotrep will be about the national average, i.e. roughly 100.

A democratic extremist will probably not be satisfied with this arrangement. Even if the Lotreps represent the population very well when selected, their position and the interaction between them might gradually change their ideas. Within a year or so, they may have 'gone native', i.e. become professional politicians, as alienated from the people as the elected politicians that rule the US, the UK and so on (see Sutherland, 2008: 147). The latter may still try to serve the interests of the people, as they usually want to be re-elected. But the Lotreps cannot be elected or re-elected, so why should they care about the opinions and interests of the people? In this light, Aleatoria looks like another mixed regime – a democracy from the outside, but a curious kind of oligarchy from the inside. In order to make it truly democratic, at least some reforms would have to be introduced. Terms should be reduced, say to one year instead of five, and/or political power should be spread more widely, through a process of radical territorial or functional decentralisation. This would raise the chances that a citizen will substantially participate in decision-making. Then, Aleatoria would have been transformed into a demarchy, the utopia of John Burnheim.

John Burnheim's demarchy

John Burnheim, born in 1927, was an ordained priest in the Catholic Church, but later parted from his flock and joined the Philosophy Department of the University of Sydney, Australia. When the department was split up into a radical Department of General Philosophy and a more conservative Department of Traditional and Modern Philosophy, he joined the former – though he was seen as a moderate among the radicals (Franklin, 1999). In 1985 he published *Is democracy possible?*, a short eloquent argument for radical decentralisation as well as sortitionist democracy – a combination he labelled 'demarchy'. In 2006 a second edition appeared with a new preface and a few self-critical comments from the author. He discarded the Marxist class analysis that had inspired the first edition, but continued to defend his libertarian critique of the state as well as his demarchy. In his view, the state is 'literally a protection racket' and 'meant to suppress violence by monopolizing it, the supreme constraint on our liberties that is meant to guarantee liberty, the provider of goods with an inexhaustible appetite for taxation.' (Burnheim, 2006: 16).

The Australian philosopher offers a simple alternative: state authority should be dispersed to functional agencies with limited powers. All decisions now taken by state agents should be taken by 'autonomous specialized agencies that are co-ordinated by negotiation among themselves or, if that fails, by quasi-judicial arbitration, rather than by direction from a controlling body' (Burnheim, 2006: 5). Education, health, welfare, public transport and industry should be regulated by different bodies with a limited geographical scope – local, regional or national. Burnheim rejects all forms of communalist anarchism, no doubt including Bookchin's libertarian municipalism, which was discussed in the previous chapter, because they would concentrate too much power in one local body. The local body, whether a people's assembly or an elected parliament, would probably be dominated by 'entrenched interests' and local elites, rather than by the people at large (Burnheim, 2006: 6, 47).

Burnheim does not share Bookchin's faith in assembly democracy. Modern society is too complex, even at the local level, to be governed by 'the people' in a general assembly. Perhaps in a classless society the notion of the people might acquire real meaning, but that seems a very distant utopia – to the Burnheim of 2006 even more than to the Burnheim of 1985. In modern society, most citizens lack the knowledge, the time and the will to deal with all political problems at the local level – let alone at the national or international levels. A popular assembly would be attended only by citizens with strong particular interests, and even then it might be manipulated by demagogues. Deliberation in a large assembly is impossible anyway, as people can only accept or reject the proposals drafted by experts or interest groups (Burnheim, 2006: 2).

Instead of one large general assembly deciding all kinds of issues, Burnheim advocates a multitude of smaller specialised bodies or councils with limited powers. Of course, they should not be controlled by special interests and technocrats, which could happen if the members were elected by the people or appointed by another body. Burnheim hopes to avoid this by selecting the members of any functional body by lot from a pool of citizens who have volunteered for this public duty. Quite likely, citizens will volunteer who have some experience with the specific function of the body: people who travel often on a bus or a train could join a Public Transport Council, people who regularly borrow books from the public library can volunteer for the Library Council, and so on. With modern technology it is easy to register the users of all these public facilities. They could be contacted regularly to ask if they would participate in the selection of the council that administrates the facility. When renewing your membership card for the library, you would be asked if you would be willing to sit on the Library Council. If you replied 'yes', your number might be drafted into the annual lottery.[1] So, the functional bodies or councils will be composed of a variety of citizens from different backgrounds – young and old, male and female, white and coloured, rich and poor – who share only a certain interest and experience in the facility to be governed by the council. Not only consumers, but also producers of the services should be selected by lot to sit on the council (Burnheim, 2006: 82). The councillors should be compensated for their time and effort, yet remain amateurs. If they desire, they could consult experts. As experts tend to disagree among themselves, they will not easily manipulate the councillors (Burnheim, 2006: 128). To avoid dominance by bureaucrats, the councils should not depend on one agency alone, but should be able to draw on competing agencies. Decentralisation would reduce the power of bureaucracy at any rate. Of course, moneyed interests might try to bribe the councillors, and so they should be scrutinised rigorously at the end of their term, like the members of the Athenian Council of 500 (see below).

Burnheim does not insist that demarchy equals pure democracy, but he does consider it superior to the 'electoral aristocracy' that passes for democracy in most parts of the world today (2006: 14). At least in a demarchy decisions would be taken by the people directly affected by them – whether as consumers or as producers – rather than by professional politicians with different interests. According to liberal theory, those politicians are accountable to their electorate. Yet in practice, Burnheim argues, they are controlled by party leaders and professionally organised lobbies (2006: 72–73). Issues tend to be mystified in election campaigns. Moreover, issues have to be packaged into more or less coherent party programmes, so a vote for a particular party cannot be interpreted as a clear opinion on a particular issue. Voters can only accept or reject a party or a candidate (depending on the prevailing electoral system); they cannot specify their reasons for doing so. If politician X loses her seat to politician Y, this could mean that she has failed in the eyes of her electorate, but it could also mean that X was not as wily or as wealthy as her successful rival, or that she received only lukewarm support from her central party office. Though at first sight elected politicians may appear more accountable to the people than the demarchs selected by lot, in fact the reverse may be true. Demarchs are more affected by their own decisions. Moreover, as they often do not have professional interests in their public function and serve only a short term, they will be more open-minded and sensitive to public opinion as well as to expert opinions. Environmental problems in particular would be better solved in a demarchy than in a liberal democracy where 'power-trading' tends to neglect long-term and diffuse interests (Burnheim, 1995). For all of these reasons, Burnheim preferred sortition over election.

Burnheim's book was not exactly a bombshell in the political and philosophical debate of the 1980s, yet it did attract the attention of some respected scholars who reviewed it in subsequent years. Most positive was Brian Martin, an Australian social scientist, who concluded with some satisfaction that Burnheim's project 'fits neatly in the anarchist tradition' (1990: 79). Lyn Carson, a political scientist who co-authored a book on random selection in politics with Martin and was actively involved as a local councillor in sortitionist experiments, acknowledged that Burnheim had inspired her (Carson and Hartz-Karp, 2005: 121). Tony Lynch, affiliated with the 'rival' Department of Traditional and Modern Philosophy at the University of Sydney, was more critical (1989). He rejected the basic assumptions of Burnheim: the idea of a total and global moral community in which differences will be settled without recourse to violence, purely as a 'demand of reason' (Lynch, 1989: 119). In his view, even barring violence, the decentralised decision-making advocated by his Sydney colleague might 'create a nightmare world of conflicting decisions and potentially never-ending appeals and counter-appeals' in ubiquitous mini-bureaucracies, 'an all-pervasive bureaucratic weave with ideally no thread that can be pulled to begin the process of unravelling it' (Lynch, 1989: 115, 116).

Janet Ajzenstat, a Canadian political scientist, was more nuanced. She compared the book to 'the best utopian writings': 'persuasive', 'illuminating', but not entirely feasible (1986: 637–638). Demarchy might work 'on a humble scale', but not worldwide. She singled out three problems. Because demarchy requires drastic decentralisation, it will 'yield less of justice defined as equal treatment for similar cases' (Ajzenstat, 1986: 639). Moreover, the institution of the political lottery seems at odds with the growing desire in contemporary society for control over every aspect of human life. And finally, she argued that Burnheim failed to provide any outlet for political ambition, as political careers would be impossible in a demarchy.

The (originally) Hungarian philosopher Agnes Heller regarded aspects of demarchy as quite reasonable, but rejected the model as a whole (1986). Its functionalism was too radical in her eyes: sensitive issues such as euthanasia or genetic engineering cannot be divided in a functional way, she argued. Moreover, the allotted councils would not be accountable to anyone. At the very least, citizens should be able to correct their decisions through a referendum.

The British scholar Paul Hirst also praised the book ('worthwhile', 'interesting'), but concluded that demarchy was 'a single bright idea carried to monomaniacal lengths' (1986: 669, 673). Burnheim's 'immodest proposal' did not follow from his argument for functional democracy and radical decentralisation, according to Hirst. Abolishing the state, as Burnheim advocated, would be impossible today, but also unnecessary for the implementation of his demarchic ideal. If Australians were to do away with the state apparatus (the army, the police and so on) they would soon be subjected to the power of regional competitors. Burnheim, in Hirst's eyes, underestimated the effectiveness of the centralised state. So did Guild Socialists such as G.D.H. Cole, who advocated a similar form of functional democracy at the beginning of the twentieth century. Perhaps Burnheim should try to learn why this movement fizzled out. Like Cole, the Australian philosopher seemed far too optimistic about the prospect of demarchs co-ordinating their different functional activities by negotiation and arbitration. It would have been instructive for Burnheim to consider Cole's difficulties in devising a means of coordination for his pluralist system 'and his subsequent abandonment of the functional democratic doctrine' (Hirst, 1986: 671).

Sortition might be tried without radical decentralisation, however. Yet this, too, is problematic to Hirst. He reminded Burnheim of the objections to sortitionist democracy raised by Robert Dahl, the leading American expert on democracy. The rotating councils could be dominated or manipulated by 'busybodies' with particular interests but no particular expertise. Or the incompetent demarchs could be at the mercy of their professional staff. Far from increasing people's power, sortition would very likely increase the influence of skilled bureaucrats (Dahl, 1970: 151). Moreover, Dahl argues that a representative sample from the population would be too large to act as an effective legislative body. An effective legislature would consist of 500 or 600 citizens at most, and might deviate substantially from the mean of the population. In Athens this was not a problem, not only because of the modest size of its population but also – and more importantly – because the allotted Council of 500 was an executive rather than a legislative body. It was subject to the authority of the popular assembly. Thus, Dahl concluded that sortitionist democracy clashes with the Criterion of Personal Choice, and would discredit rather than strengthen democracy (1970: 152–153). Even so, he proposed that elected representatives might benefit from randomly selected advisory councils of ordinary citizens (Dahl, 1970: 149).

Dahl's critique is fundamental and relevant to all advocates of sortition, not only Burnheim. In fact, only one argument seems less relevant to demarchy: the Australian theorist does not claim that the various functional allotted councils are representative samples from the total population of the area they cover – which would be a modest area in his decentralised utopia anyway. Burnheim also dismisses the argument that experts and bureaucrats would dominate incompetent councillors, as we have seen above. Competition between experts and agencies should solve that problem. Yet Burnheim did not take the Criterion of Personal Choice very seriously. Only public opinion and social control could check the power of the allotted bodies.

In 1990, Burnheim summed up his proposal in a slightly more modest frame: 'a way of dealing with the problem of public needs and at the same time whittling away the power of the state, even if that power is never finally abolished' (1990: 27). Moreover, he wants to offer 'the possibility of a society where the tomfoolery and corruption of our present political parties is supplemented by rational discussion of public issues in which everybody who wants to can take a significant part' (Burnheim, 1990: 27). Though he considers it a revolutionary project, he advocates a gradualist, reformist strategy: 'One might start with specific temporary bodies such as investigative or consultative committees and then press for such bodies to be made permanent and to be given executive powers' (Burnheim, 1990: 27). With respect to the coordination between the functional and representative bodies, he suggests 'higher level bodies which would allocate resources, adjudicate disputes, hear appeals and so on [and which] would be chosen by lot from a pool of people nominated by their peers on lower level bodies as having the qualities necessary for these more difficult tasks' (Burnheim, 1990: 26). These second-order groups would provide a legal or constitutional framework for the first-order councils (see also Burnheim, 2006: 87; Carson and Martin, 1999: 108–109). Perhaps this was his way of meeting critics halfway.

The discussion about demarchy may have fizzled out after 1990, but it has been revived in recent years (see also Carson and Martin, 1999: 102–114). No doubt the republication of Burnheim's original work contributed to this. In 2010 his ideas were discussed by the 'kleroterians', an informal network interested in the 'deliberate use of randomness (lottery) in human affairs' (Kleroterians, no date). Yoram Gat, a statistician and software engineer working at the University of California and co-editor of the blog of the Kleroterians, who initiated the discussion, agreed with representation by lot rather than by election, but questioned the 'localism' of Burnheim.² Most citizens would be reluctant to spend much time and energy on local issues, so local councils would mainly attract 'busybodies' without much expertise. Burnheim disagreed: if citizens are directly affected by decisions at the local level, they will be motivated to get involved and participate in the decision-making process. The work on local councils would be part-time and be paid like average clerical work. Participation should not be imposed as a burden like jury service (in countries such as Australia or the US). He continued to argue for coordination by voluntary agreements, but seemed more willing than before to let higher-level bodies play a role in the process. A global authority might even be desirable, to solve problems such as climate change and the international financial crisis. The members of the global authority should be 'chosen by lot from a large pool of people nominated by states and relevant scientific bodies, with very clearly defined powers'.³ Yoram Gat, the Kleroterian, objected to this 'elitist argument': 'such filtering would produce a governing elite whose interests would be different from those of the average person'.⁴ Indeed, it would defeat the whole purpose of sortitionism, i.e. to replace electoral representation by a more egalitarian and democratic system.

In spite of its ambiguities, Burnheim's demarchy might inspire democratic experiments, particularly at the local or regional levels. Gat's objections might be lifted if the allotted members were rewarded well – not necessarily in cash, but in kind. One could award Library Council members free books, Transport Council members a free railway pass or bus passes, and so on. For some councils, such as the Prison and Security Council, this might require some creativity – few people would consider a free sojourn in a prison a fair reward for their efforts, but if prisoners produce certain household goods, the councillors might be rewarded with some of these goods.

The example of a Prison and Security Council might raise another objection to demarchy, however. What constituency would be represented here? Should convicted criminals and prison inmates be allowed or even encouraged to volunteer? A quota system might provide a solution to this question, e.g. one-third of the council could consist of (former) prison inmates, one-third of prison wardens and other security personnel, and the remaining third of concerned citizens. This pragmatic solution may not satisfy sceptics who question the fundamental principle of representation by sortition and single out the Prison and Security Council to expose the absurdity of the whole idea. Prison and other punitive institutions are meant to increase the security and satisfy the sense of justice of all citizens, not merely a particular group. The specific interests of prison wardens and prison inmates should not prevail over this general public interest. So, important decisions about prison regimes, parole and rehabilitation should be taken by a body representing the citizens at large and not just 'concerned citizens' – a group that might end up consisting of former prisoners and their relatives, who may have a particular axe to grind rather than a contribution to make to public safety. Here we come back to the problem of corporatism and Guild Socialism raised by Hirst. In order to solve that problem, the functional councils based on a random selection from a particular group should be subordinated to a body representing the general interest. This body could be elected or allotted. The former option would be a weak and hybrid form of sortitionism. In either case, we move away from demarchy. I will first discuss the stronger forms of sortitionism, and then the hybrids.

Strong sortitionism: the citizen juries of Simon Threlkeld

In 1998 the Canadian lawyer Simon Threlkeld published a 'blueprint for democratic law-making'. In a short article in the journal *Social Policy* he criticised the dominant electoral democracy where 'elected governments are free to impose laws that are contrary to the informed will of the citizens. The democratic way is for the citizens, not the politicians, to have the final say about which laws go into effect' (Threlkeld, 1998: 9). One way to realise this would be via referendums; but referendums are ill-suited to informed decision-making and 'heavily skewed in favor of wealth and power' (Threlkeld, 1998: 5). Therefore, Threlkeld suggests citizen juries randomly chosen from the citizenry that would meet face-to-face for days, weeks or months in order to deliberate and decide on all laws proposed either by the government or by citizen groups. Supporters and opponents of the proposed law would present their views, and then the jury would come to a decision by a majority vote. Each proposed law would require a new jury, so over the course of time large numbers of citizens would gain legislative experience. The size of the jury could vary from between 100 and 1,000 – also to be decided by a jury – and jurors could break into smaller groups to discuss details. Jurors would receive payment. Threlkeld did not make clear whether jury service should be mandatory or voluntary, but given his emphasis on representativity, some element of compulsion would make sense.

Many other details were not elaborated in the five-page article. Threlkeld assumes a government that would propose and presumably execute the laws passed by the civil juries, but does not specify where this government comes from: elected directly by the people, like the Athenian *stratégoi*? And what would happen if citizen juries approved of inconsistent, unconstitutional or inhuman laws? Perhaps Threlkeld, writing in a North-American context, assumes some form of judicial review by a Constitutional Court? The extreme simplicity and incompleteness of his proposal makes it too easy a target for criticism. This may explain the scant attention his radical idea has received from academics: the American constitutional expert Ethan Leib mentioned Threlkeld only briefly (2004: 97), as did John Gastil, a specialist in communication arts (2000: 162).

The Canadian lawyer is not the only one to defend pure sortitionism. Similar ideas have been articulated by the Spanish (or Catalan, if you prefer) philosophy professor Carles Ferrer i Panadès (2011), the French high school teacher Etienne Chouard (2011) and the Australian scientist George Christos (2011), as well as by a small Spanish party, the *Partido Azar*.

Strong sortitionism: the Partido Azar

In the spring of 2011 a new party was founded in Spain, inspired by the democratic protest movement that had filled the streets of major cities since 15 May.[5] The *Partido Azar* (Chance Party) distinguished itself from all other parties by its radical proposals for a new political system 'without professional politicians' (Partido Azar, 2011). The elected parliament should be replaced by a citizens' assembly (*Asamblea de ciudadanos*) selected every six months by sortition from all citizens above a certain level of competence. It should be a stratified sample of the population, based on a balanced representation of age, gender, region, income category, education level and ideological position. Selected members should receive a standard salary and sign an agreement to the effect that they would not pursue a political career. They would be trained for a month before entering the assembly. The citizen assembly would be the only sovereign body in Spain. Citizens would be able, however, to introduce legislation through a popular initiative.[6] The assembly would also elect an executive body or government, presumably prestigious experts in different areas rather than politicians.[7] Only the judiciary would remain independent of the assembly. The party expected that the allotted citizens' assembly would be considerably less corrupt and more responsive to citizens' interests than an elected parliament, as well as more efficient, due to a lack of partisan conflicts.

This model would qualify as democratic extremism, even if the minimal competence required of the allotted citizens seems an aristocratic blot on the democratic escutcheon. The *Partido Azar* did insist that it would be 'a simple objective test' (*una sencilla prueba objetiva*), yet did not specify exactly what would be tested: mere literacy, or also a basic understanding of political processes? (Partido Azar, 2011). The former seems practically superfluous in modern society, the latter would be inviting ideological bias. Similar problems might complicate the stratification of the sample. If gender is considered a relevant variable, why not also homosexuality? What about religion, non-regional ethnic minorities (like Roma or Sinti) and immigrant groups? And how should ideological positions be measured objectively? Party preference would not do, as political parties would lose their main raison d'être in this system without elections. Obviously, the proposal of the *Partido Azar* could do with some more elaboration – not surprising, given that the party has just been founded. It intended to present candidates in the Madrid district at the 2011 general elections, but failed to collect the 5,000 required signatures.[8] The party might do better at the next elections. However, its project may be too abstract and too extreme to attract mass support, unless people become so desperate that they are willing to try anything. For the time being, more moderate reforms of the existing system may stand a better chance, like combinations of sortition and election.

Sortitionism balanced with electoralism: Callenbach and Phillips

Pure sortitionism appears to be a rare bird. Most advocates of political lotteries propose combinations of allotted and elected bodies sharing the sovereignty in their political system. Some may do so for tactical reasons, hoping to make their package more palatable to public opinion and pacifying the powers that be by allowing political parties to retain some power. Others present more principled arguments for checks and balances between the different bodies. As the former may still be democratic extremists at heart, while disguised as moderates, they should be discussed here first.

The writers Ernest Callenbach and Michael Phillips very likely tried to avoid extremism when they published their proposal for a 'citizen legislature' in 1985.[9] They began by piously quoting the American founding fathers James Madison and John Adams. Yet the quotes were quite radical: the legislature ought to be 'the most exact transcript of the whole society' or 'an exact portrait, in miniature, of the people at large, as it should think, feel, reason, and act like them' (Madison and Adams, respectively, quoted in Callenbach and Phillips, 2008: 17). Representative bodies in modern industrial societies, including the US, clearly deviate from this ideal. They are usually dominated by powerful interest groups. Women, manual workers and ethnic minorities tend to be under-represented. As a result, the views of the people at large and the actions of their supposed representatives diverge more and more. Increasingly, citizens avoid the voting booth. Elections are decided by money. Even if the elected politicians do not act directly as agents of their sponsors and benefactors, they are inclined to lend them a willing ear and neglect other interests. Callenbach and Phillips did not expect that campaign funding reforms would end this subtle and diffuse corruption: 'Political money is a hydraulic system: if you stop up a leak in one place, the level rises and causes a break someplace else' (2008: 49). Referendum and people's initiative would not help the under-represented very much either, as money tends to defeat most initiatives that threaten corporate interests (Callenbach and Phillips, 2008: 51–52). The only way to guarantee representation in the legislature for all sections of society would be to draw a representative sample from the population.

A random sample really would be an 'exact portrait' of the people at large. In the US, 435 names could be selected at random from potential juror lists. With a margin of error of 2.5 per cent, all groups over 400,000 would be represented most of the time, and they would be represented more or less in proportion to their real numbers. In around 1985 about 218 of the allotted representatives would be women, 52 African Americans, 26 Latinos, and 108 blue collar workers. Thus the House of Representatives would become a truly Representative House. Callenbach and Phillips did not suggest a minimal competence test, only a minimum age (25) and at least seven years of citizenship – the same requirements that apply to the elected House (2008: 37). Every year, one-third of the House should be renewed. New members should follow a total-immersion training period of three months in order to familiarise themselves with legislative procedures, debating and decision-making techniques, as well as with major political issues. Factions or caucuses might develop, such as a women's caucus or a caucus of the unemployed. Natural leaders would emerge. Some representatives might be manipulated by lobbyists or staff members – but so are elected members of the existing House. The latter may be more malleable, as they want to be re-elected and need the support of their sponsors, whereas the allotted members of the Representative House cannot be re-elected. Some might prefer to stay home rather than attend the meetings of the House and its committees – but so do elected members, usually because they want to address their voters or placate their fund-raisers. The allotted representatives would receive the same salary as elected members of the House today. Like the present House, the allotted Representative House would review and approve or reject bills from the Senate and generate bills itself – though perhaps the latter not so much, at least in its first years. Callenbach and Phillips expected that the Representative House would be more co-operative and more responsive to the needs of the people than the present House of Representatives.

Yet their enthusiasm about sortition did not extend to the Senate, or to the President. Senators would continue to be elected, state by state, 'so they would go on representing the special interests of their respective states – especially the corporate interests in those states' (Callenbach and Phillips, 2008: 63). Why not select senators by lot, on a state by state basis? Thus they could also represent the interests of their state, and act as check on the power of the Representative House. Callenbach and Phillips implicitly rejected this option but did not present any substantial arguments for election. The reader is bound to infer that they want to maintain the elected Senate as it is merely to placate the powers that be and dispel fear that they would 'completely overhaul Washington' (Callenbach and Phillips, 2008: 35). They argued that their 'pragmatic bicameralism fits in well with the history of American representative institutions' (Callenbach and Phillips, 2008: 35). Yet they did hope for a gradual but radical evolution of society. Sortition should become a 'normal way of distributing many goods, including political power' (Callenbach and Phillips, 2008: 70). Distribution should become more equal and fair. The Representative House might also encourage 'worker ownership, worker representation on boards of directors, and more equable distribution of income' (Callenbach and Phillips, 2008: 65). In other words, Callenbach and Phillips were striving for a fairly radical type of democratic socialism. This is not surprising: after all, ten years before the publication of *A Citizen Legislature* Callenbach had already expressed equally radical egalitarian – though not sortitionist – political ideals in the utopian novel *Ecotopia* (1975).[10]

The proposal of Callenbach and Phillips provoked criticism from many sides. The authors had sent their text to political activists and politicians and published eight reactions in an appendix to the book. Some of them did not mince their words. John Vasconcellos, a progressive member of the California State Assembly at the time, considered the ideas 'simplistic, unwieldy and unrealistic'

(Callenbach and Phillips, 2008: 89) and quoted George Bernard Shaw: "Why should the people not write their own plays?" (Callenbach and Phillips, 2008: 89, 87). The writer Malcolm Margolin regarded the idea of government by lottery as 'utterly silly and unworkable' (Callenbach and Phillips, 2008: 80). Some of the general criticisms of sortition have already been discussed in the preceding section on Burnheim's demarchy. The allotted representatives would lack the competence and the motivation to produce solid legislation; too many of them might prefer to stay home rather than spend long days in committee rooms and assembly halls. Margolin added an insightful psychological aspect: many, if not most of the representatives would encounter 'grave personal problems, their lives in total disarray caused by a sudden influx of money that they don't know how to handle, a change of occupation, a move to a distant city, and separation from family and friends' (Callenbach and Phillips, 2008: 81). Peter Stone, who defended a PhD thesis about sortition in 2000, made a more theoretical point in his critical introduction to the 2008 edition of *A Citizen Legislature* (Callenbach and Phillips, 2008: 9–15). Clinging firmly to a descriptive notion of representation, Callenbach and Phillips seem to overlook the more substantive meaning of representation of interests. The members of the Representative House would automatically represent the American people, even if they choose to 'move to Hawaï and become beach bums' (Callenbach and Phillips, 2008: 47). This suggests a total lack of concern with the quality of legislation to be expected from the Representative House. Yet Callenbach and Phillips are not consistent, as they want to exclude convicted felons and mentally ill citizens from the lottery (Callenbach and Phillips, 2008: 27). If they opted for pure descriptive representation, this exclusion makes no sense. Their position, therefore, is not entirely clear.

The distinction between descriptive and substantive representation goes back to Hanna Pitkin's classical analysis of the concept of representation (1967). She regarded descriptive representation as a rather one-sided and dangerous notion. Representatives have to 'act for' – rather than 'stand for' – their constituents by deliberating, negotiating and governing. Iris Marion Young elaborated the distinction (2000). She argued that representation requires 'active relationships of authorization and accountability between constituents and representatives' (Young, 2000: 143). These relationships not only involve interests (material resources) but also opinions and perspectives, i.e. knowledge, experience and sensibilities resulting from a particular location in society (Young, 2000: 134–141). Descriptive representation might make sense with respect to perspectives even more than opinions or interests. In most contemporary democracies the perspectives of women, ethnic minorities, manual workers and the poor are often excluded from decision-making processes as they are under-represented in legislative and executive bodies. And even if those groups are included nominally, they may be ignored in the decision-making process if they fail to adapt to the rational mode of deliberation, formal speech, applying general principles to individual cases, avoiding emotion and figurative speech (Young, 2000: 37–40, 141–142). Jane Mansbridge adds that descriptive representation might benefit disadvantaged groups in particular when their interests are not clearly crystallised, when their 'ability to rule' has been questioned within a long history of political subordination and when communication between them and the dominant groups is impaired by distrust (1999). She points out, however, that the costs of sortition – the waste of the political talent and acquired skill of professional law-makers – might outweigh the benefits, at least at the macro-level of the national state (Mansbridge, 1999: 632).

Sortitionism balanced with electoralism: Sutherland and the Kleroterians

The British writer (and printer) Keith Sutherland tried to incorporate the critical arguments of Pitkin, Young and others in his own defence of a hybrid utopia (2008; see also 2011b). Randomly selected representatives should only vote on proposals presented by elected officials, either ministers or 'Lords Advocate' – the new House of Lords, consisting of appointed experts as well as elected members of political parties. In Sutherland's sophisticated system, the House of Commons would consist of citizens selected at random from the electoral roll for a limited time. The procedure could be copied from the selection of juries. Only convicted criminals and mentally incapacitated citizens should be excluded, as well as the very young. Sutherland did consider further restrictions, based upon intelligence or political competence and age, but realised that this elitism might go against the grain for most democrats. Like a jury, a parliament should be selected for a specific case, for a short period only. Rather than a house with more or less permanent residents, the House of Commons would be a hotel with transient guests. The parliamentary jury would study a new bill, listen to the pro and con arguments from ministers, Lords Advocates and other experts, then vote – anonymously, to avoid possible corruption – and go home. It should not engage in discussions about the bills presented to it, in order to retain its purity as a representative sample from the population. In Sutherland's eyes, discussion would foster consensual 'group think' and manipulation by the more educated, prestigious and eloquent members of the group. It would spoil the 'wisdom of the crowd': when asked to predict objective events or estimate the weight of an animal, crowds of laymen prove better predictors and come closer to the truth than experts, provided they remain independent of one another. Sutherland refers here to the work of James Surowiecki and Philip Tetlock, as well as to the Jury Theorem presented by Condorcet – who figured prominently in Chapter 4 – in 1785 (2008: 73–84). If one rejects moral relativism and assumes that 'moral truth' is a meaningful (even if not very precise) concept, then a randomly selected jury of laymen would come closer to moral truth through a simple majority vote than a group of experts trying to reach a consensus. The jury would also do better than an elected parliament, as elections imply party discipline (at least in modern times) and dependence upon campaign fund-raisers.

Sutherland realised that his modern version of the Athenian *nomothetai* 'would make legislation a somewhat lengthy process as Advocates would need to explain every new bill from first principles' (2008: 149). Quite likely this would 'diminish the flood of legislation we have become accustomed to' (Sutherland, 2008: 149). Sutherland welcomed this consequence, but in doing so might have alienated potential supporters who did not agree with his libertarian kind of conservatism. He did not appear entirely convinced himself, as he discussed other options for the allotted House of Commons quite seriously, too: terms of one year, ten years or even longer. The longer the term, the more competent the members of the House would be, but also the more likely they would 'go native' and lose their representativeness. Moreover, longer terms would require a voluntary commitment, whereas a participation in a short ad-hoc legislative jury could be imposed upon citizens, like participation in a criminal jury. Voluntary commitment would also undermine the representativeness of the allotted House, and therefore its independence from particular interests. Moreover, ad-hoc juries would provide more citizens with an opportunity to learn about politics and exercise power. However, by the same token one might object that the ad-hoc jury members might be more easily manipulated by lobbying experts and bureaucrats – but Sutherland does not deal with this objection.

In Sutherland's system, the allotted House of Commons has a clearly restricted but vital function. It cannot initiate legislation nor set its own agenda, but it holds veto power over all legislation proposed by the government or by the Lords. The Lords Advocate – as he liked to call them – 'examine the merits (or otherwise) of government legislation in front of the "jury" of the people (the Commons). The Lords propose/support/amend/oppose, but only the Commons vote' (Sutherland, 2008: 133). The Lords Advocate would meet in the same room or hall as the House of Commons; they do not need a separate House. The Lords explicitly represent particular interests, such as trade unions, business, environmentalism, sports, finance, religion, arts, sciences – perhaps even political parties, though again Sutherland seems rather wavering here. The election process 'would enable the representation of interests in the same way as present, but via the *upper* house', but this would 'unfortunately mean a reduction in the power of informed advocacy and also that the partisan, factional and demagogic influence of electoral politics would remain – a high price to pay for the representation of interests (factional, by definition)' (Sutherland, 2008: 158, 159). Alternatively, the Lords Advocate could be nominated by the various interest organisations, but elected by the House of Commons – for life. Or, by way of compromise, perhaps eighty Lords could be elected by the people (via political parties, necessarily) and the rest by the Commons (Sutherland, 2008: 160). Though Sutherland did not argue this explicitly, the two categories of Lords and the allotted Commons seem to correspond with the three types of representation distinguished by Young: the partisan Lords elected by the people would represent the opinions, the Lords nominated by interest groups the interests, and the Commons the perspectives of the people.

The two legislative bodies would be interdependent: the Lords Advocate depending on the vote of the Commons, with the latter depending on the Lords for advice and expertise. The third branch of government, the ministers, would be experts appointed by the Crown but approved by parliament – i.e. the House of Commons. Sutherland's utopia is a (constitutional) monarchy; he does not deal with the question of how a republic should select its head of state (2008: 115–132). Sutherland hopes to create a pluralist system of checks and balances, in the spirit of Madison and James Harrington – the seventeenth century creator of another political utopia, the Commonwealth of Oceana. Of central importance to Sutherland is the separation of executive, advocacy and judgment powers, preferably instantiated by their own unique mechanism: appointment, election and sortition. In his book and in his contributions to the Kleroterians' weblog, Sutherland has always insisted on this separation, while showing flexibility concerning the institutional forms and details. In his blog he developed another model, 'Athenian Democracy Reincarnate', wherein policy proposals would be initiated by randomly selected advocates from various interest groups, then ranked by a public vote or referendum, and finally approved or rejected by a randomly selected legislative jury (Sutherland, 2011a). The three stages would correspond to the *boulè, ekklèsia and nomothetai* (respectively) in ancient Athens (see also Chapter 3 and the next section in this chapter).

Sutherland's book received a fairly benevolent but short review in the *Times Literary Supplement* from the hand of the well-known British constitutional expert Vernon Bogdanor. He concluded that the book raised important issues but did not 'fully succeed in resolving them' (Bogdanor, 2008). In his opinion, Sutherland was too radical. Sortition might work at the local level, but not in Westminster. Some Kleroterians, however, argued that Sutherland was not radical enough. The amateurs of the allotted House of Commons would be manipulated by the professional Lords Advocate, especially if they could not control their own agenda nor amend the bills they had to vote on. Power would be concentrated in the hands of the elected and appointed Lords Advocate and the cabinet. Sutherland's utopia would be practically as elitist as the present system.

At a more theoretical level, some Kleroterians questioned the incompatibility of descriptive and substantive representation. The allotted representatives could listen to various experts and lobbyists articulating and interpreting the interests of their own groups. Given some time (and effort) they would be able to represent the interests of these groups in every sense of the term. They would not only share the social perspective of the groups, but also interpret their (material and social) interests – in a more active and sophisticated way than most members of these groups might do, as the representatives would have spent more time reflecting on their interests and digesting the information provided by the experts and lobbyists. In the process, they might have developed and changed their opinions on issues. This need not be a problem, one might argue, if the representatives could explain their development to the public.

The complexity of Sutherland's institutional design and his almost bewildering willingness to consider alternatives make a straightforward assessment far from easy. One might wonder if he does not leave too much power in the hands of ministers and civil servants. Ad-hoc juries might remain rather weak institutions, dependent on their environment. Obviously, this criticism would also affect Threlkeld's proposal. It does not apply to the weaker forms of sortitionism that will be discussed in the next section.

Sortitionism subordinated to electoralism: Zakaras, O'Leary and Leib

Alex Zakaras, a political scientist at the University of Vermont, published a 'modest proposal' (his words) which looks like Callenbach and Phillips reversed: an allotted Senate combined with an elected House (2010). However, his Senate would exercise only limited powers: it would review, approve or veto legislation passed by the elected chamber, but not amend or initiate laws. Moreover, it could compel the House to vote on bills that were 'languishing in committee' and it could redraw legislative districts, removing this sensitive task from the hands of elected officials (Zakaras, 2010: 457–458). Terms would be short (one legislative session) and membership voluntary. Zakaras wants to introduce the same dual system at all levels: allotted chambers should co-exist with elected legislatures not only at the federal, but also at the state and local levels. The latter represent citizens in a different way than the former: whereas elected representatives act (ideally) in response to the needs and demands of their constituents and can be held accountable to them, the allotted representatives share the general attitudes of their constituents. Following Philip Petitt, Zakaras refers to 'responsive' and 'indicative' representation (2010: 462). In his opinion, the two principles would complement each other very well. By monitoring (and if necessary) vetoing decisions of elected representatives, the allotted chambers would make the latter more accountable to the public. Moreover, in his design more and more citizens would participate in decision-making, while acquiring greater political knowledge and interest in public affairs (Zakaras, 2010: 464). This may redress, at least to some extent, the 'unenlightened self-interest' of many American voters who often support legislation which they erroneously perceive as serving their interests, such as regressive tax cuts (Zakaras, 2010: 460–461).

Both Kevin O'Leary and Ethan J. Leib call for an allotted body as an addition to rather than the replacement for an elected legislature. Both Americans graduated from Yale and could be considered as members of the 'Yale School of Democratic Reform' (Snider, 2007). Following the tracks of Robert Dahl, this (informal) school has tried to graft sortition onto representative democracy through a dialogue with the Founding Fathers of the United States. At first sight the reforms they advocate seem rather modest, yet in the long run they might give substantially more power to the people and make not only the political system but also society at large more democratic.

Leib, an expert in constitutional law teaching at Fordham University School of Law in New York, proposed a 'fourth branch of government' consisting of civic juries composed of stratified random samples of 525 eligible voters (2004: 12–13). Like Sutherland's and Threlkeld's parliamentary juries, they would meet for a limited time to discuss specific issues, such as drug policy or gay marriage. They would gather first in small groups and then take a decision collectively (by a two-thirds majority). The (elected) legislative branch of government should develop this decision into a coherent written statute – or alternatively it could veto it, at its own political peril. The decision could also be vetoed by the executive branch or struck down by the judiciary. The issues to be discussed would be either proposed by one of the branches of government or by a group of citizens; already 10 per cent of the population could place a proposal on the agenda. Service on the civic jury should be compulsory, like service on a legal jury (Leib, 2004: 18–19). Thus, self-selection would be avoided and representativity guaranteed.

Leib expects his popular branch will enhance political participation and deliberation and reduce power inequality, political alienation and ignorance (2004: 8). It should also help to break legislative deadlock and bring back onto the agenda issues that have been shelved by legislatures. The popular branch would fulfil the functions of popular initiative or referendum in a more effective way, adding the element of deliberation which these institutions lack (Leib, 2004: 12). Though Leib emphasises that his proposal fits in with American traditions – 'democratic experimentalism', separation of powers, popular sovereignty – he also feels that it could be adapted to other systems (Leib, 2004: 69).

O'Leary, a political scientist, proposed 435 local assemblies, consisting of 100 members each, randomly selected from the (adult) citizens of a congressional district. In a first stage, the assemblies would merely advise the elected congresswoman or congressman representing the district in the House of Representatives. In a second stage, O'Leary hopes the assemblies will form a virtual national assembly– the People's House – with the power to initiate bills as well as to amend or veto legislation passed by Congress (2006: 98–99). The bills it initiates would have to be discussed and refined or amended by Congress, whereas bills approved by the House and the Senate could be vetoed by the People's House. O'Leary expects the new institution would curb the power of special interests, speed up legislation and break gridlock – in certain cases – and provide growing numbers of citizens with opportunities to take part in political decision-making and deliberation (2006: 107–112, 113–138, 146–150). Moreover, legislators would benefit from the 'wisdom of the crowds' and the everyday life experiences of citizens (O'Leary, 2006: 153–156).

Unlike Leib, O'Leary does not advocate compulsory service in the assemblies and allows selected citizens to opt out if they wish (2006: 89). He expects that a sufficient number of citizens will be motivated by civic spirit and a modest per diem to sacrifice a significant portion of their time – comparable to a busy city councillor – over two years, once they have been selected. In a critical review, J.H. Snider questions the plausibility of this expectation (2007: 4), as does Sutherland in his book discussed above (2008: 56–72). Why would 43,500 people devote so much energy to (often tedious) legislative work if their chances of making a difference are so small? The large size of the People's House makes for strong representativity, provided the samples are cleverly stratified in order to prevent over-representation of the usual suspects – the highly educated white males that tend to volunteer for political activities. Yet it also makes for complicated procedures. Legislation might first be prepared in a small task force, then discussed and voted upon in the plenary local assemblies, before finally votes are aggregated at the national level. However, aggregation might not always result in a clear majority. So, in the end, the addition of a new legislative body might slow down rather than speed up legislation. Snider would advise O'Leary to reduce the size of the People's House, though admittedly this would also reduce political participation and equality. The problems mentioned so far seem peculiar to O'Leary's proposal. A more general weakness of all sortitionist proposals might be the vulnerability of randomly selected citizens to corruption and manipulation, and their lack of accountability (Snider, 2007: 4). We will see below how the ancient Athenians dealt with this problem.

Hybrid forms of sortitionism, combining elected and randomly selected legislatures, have been designed not only in the US and UK, but also in Denmark, France and Germany. The Danish political scientist Marcus Schmidt advocated an electronic chamber of parliament of 75,000 Danish citizens selected by lot, which would vote on all legislation approved by the elected chamber of parliament. Given the average life span in Denmark (about 75 years), every Dane would quite likely be selected for this body once in her or his lifetime (Buchstein, 2009: 415–416). The French political scientist Yves Sintomer proposed a Senate selected at random rather than elected indirectly, as is the case with the French *Sénat* at present (2007: 163–164). The German political scientist Hubertus Buchstein suggested a 'House of Lots' as second chamber of the European Parliament, with the right to initiate as well as veto legislation in order to reduce the democratic deficit in the European Union (2009: 445–453). And one should also mention the American economists Dennis Mueller, Robert Tollison and Thomas Willett, who published a pioneering plea for sortition in 1972, though without advocating a particular institutional design (1972). However, discussing the details of these proposals may be repetitive and probably boring for most readers – so we will skip them here.

Pros and cons of sortitionism

Clearly, sortitionists differ in terms of the functions and the power they want to allocate to allotted bodies, as well as the time period the bodies should exist. Extremists such as Burnheim, Threlkeld (if I understand him correctly) and the *Partido Azar* would concentrate all power in the hands of the Lotreps and do away with elections altogether. More moderate sortitionists such as Buchstein, O'Leary, Leib, Sintomer, Sutherland and in fact (possibly *contre coeur*) also Callenbach and Phillips argue for a balance of power between elected and allotted legislatures. Whilst O'Leary's People's House and the Representative House of Callenbach and Phillips serve terms of a few years, the parliamentary juries of Threlkeld and Sutherland and the civic juries of Leib meet only for a few days or weekends to decide on a particular bill. However, they all roughly agree about the benefits of sortition.

In the first place, sortition would contribute to political equality and inclusiveness. Every citizen has an equal chance of being selected for the legislature, with very few exceptions (such as convicted criminals and the mentally or physically very ill). No professional political elite will dominate the population. Women, manual workers, ethnic and religious minorities, homosexuals, and other groups that are usually under-represented in elected bodies will have equal chances of being selected. Some of them might feel a little uncomfortable at first, if they are used to being discriminated against and excluded from privileged positions in society, but they will be encouraged and coached to fulfil their duty as citizens by professional facilitators and coaches. In the long run, their participation might reduce social exclusion and discrimination in civil society at large. By definition, all statistically significant social groups and opinions will be (roughly) represented in the House of Lots – depending on the size of the sample and the size of the population, of course. This statistical representation does not imply that Lotreps shall speak 'on behalf of' certain categories – after all, they have not been selected by an organisation to articulate its interests. They are free to express their personal opinions, and to adapt them in the course of their deliberations. Yet presumably they will be able to understand the problems of their own groups better than others. They will add their perspectives, which are usually ignored or misrepresented by elected representatives belonging to the dominant classes or groups.

In the second place, sortition might improve the quality of decision-making and reduce the corruption and costs of professional politics. In view of the rising costs of election campaigns in the US, Ernest Callenbach and Michael Phillips argued that sortition would be a much cheaper and less corruptible mechanism than election (1985: 33–36). They, as well as Goodwin, also expect more open-mindedness and common sense, and less polarised ideological debates from Lotreps than from professional politicians: their lack of political experience might be compensated by 'personal knowledge' and a variety of experiences in civil society.[11] Groups or categories that are now clearly under-represented in most legislatures – such as women, ethnic minorities, low-income groups and manual workers – would bring their experiences and perspectives to the table, thus enlarging the 'epistemological diversity' of the bodies (Burgers, forthcoming). The lack of party discipline might enhance rather than reduce the quality of decision-making. Ad-hoc factions or caucuses might emerge only to disappear again in short order. In one session, rural folk might clash with urbanites over environmental policies, yet the next day, old-age pensioners might face young workers when a pension plan or tax reforms are discussed. Social conflicts will be reproduced within the House, but might be reconciled there as well, as Lotreps are trained to listen to each other and accommodate diverse interests. Common sense, personal knowledge and empathy might play a larger role and lead to better decisions, as Sintomer argued (2007: 139–144).

In the third place, participation in the House of Lots (or similar bodies at a regional or municipal level) would socialise citizens in a spirit of equality and commitment. As a consequence, society at large might become more democratic and public-spirited. This effect would be rather modest if these bodies are small, but might be significant if the proposals of Burnheim, Leib, O'Leary or Schmidt were tried. And – this might be seen as a fourth argument, but closely related to the other ones – the random selection of political leaders will reduce the power of closed political elites but also prevent polarisation of the community into opposing parties or factions (Carson and Martin, 1999: 35). Prevention of factionalism as well as oligarchy may have been the main reasons why city-states in Greece and Italy used sortition, according to Dowlen (2008: 50, 56, 64–65, 117).

Naturally, there are disadvantages to sortition. Critics have pointed out at least five problems. First, there is the question of whether selection should be compulsory or voluntary: if the former, the Lotreps might lack commitment and neglect their duties; if the latter, self-selection might detract from the representativity of the sample and produce over-representation of 'the usual suspects' – highly educated white males of a certain age, as well as ambitious 'busybodies'. However, there are ways to prevent or at least mitigate this distortion, such as sufficient monetary rewards, stratified sampling or sub-samples from under-represented groups.

Second, even if the sample is perfectly representative of the population at large, it may be dominated and manipulated by 'logocrats' who tend to be more eloquent and committed than the average member. In other words, social inequality will be reproduced within the allotted legislature. Again, to some extent this problem could be solved by carefully trained moderators and facilitators, allocating less eloquent or less educated participants and 'logocrats' to separate subgroups or by allowing all members equal speaking time.

Third, even if all opinions were expressed freely and received equal attention in the legislature, its members might gradually change their ideas, being exposed to expert opinions and information that average citizens are not familiar with. The longer the terms they serve, the more likely it is that they will 'go native', as Sutherland put it – for good or bad reasons, either enlightened or manipulated by the experts and professional staff members. While doing so, they may lose legitimacy in the eyes of the ordinary citizens they are expected to represent.

In fact, their legitimacy seems problematic to many critics, in principle, as the Lotreps are not accountable to the people in any way. Political representation requires accountability, according to several theorists. Accountability can be provided by the process of election and (non-) re-election but not by sortition, as Lotreps need not worry about re-election (Delannoi, 2010: 29–30; see also Pitkin, 1967: 60–91; yet cf. Sutherland, 2011b; Carson and Martin, 1999: 35). This criticism would apply more to the stronger forms of sortitionism than to the hybrid proposals of Zakaras, Sutherland, Leib and O'Leary.

And finally, Lotreps lack the political experience and competence of elected and professional politicians. The talents of the latter are wasted when they cannot run for election. Instead they have to wait for a (relatively small) chance of being selected by lot. So, most political talents will presumably be forced to choose a different career.

As long as the institutional designs remain on the drawing-board, we can only speculate about their pros and cons. However, sortition has been practiced in different circumstances, in ancient Athens, in British and American juries and most recently in experiments with citizen assemblies and citizen juries. These practices might tell us a bit more about the advantages and disadvantages of sortitionist democracy, if only indirectly.

PRACTICE

Sortitionism has inspired few political projects in modern times. In ancient democracy, it was quite important, as will be shown in the following section. Lotteries were also used to select executive bodies in medieval Italian city-states such as Venice and Florence, though not within the same egalitarian setting as in Athens (Dowlen, 2008: 67–136; see also Buchstein, 2009: 155–189). Modern democratic movements did not follow the Athenian example (see also Manin, 1997: 42–93). In the First French Republic and in the United States, executives and legislatures were elected rather than allotted. Only in the judicial branch has sortition been applied to select juries – especially in recent times. Even more recently, randomly selected citizen juries or citizen panels have been invited to take part in democratic planning and problem-solving experiments in several European countries as well as in Canada and the US.

Though there is no direct link between the theories and utopias discussed above and the practice of criminal juries and citizen panels, the latter may tell us something about the pros and cons of sortition in different situations, and indirectly about the feasibility and desirability of an allotted legislature such as the House of Lots or the Representative House. More specifically, the practice may provide at least a partial answer to questions about the competence and motivation of randomly selected citizens.

The Council and the courts in Athens

To the ancient Greeks, selection by lot seemed the only way to guarantee all citizens an equal chance to participate in decisions outside of the assembly. Hence, most important offices were allocated by lot in ancient Athens, including the courts and the Council of 500.

The main co-ordinating and executive body in the Athenian polity must have been the Council of 500, usually called simply 'the Council' (*Boulè*, βουλη). Some experts regard the Council as the 'lynch-pin' or chief organ of government, and the only body that could restrain the powerful assembly (see Sinclair, 1988: 84; Starr, 1990: 61; Stockton, 1990: 94; Dowlen, 2008: 35). Others stress the subordinate and administrative role of the *Boulè* (Hansen, 1991: 140; Hornblower, 1993: 15; Jones, 1957: 105–108). There is broad agreement, however, about the functions served by the Council.

In the first place, the Council prepared the agenda and the decisions of the popular assembly. Formally, the assembly could only vote on decrees prepared and discussed by the Council (*probouleumata*), though it could amend them or vote for alternative proposals. Mogens Hansen, the famous Danish expert on Athenian democracy, estimated that about half of the decrees passed by the assembly in the fourth century were ratifications of proposals drafted by the Council (1984: 42). Moreover, the Council could pass certain decrees without the approval of the assembly (*boulès psephismata*), albeit in minor or routine matters only (Hansen, 1991: 255–256).

In the second place, members of the Council chaired the assembly.

In the third place, the Council had to execute the decisions taken by the assembly. It co-ordinated and supervised the collection of taxes and tributes from allied states, it inspected public buildings, naval yards, ships and even the horses of the cavalry, it could impose fines and imprison offenders (Hansen, 1991: 259–265; Sinclair, 1988: 73–75; Stockton, 1990: 84–95).

In the fourth place, the Council represented Athens in relations with other states. Its chairman-of-the day – also selected by lot – acted as head of state and would receive foreign ambassadors (Sinclair, 1988: 74).

Not all of these functions were performed by the Council in plenary sessions. Some were delegated to commissions, others to the standing (executive) committee or *prytaneis*. The standing committee consisted of fifty councillors from a particular tribe (*phyle*) and rotated every *prytaneia* – one tenth of the year – so that every councillor would be a member of the committee at some point (Thorley, 2004: 28–32).

The term 'tribe' may be somewhat misleading as it suggests a primitive ethnic unity, whereas the Athenian *phylai* were artificial constructs based on residence, created by the great statesman Kleisthenes around 500 BCE to replace the older, traditional tribes (Hornblower, 1993: 7). Each tribe consisted of a fixed number (around 14) of *demes* (districts), which nominated the candidates – in proportion to their number of residents – for the Council. Some districts may have nominated just enough candidates to fill the positions, so sortition was not necessary (Thorley, 1996: 31; Jones, 1977: 105–108). If there were more than enough candidates, they would put their personal bronze plaques in the allotment machine (*klèroterion*) in order to select the required number (Hansen, 1991: 246–247).

Once selected, the future Councillors had to be scrutinised by a people's court to prove that they were law-abiding citizens who had paid their taxes, treated their parents well and worshipped the gods (Sinclair, 1988: 76–79). All other public officials also had to pass this *dokimasia* as a kind of entrance exam, even though it may have been a formality in most cases. In the fifth century only citizens with property or income above a certain level could join the Council, but this requirement seems to have been relaxed (if not abolished) in the fourth century, when councillors received an allowance from the state (Stockton, 1990: 84–86; Hansen, 1991: 248–249, 253–255). They had to work fairly hard: the Council met practically every day, except for festivals (which were quite frequent, however). At the end of their one-year term, the Councillors had to again appear before a people's court to prove that they had not unduly enriched themselves or abused their office in any other way. If they failed this final exam, or *euthyna*, they could be prosecuted by the court.

The courts (*dikastèria*) were hardly less important than the Council. They were manned by randomly selected citizens, rather than professional lawyers.

The members were selected from a pool of about 6,000 citizens who had sworn a solemn oath (in the name of the gods Zeus, Apollo and Demeter) that they would act in a just and impartial manner (Hansen, 1991: 181). The courts mainly dealt with criminal and public offences. Private conflicts were often left to arbitrators and minor offences to local judges (Stockton, 1990: 96–103; Hansen, 1991: 178–180). Public offences were interpreted rather broadly, however. Even citizens who had advocated a law (in the assembly) that was regarded by other citizens as 'unconstitutional' or 'undesirable' could be prosecuted (*graphè paranomon* or *graphè nomon me epitedeion theinai*) and occasionally convicted (Hansen, 1991: 205–212). Public officials were often accused of 'conspiracy' or 'treason', and even successful generals could be condemned to exile or death. For each case, a jury would be convened, often for a whole day, consisting of 201, 401 or even more citizens (Thorley, 1996: 35). The jurors would listen to the speeches of the prosecuting and defending citizens, and then decide on a verdict and possibly a penalty. Decisions were not deliberated, merely voted.

The same pool of jurors may also have produced the *nomothetai* – lawgivers or legislators. After 402 BCE they would review existing laws and pass new ones when asked by the assembly (Hansen, 1991: 161–177; Stockton, 1990: 102; Thorley, 1996: 58). In a trial-like procedure, they would decide between the existing law and a new one proposed by citizens (Sealey, 1987: 32–52).

Hansen estimated that many other officials were also selected by lot; probably about 600 (1991: 218). Only officials performing rather specialised or sensitive functions were elected (usually by the assembly): the military leaders (*stratègoi*) as well as certain financial and technical specialists such as architects and superintendents of the water supply (Starr, 1990: 39–48; Stockton, 1990: 103–109).

One might expect that sortition mainly produced incompetent officials who would cash their payment and neglect their duty, as they were not pursuing a career in politics or public administration. Yet the records suggest incompetence was not perceived as a major problem. When public officials 'failed' their final exam (*euthyna*), it was usually because of bribery or corruption, rather than incompetence or laziness (Hansen, 1991: 239). Though the principle of sortition was not uncontested in Athens, there seemed to have been widespread support for the practice, mainly because of fear of corruption, factionalism and accumulation of power – the main disadvantages of the principle of election, in the eyes of the Athenians (see Hansen, 1991: 236).

Sortition must have worked fairly well, in the perception of the ancient Greeks. From a modern perspective, it was far from flawless. The *klèroterion* might have been an efficient sampling device, but the samples were drawn from a small section of the population: only free adult males, born from Athenian parents and who had volunteered for selection. So the allotted members of the Council and courts did not constitute a representative sample of all Athenians – and perhaps not even all of Athenian citizenry, as we do not know who volunteered and who did not. Of course, the modern idea of a random representative sample was unknown to the ancient Greeks. However, equality was an important value to the Athenians, even if applied only to citizens. The procedures within the *dikastèria* guaranteed a certain equality, in so far as all members had equal rights: one man, one vote was the rule when votes were taken. As there was no deliberation, the jurors could not be manipulated or intimidated by eloquent or prestigious fellow members. Yet in the Council, some deliberation and hence some manipulation might have taken place – we do not know. All in all, Athens remains an important source of inspiration for all sortitionists, but they need more practical experience and empirical evidence to build a convincing case.

Sortition and the jury system

With the demise of the independent city-state at the end of the fourth century BCE, sortition lost its political importance in Greece. Autocratic regimes replaced democracy. Lotteries continued to play a role in the Roman republic as well as in Italian city-states in the late Middle Ages, but mainly to distribute offices among a political elite rather than to select office-holders from the people at large (Dowlen, 2008: 67–97; Buchstein, 2009: 112–133, 150–154). In Venice, lottery was combined with election of officials – selected from a restricted class of less than 2,000 citizens – from the thirteenth until the end of eighteenth centuries (Buchstein, 2009: 155–164). In the American Revolution and the French Revolution sortitionist ideas were discussed, but never implemented (Dowlen, 2008: 188–214; Buchstein, 2009: 207–215).

Yet while sortition was refused entry at the front door, it returned through the back door. According to Oliver Dowlen, in parts of England and in some American states criminal and civil juries have been selected at random since the late seventeenth century (2008: 176; see also Burgers, 2013: 25–26). Even if those jury members were often appointed by a sheriff or constable, they were supposed to constitute a cross-section of the local community (Pole, 2002: 108; King, 2000). Sortition was prescribed by law only in fairly recent times: 1972 in the United Kingdom, 1968 in the United States (Lloyd-Bostock and Thomas, 2000: 68–72; Abramson, 2000: 99–100, 117–118). Jurors are now selected at random (by computer) from electoral registers or voter lists, supplemented in the US by driving license lists, telephone directories or tax rolls. Their occupations match those of the population fairly closely, but white males are still somewhat over-represented in Britain as well as in the US (Lloyd-Bostock and Thomas, 2000: 71; Abramson, 2000: 129–130; King, 2000: 110–114). The original idea was not that all groups in society should be represented on the jury. Instead, the idea was that random selection would guarantee impartiality and objectivity within a trial setting. Abramson laments that in the US in recent years the pursuit of a common truth through deliberation and consideration of different perspectives has been supplanted by a relativistic notion of representation of different group views, ending in a majority vote rather than agreement (2000: 241–250). Meanwhile, representativity is undermined by the practice of 'peremptory challenges': lawyers try to eliminate jurors who might be biased against their clients – though fortunately they often fail to predict the behaviour of the potential jurors (Abramson, 2000: 127–128, 143–176).

The invention of the jury system seems lost in time. It is not clear whether the practice may have been a Norman or Scandinavian invention introduced to England in the eleventh century or developed there spontaneously in the twelfth or thirteenth centuries (Mulholland, 2002; Lloyd-Bostock and Thomas, 2000). According to Sally Lloyd-Bostock and Cheryl Thomas, criminal juries were firmly established after the ordeal of fire and water was banned by Pope Innocent III in 1215 (2000: 53). Members of the community of a suspected wrong-doer were put under oath – hence the name 'juror' – to tell the truth about the affair. They were usually twelve men, freeholders or noblemen, assembled on a temporary basis to decide whether the accused person was guilty of a criminal act. In civil disputes, juries were expected to decide which side should prevail. The institution of the criminal jury spread from England to its colonies and quite a few other countries – more than fifty altogether, according to Neil Vidmar (2000: 2–3). Though an increasing number of criminal cases are no longer submitted to a jury in both the US and the UK, juries continue to deal with important cases like capital crimes.

In feudal systems, judicial and legislative functions were not clearly separated, so juries could occasionally influence legislation, too. Even in the nineteenth and twentieth centuries, American juries could 'nullify' a law and pardon lawbreakers, especially dissidents, though according to Jeffrey Abramson this practice has become more controversial and less frequent (2000: 57–95). Also in England, juries tended to protect political freedom against the state (Dowlen, 2008: 181). Even so, neither the English nor the American jury has exercised formal legislative functions like the Athenian *dikastèrion*.

Critics have questioned the competence and rationality of jurors. Yet experimental research suggests that jurors and professional judges tend to agree in most cases. In less than a fifth of cases the jury would have acquitted a defendant that the judge wanted to convict (Simon, 1980: 49–50). Generally, the juries applied even more rigorous standards than the judges. Jurors tend to favour defendants or plaintiffs of their own sex and occupation, but the evidence is not very strong here, concluded Rita Simon in her study of the American jury's role in society (1980: 29–47). Abramson observed that juries are influenced by experts and newspaper reports, but only to a modest degree (2000: 109–121). In the 1940s and 1950s they conformed more often to the ideological climate (the Cold War), but less so since the 1960s (Abramson, 2000: 123–149).

We may conclude that the jury system provides some evidence that randomly selected citizens can take reasonable decisions about matters of life and death.

Opinion polls, citizen assemblies and juries

In the 1970s and 1980s, the idea of a randomly selected group of citizens reaching an impartial and just decision after serious deliberation travelled from the legal realm to other sectors of society. Their names and characteristics varied: 'citizens juries', 'citizen panels', 'consensus conferences', 'policy juries', 'citizen assemblies', 'deliberative opinion polls', 'mini-publics' or 'planning cells' (*Planungszellen* in German). They were usually organised on an ad-hoc basis in order to assist and advise local, regional and occasionally national governments in solving social and political problems or to influence public opinion and educate citizens.

Sintomer attributed the growing popularity of random selection in politics to two phenomena: the call for more citizen participation, and the refinement of statistical techniques and theories of random sampling (2007: 104–108, 110–111; see also Carson and Martin, 1999: 65–78, 97). Perhaps it was a two-step process. The first step was the development of sophisticated opinion polling and market research. The modern technique of random and stratified sampling had already been applied in the US in the 1930s by George Gallup and his associates, becoming widespread in the 1940s and 1950s (Gallup and Rae, [1940] 1968: 44–76). In that period, however, deliberative experiments seemed to decline rather than grow, as John Gastil and William Keith observed, probably due to the Cold War and to waning localism (2005: 13). The first 'planning cells' were set up in the 1970s by Peter Dienel in Germany, and the 'citizens juries' at about the same time by Ned Crosby in the US, while James Fishkin organised the first 'deliberative opinion polls' in the late 1980s.

So, there appears to be a time lag between the development of sophisticated opinion polling and the introduction of randomly selected citizen panels. Yet as Sintomer pointed out, opinion polls gradually acquired a stronger influence in politics – and in society at large – as the faith in sampling and statistics increased. Pollsters, journalists and politicians came to identify the sample with the population. If 77 per cent of a sample answered 'no' to the question 'Should divorce be easier to obtain in your state?', as posed by the American Institute of Public Opinion (in December 1936), it was assumed that the American people did not want to make divorce easier. Newspapers would report the results of polls as if the people had spoken. Gallup and Rae argued that public opinion polls might bridge the gap between the people and the decision-makers [1940] 1968: 14). After all, democracy meant that 'the attitudes of the mass of the people determine policy', not only through elections but also directly (Gallup and Rae, [1940] 1968: 6). In their eyes, opinion polls were a more reliable articulation of the people's will than petitions, mass meetings and the competing voices of pressure groups, and they were less costly than referendums.

This ardent defence of opinion polls has not gone unchallenged, however. As early as 1948 the sociologist Herbert Blumer argued that 'public opinion is organic and not an aggregate of equally weighted individual opinions' (1948: 554; see also Bishop, 2005: 1). In a broader historical context, his German colleague Jürgen Habermas described how the concept of 'public opinion' had developed. In the eighteenth and nineteenth century public opinion had been formed through discussions in coffee houses, parlours, clubs and associations, as well as newspapers, even if participation was restricted mainly to middle-class bourgeois males. Authorities and privileges were questioned and traditional opinions challenged in a critical and rational spirit. In the twentieth century this critical dimension was lost, in the 'socio-psychological dissolution' of public opinion by polls and survey research (Habermas, [1962] 1968: 260–271).

A few decades later, political scientists like James Fishkin resumed this critique of public opinion polls as aggregating unreflected and often poorly informed individual opinions (1995: 80–84; also Fishkin, 1991: 19). In real life, people would form an opinion while discussing a topic with colleagues during a coffee break, with friends at a bar or with family at the dinner table. There they would be exchanging information and adjusting opinions in the course of a conversation, as had happened in the parlours and coffee houses of the eighteenth century. In a poll, however, people are suddenly confronted with topics they may never have thought about and invited to react immediately to certain statements: 'Do you support or oppose stem cell research?' Experiments have shown that many people feel obliged to answer the questions of the pollsters rather than admit ignorance or indifference (Bishop, 2005: 19–45). Many people even express opinions on faked issues and fictitious subjects. In an academic experiment in the 1940s, many students seriously considered the question of whether 'Pireneans' should be admitted to the US – and most of them appeared to dislike this imaginary nationality (Fishkin, 1995: 81). If the respondents have not formed an opinion, they follow cues and venture an opinion on the spot. If the question is worded differently, the ill-informed respondent will give a different answer. More sophisticated questioning and neutral wording can filter out these pseudo-opinions, thus improving the validity of the poll – but not the quality of public opinion.

To improve the quality of public opinion, Fishkin and his colleagues advocated a second step: combining the sampling technique of the pollsters with a critical and rational discussion of the questions in small groups. Thus, they reproduced a 'real life' situation, as in the coffee houses and parlours of old, or in contemporary bars and at dinner tables. Participants in these deliberative opinion polls – as Fishkin called his method, which he registered as a trademark in the US – were selected at random by telephone (random digit dialling) or letter (Fishkin and Farrar, 2005: 74). They were paid a small sum like $75 a day or $200 for two and a half days. The size of the poll varied from 130 to 450 members, divided into smaller groups of eighteen. In some cases the topics were selected by the organisers. On other occasions the groups had a voice in the selection as well. The groups would discuss among themselves, listen to experts and question politicians. At the end, participants developed more informed and nuanced – though not necessarily radically different – opinions on the subjects. They arrived at 'the conclusions people would come to, were they better informed on the issues and had the opportunity and motivation to examine those issues seriously' (Fishkin, 1995: 162). The experience often seemed to have 'a galvanizing effect on the participants' interest in public affairs' (Fishkin, 1995: 174).

Some deliberative opinion polls had an immediate impact upon local government, particularly in China. The Zeguo township organised several polls to consult the citizens about infrastructural projects and other budgetary priorities in 2005, 2006 and 2008. The local People's Congress implemented practically all of the recommendations of the citizen panel (Fishkin, *et al.*, 2010: 437, 447). Possibly, sortitionist democracy will provide the Chinese political elite with a way to broaden popular support without undermining the monopoly of the Communist party – but this is speculation.

Anyhow, most deliberative opinion polls seemed intended to educate and inform public opinion and voters rather than decide policies. Here they differed from the planning cells. Peter Dienel developed the *Planungszelle* when he was a member of the planning staff of the government of North-Rhine/Westphalia – the most populous state of the Federal Republic of Germany – in the 1970s (Vergne, 2005: 1; see also Carson and Martin, 1999: 71–75). Later his model would be copied in other countries, such as Austria, Spain and the US, while the term 'planning cell' would be replaced (also in Germany) by 'citizens' report' – to avoid a confusing association with prison cells, presumably (Hendriks, 2005: 90). A cell consists of twenty-five randomly selected citizens, who would spend four days digesting and discussing information about a (pre-selected) complicated planning problem. They may not be representative in a strict statistical sense, but they represent different social groups. Aided by two process-facilitators or process stewards (*Prozeßbegleiter*), they would try to solve the problem and draft a 'citizens' report' (*Bürgergutachten*) following discussions in smaller groups, briefings, interviews with academics, civil servants and interest groups and occasionally a field trip. Remuneration would be modest, e.g. € 130 (about $165) for a four-day planning cell about consumer protection commissioned by the Bavarian government in 2001 (Hendriks, 2005: 86, 102). Often six or even ten cells would work on the same problem at different locations – thus creating a more representative sample of the population. According to Carolyn Hendriks, planning cells tend to have a substantial impact at the local level and a lesser impact at the regional level (2005: 92–93). After all, they are usually commissioned by local or regional governments. They require mutual trust, as manipulation by process-facilitators cannot easily be prevented. Hendriks cites one example of a planning cell in New Jersey that rebelled against the organisers and presented a different report without the help of the process-facilitators (2005: 93).

The citizen juries introduced by Ned Crosby in the US operated in a similar way. Crosby had developed the idea while working on a doctoral dissertation on social ethics in 1971 (Crosby and Nethercut, 2005: 112; see also Carson and Martin, 1999: 67–71). In 1974 he set up the Jefferson Centre in Minneapolis, which would organise more than thirty citizen juries in the US, at local and regional levels, and occasionally at the national level. 'Citizen jury' was registered as a trademark in the US. A jury consisted of twenty-four randomly selected citizens. The sample would be stratified in terms of age, gender, education level, race and sometimes also with respect to attitudes. In the national citizen jury organised in Washington DC in 1993, eleven of the twenty-four jurors had given an affirmative answer to the question of whether federal taxes should be reduced, corresponding to 45 per cent of the population in a nation-wide opinion poll on this topic (Crosby and Nethercut, 2005: 111). The attitudes changed, however, in the course of the deliberation: in the end, only seven jurors voted against a tax increase. According to Crosby and Doug Nethercut – who had served as an executive director of the Jefferson Centre – the impact of citizen juries on policy-making was modest, compared to that of professional lobbyists, while the costs were fairly high (2005: 116). For this reason the Jefferson Centre closed down in 2002, though citizen juries are still organised elsewhere and Crosby has been working on a new but related project: citizen initiative reviews (Crosby and Nethercut, 2005: 117–118). Citizen juries or citizen panels – the more generic term – of a similar kind have been organised in Australia, Canada, France, Germany, the Netherlands, Spain and several other countries. In Denmark, the Board of Technology, established by the government to stimulate public debate about the social consequences of technology, has organised 'consensus conferences' along similar lines as the German planning cells (Hendriks, 2005: 83–84, 89).

In the German Westphalian city of Emsdetten as well as in the French Pont-de-Claix – a small town in the French Alps – citizen panels have been institutionalised as advisory bodies that are annually consulted before the municipal budget is decided upon (Röcke, 2005: 121–125; Sintomer, 2007; see also Stadt Emsdetten, 2011; Ville Pont de Claix, 2007). In Emsdetten, 500 randomly selected citizens are invited to attend the *Emsdettenkonferenz*, of which usually 60–70 actually turn up (Stadt Emsdetten, 2011: 13; Antwort 4). In Berlin, *Bürgerjurys* were even given formal power in 2001: in two years they could allocate € 500,000 in seventeen (relatively underprivileged) neighbourhoods (*Quartiere*) of the city (Röcke, 2005: 105–107). About half of the 15–30 members of the citizen jury would be randomly selected from the register; the other half were representatives of parents, and of businesses and voluntary associations. In 2001, 16 per cent of the 4,000 invited citizens actually participated in the decision-making process (Röcke, 2005: 110). However, the budget has been cut drastically since a new city government was elected in 2003 and many *Bürgerjurys* have disappeared (Sintomer, 2007: 117–120). Yet in the district of Lichtenberg it has survived, with a modest budget – thirteen neighbourhood juries could spend € 6,000 each in 2012 on small projects proposed by citizens. There, the citizen juries are selected completely at random – provided sufficient citizens volunteer (Bezirksamt Lichtenberg von Berlin, 2012).

In Canada, citizen assemblies were convened by the provincial governments of British Columbia (2004) and in Ontario (2006) to draft a proposal for a new electoral system. In both provinces, assembly members were randomly selected from voter registration lists. In British Columbia, 158 members were drawn by lot from the 964 citizens who had attended a first meeting; a man and a woman from each riding or constituency, with some stratification for age, because young voters tend to be under-represented in the registers (Warren and Pearse, 2008: 10–11; James, 2008). When it turned out that no Aboriginals had been selected, two who had been at the first meeting joined the assembly. Members were paid Can$150 (and travel expenses). In Ontario, 103 citizens were selected from the voters in the 103 provincial constituencies, including one native member (Leduc, 2011: 554). Here also, stratification ensured a balanced age distribution.

Unlike other citizen panels, the citizen assemblies met not once or twice, but spent more than a dozen weekends together over the whole year. The British Columbia Citizens' Assembly started in January 2004 and presented its final report in December 2004. After extensive and intensive deliberation, a majority of 123 (out of 160) had voted for a single transferable vote system (STV). As promised, the provincial government submitted the proposal to a referendum in May 2005. It had specified that the existing single member plurality or 'first past the post' system would be replaced only if a majority of 60 per cent of the voters and 60 per cent of the constituencies agreed. As slightly less than 58 per cent voted for STV, the proposal was not accepted.[12] Yet a clear majority of the population (according to an opinion poll) expressed trust in the judgment of the assembly 'because the Citizens' Assembly are people like me' (Cutler *et al.*, 2008: 179).

The Ontario Citizens' Assembly recommended a mixed member proportional system – similar to the electoral systems of New Zealand and Germany. The media almost uniformly opposed the proposal which probably contributed significantly to its defeat in the October 2006 referendum: only 37 per cent of the voters agreed with the Citizen Assembly's recommendation (Leduc, 2011: 558–562).

Inspired by the British Columbian Citizens' Assembly, the government of the Netherlands convened a citizen panel (*burgerforum*) in 2006 to discuss changes to their own electoral system, which is based on pure proportional representation. The panel was selected in two rounds: first a random sample of about 50,000 citizens was drawn from the municipal administrations and invited to attend an informative meeting. From the roughly 2,000 people who attended the meeting a second sample of 143 citizens was drawn (Leyenaar, 2009: 15; Van der Kolk and Brinkman, 2008: 19; Burgerforum Kiesstelsel, 2006; Rose, 2009: 219).[13] The sample was stratified according to gender and province. As in other citizen panels, the members were somewhat better-educated than average citizens. They were also more interested in politics and voted more often for Democrats 66 – the leftwing Liberal party that had most emphatically pushed for this experiment and that considered electoral reform one of its core issues (Leyenaar, 2009: 21). After ten meetings (on Friday evenings and Saturdays) the panel recommended a few modest changes to the electoral system, allowing voters more influence over the selection of members of parliament and a free choice of a polling station within their municipality. However, by the time the panel had completed its report, Democrats 66 had left the coalition and the government had collapsed. The next government rejected all of the recommendations of the panel except the last one, regarding the free choice of a polling station (Rose, 2009: 215; Tweede Kamer der Staten-Generaal, 2008).

Careful evaluations by different authors suggest that the citizen panels in different countries shared strengths as well as weaknesses. In the first place, random selection (as expected) produced considerable diversity in the panels, even if it could not ensure that they were representative of the population in a statistical sense. As participation was voluntary, self-selection of the more educated and politically involved citizens could usually not be prevented (Font and Blanco, 2007: 564–568; James, 2008). In some Dutch citizen panels, not only women and youth but also Christian Democrats were under-represented and leftwing Liberals and Social Democrats over-represented (Huitema *et al.*, 2007: 306–309; see also Leyenaar, 2009: 20–21). Stratified sampling can reduce skewed tendencies, but may create 'false essentialisms', as Graham Smith and Corinne Wales argue (2000: 56–57). Women, youngsters or immigrants may be perceived or see themselves as representatives of a group rather than as autonomous individuals. Therefore, Smith and Wales prefer 'inclusiveness' to 'representativeness' as the criterion for citizen panels: they should include a variety of perspectives that can be found in the population from which they are selected, but not necessarily in the same proportions (see also Brown, 2006).

In the second place, even within the panel, the participation of the less educated and less eloquent members tended to be smaller compared to that of college graduates and more talkative persons. Discussions often followed dominant patterns, such as the presentation of rational arguments and references to 'scientific facts' and expert opinions. To some extent, the status and power differences of a society were reproduced within the panels, as Iris Marion Young had warned (2000: 16–51; see also Kadlec and Friedman, 2007; Huitema *et al.*, 2007: 305; Smith and Wales, 2000: 58). However, careful design by non-partisan agents, as well as the involvement of skilled and experienced facilitators, might reduce these differences. By promoting alternative forms of communication such as story-telling – with which less educated people may be more familiar – or by allocating equal speaking time to all participants, the less educated and less eloquent members could be encouraged to express their opinions (Kadlec and Friedman, 2007). Another way to deal with this problem might be to organise separate panels for disempowered groups. Christopher Karpowitz, Chad Raphael and Allen Hammond describe a successful experiment with a consensus conference on municipal broadband and digital inclusion in California, which consisted of three African Americans, four Hispanics, three Asian Americans or Pacific Islanders and only three white persons; besides which, three members had physical disabilities and almost all earned a below average income (2009: 589). Participants came to know the important facts about broadband technology and drafted a report that was evaluated fairly positively by experts and stakeholders. In the British Columbia Citizens' Assembly, members from the rural northern part of the province took the initiative themselves to meet in a separate 'Northern caucus' and did have some impact upon the agenda (Lang, 2008). Generally speaking, citizen panels have limited influence on their own agenda, as they are usually commissioned by a government or non-governmental organisation and dependent upon financial sponsors.

In the third place, most observers are impressed by the quality of the deliberations in citizen panels. Citizens 'proved to be willing, capable, and valuable deliberators', according to Hendriks (2005: 98). They acquired considerable competence, Smith and Wales noted (2000: 60–61). 'Experts are often surprised and impressed by the quality of the public's deliberations, judgments and actions', Peter Levine, Archon Fung and John Gastil concluded, provided that the questions are clear and the discussion is well-organised (2005: 273). Panel members thought more in terms of a common interest and showed more political involvement than before (Leyenaar, 2009: 21–23; Huitema *et al.*, 2007: 306; also Fishkin, 1995: 174). Their views became more nuanced (Fishkin, 1995: 167–168). Polarisation and 'groupthink' or conforming to group pressure rarely occurred, even in the relatively homogeneous consensus conference in California (Karpowitz *et al.*, 2009: 595–600). In a way, citizens became experts, Jonathan Rose concluded (2009: 230). Without changing their personal values, they developed deeper understanding and reduced distortions in their opinions, Simon Niemeyer asserted (2011: 125). Participants in the Australian Citizens' Parliament showed a 'genuine increase in knowledge, understanding, and judgment' (Felicetti *et al.*, 2012: 12). Analysing a dozen citizen juries in Spain, Joan Font and Ismael Blanco concluded that the quality was quite good, provided that the topics were well-framed, the presentations were well-adapted to the participants and the moderators were unbiased (2007: 568–571).

In the fourth place, the impact of the panels upon policy decisions seems generally rather modest. The citizen juries in Berlin seem exceptional, as they were given real spending powers. Other citizen panels have no real power but can pass recommendations to a legislative body such as the city council or regional government; governments may then 'cherry pick' the recommendations that suit them and shelve the others (Smith, 2009: 93). And if the government is willing to submit the proposal to the people in a referendum, the people may lack the enthusiasm or knowledge of their randomly selected representatives and reject their proposal, as happened in British Columbia and Ontario. Therefore, it is difficult to disagree with the conclusion of Graham Smith about citizen panels and similar 'mini-publics': while 'the way they realise inclusiveness and considered judgement distinguishes mini-publics from traditional forms of consultation, they share the same problem: it is not always transparent how or even whether they have affected the broader political decision-making process' (2009: 110).

EVALUATION

Aleatoria and its Total Social Lottery may not be meant to be a utopia we should try to reach. It seems very doubtful if a modern society could function at all without any stable division of labour. More and more jobs require technical expertise and years of training. Aleatoria, if ever established, might disintegrate within a short time; if its inhabitants are fatalistic enough to accept any outcome of the lottery, they might even accept the death of their own society. However, one could imagine that Aleatoria's sortitionist political system would function reasonably well if detached from the rest of society. Even in contemporary polities, political representation and decision-making do not require specialist education; freshly elected members of parliament usually make do with an improvised crash course in politics and some coaching by senior colleagues. Therefore, replacement of an elected legislature by an allotted House of Lots seems quite feasible, in principle. Athens has shown that allotted bodies such as the Council of 500, the *nomothetai* and the *dikastèria* were able to serve executive, legislative and judiciary functions for more than a century. Randomly selected criminal juries have taken decisions about life and death in England, the US and other countries for many years.

The randomly selected citizen juries or political juries advocated by Threlkeld, Sutherland and Leib might function just as well as the criminal juries or the *dikastèria* they have been modelled after. Moreover, Leib and Sutherland do not want to grant them absolute legislative powers, but balance them with elected bodies – Congress or the Lords Advocate, respectively. Only in Threlkeld's rather simple model is it unclear whether the citizen juries can be checked and corrected by another body if they make a decision that goes against the basic values and moral feelings of the majority (or even a very large minority) of the population. This might create a legitimacy deficit which makes the model less viable in the long run.

John Burnheim's allotted functional councils may face similar legitimacy problems, confounded by jurisdictional conflicts between them. The higher-level co-ordinating bodies he later added to his demarchy might solve these problems to some extent, but their legitimacy depends upon a combination of sortition and nomination by the lower allotted bodies that may reproduce the problem at a higher level. Demarchy, moreover, does not appear a feasible project in the eyes of many critics because it requires drastic decentralisation on a universal scale. Like Bookchin, Burnheim has constructed a small-scale utopian society incapable of defending itself against aggressive neighbours.

Ernest Callenbach, who created an ecological utopia in the 1970s, seems less guilty of utopianism in the proposal for a 'citizen's legislature' that he defended with Michael Phillips about ten years later. Though more radical than the hybrids designed by Leib and O'Leary, their combination of an elected Senate with an allotted Representative House seems quite feasible. The fact that they combine two competing logics – sortition and election – is perceived as a weakness by the French political scientist Gilles Delannoi (2010: 29–30). Yet it could also be seen as a strength; after all, countries such as Britain and Canada have combined election with appointment – also two conflicting logics – for several centuries. In both countries the members of the upper house are appointed by the government. One might regard this as a historic compromise between the forces of modernity and tradition that has served its time and should now be replaced by a more modern construction. But in a similar vein, sortitionists might defend a compromise between election and allotment that could last for (at least) a few decades – until we are all used to sortition and can dispose of elections as outdated remnants of an aristocratic era.

Perhaps a more serious weakness of the Representative House proposed by Callenbach and Phillips is the relatively long term – three years – that a representative should serve. As a consequence, representatives might 'go native', to use Sutherland's words, and lose the legitimacy that was based on their descriptive representation of ordinary people. Due to the influence of experts, lobbyists and fellow-representatives their ideas might diverge more and more from those of their constituents. The same legitimacy problem affects the models advocated by O'Leary, by the Spanish *Partido Azar* and, to a much lesser extent, the proposal of Zakaras who argues for a shorter term. The problem could be mitigated, if not solved, by effective public relations and framing: if the allotted representatives can explain to the public how and why they changed their opinions on important issues, they might be able to convince the public and retain their legitimacy. In British Columbia the citizens' assembly seems to have been quite successful in this respect, unlike its counterpart in Ontario.

Legitimacy has an impact upon feasibility, at least in the long run, but it is also related to desirability. Every political system needs legitimacy, but a democratic system that is illegitimate in the perception of the population seems a contradiction in terms – or *in exercitu actu*: even if it is democratic on paper, it will not function in a democratic way. In Chapter 1 five other (albeit related) criteria were suggested to evaluate the desirability of a democratic project. They will be applied again below.

In the first place, a democratic regime should offer the people substantial opportunities to take all, or at least most, decisions on important matters in accordance with their needs and interests. Immediately, a problem arises when we discuss sortitionism: it is not the real people but one or more random samples from the people who take the decisions. Following the logic of opinion polling, and assuming the rules of proper sampling have been applied, one could regard the sample as a virtual reflection of the real people and their needs and interests. Even so, most citizens of a sortitionist democracy will not take part in decision-making most of the time, but find out about 'their' decisions in the media. They may feel excluded and alienated as a result. The problem may be less serious when practically every citizen will be selected for a political jury once in her lifetime, and knows from the experiences of her neighbours and relatives what it is like. In that case, a citizen can identify with the allotted representatives and accept their decisions as legitimate. The numerous temporary juries proposed by Burnheim, Threlkeld, Sutherland, Schmidt and Leib seem more promising in this respect than the single, more permanent Representative House advocated by Callenbach and Phillips, Goodwin's House of Lots, or the citizens' assembly suggested by the *Partido Azar*. O'Leary's People's House serves a fairly long term, too, but involves a larger number of citizens (435,000). Nevertheless, a classical democrat would probably want to provide the people with an 'emergency brake', such as a corrective referendum, in case they regard the decisions of their randomly selected representatives as morally outrageous or practically unacceptable.

The experience of citizen panels and similar bodies seems to indicate that even a fairly small sample of the citizens of a country (or city or region) can reflect the different perspectives and problems perceived by the population and

Aleatoria: sortitionist democracy 151

come up with reasonable solutions to those problems. The quality of the deliberations has been surprisingly good in most cases, as we have seen. So sortitionist democracy satisfies our second criterion.

The third criterion might be more problematic. Most citizen panels have had a modest impact on policy-making, as we have seen. They were often commissioned by a local government or a non-governmental organisation and could not set their own agenda. At best, they could amend the agenda, as did the British Columbia Citizen Assembly with regard to the representation of the North. The impact of the allotted bodies advocated by the theorists discussed in this chapter may vary considerably. In the most realistic proposals it would be substantial, but restrained by the power of the elected legislatures.

The fourth criterion concerns the inclusiveness or representativeness of the decision-makers. This should be a strong point in favour of sortitionism. Unlike elected representatives, who tend to belong to wealthier and better-educated groups than the average citizen, the Lotreps are randomly selected from all sections of the population – in principle! In practice, as we have seen, this depends to a large extent on the sampling technique, the way the sample is stratified, the size of the sample and the incentive structure: whether the randomly selected citizens are legally compelled to attend the assembly and/or at least rewarded generously, or motivated primarily by civic virtue and political idealism. If participation is voluntary and mostly unrewarded, it might attract mainly mavericks, fanatical activists and 'busybodies', but not the average Joan or Joe. Furthermore, participation in the citizen assembly or jury may or may not be equal, depending on the rules and procedures of the deliberation and the skill and commitment of the organisers and facilitators. However, in spite of all these qualifications, it seems fair to conclude that randomly selected legislatures will be more inclusive of various minorities – and *a fortiori* of women – than elected parliaments.

The fifth and final criterion relates to the impact of the political system upon society. Here again the sortitionist systems vary considerably among themselves. If a relatively small allotted chamber is grafted onto an existing parliamentary system, as Callenbach and Phillips argued for, the impact may be rather limited – in spite of their ambitions. O'Leary's People's House is much larger than the Representative House of Callenbach and Phillips, but its role and its influence seem more modest. The ad-hoc juries of Leib, Threlkeld and Sutherland will involve more citizens – at least over time – and hence imbue larger numbers with sortitionist values. As a result, society might become more egalitarian and perhaps more tolerant of diversity in the long run. Burnheim's demarchy could be seen as both cause and effect of a rather drastic social revolution, which goes further than the social change envisaged or advocated by the sortitionists mentioned so far. As Martin observed, demarchy fits in with the anarchist tradition. It would be difficult to reconcile it with either corporate capitalism or state socialism. However, if critics such as Lynch and Hirst are right, it could lead to a more bureaucratic society, rather than a more egalitarian one. Dozens of functional councils, controlled by an informal elite of self-selected 'busybodies', would be competing for power, while a growing number of disgruntled citizens would withdraw into a state of heightened privacy and apathy or flee the country. The views of the critics may be a bit too gloomy, but they cannot be brushed aside easily. However, Burnheim's proposal might be implemented in a less revolutionary and more modest way, such as selecting users of public transport for a council supervising the railway or bus companies at the local, regional or even national levels.

What has been said about the social revolution pursued by Burnheim could also be said about Goodwin's sortitionist revolution – except that the latter is even more drastic than the former. Her Total Social Lottery really defies our imagination. It would also defy democratic values. Aleatorian society may be more egalitarian than any society that has ever existed, as it is ruled by the dice rather than by the people. As Goodwin hints, the House of Lots takes quite a few decisions by throwing dice (or some similar device). Given the sortitionist values that permeate society, one might expect that it will do so more and more in the course of time. In order to accept their unpredictable fate, Aleatorians have to become more and more fatalistic. Personal responsibility will be a receding and rather unpractical value in Aleatoria. However, fatalism and egalitarianism are ultimately conflicting value systems, as Michael Thompson, Richard Ellis and Aaron Wildavsky have suggested. Where fatalism is endemic, democracy cannot survive (Thompson et al., 1990: 256). After a period of increasing misery, Aleatorians might accept anything, even a coup by a bunch of fanatical military officers who refuse to give up their powerful position at the next Total Social Lottery.

Yet before leaving Aleatoria forever, classical democrats could revise its constitution. A sortitionist system may be quite acceptable to them, provided that four amendments are implemented. In the first place, the Total Social Lottery should be abolished and a normal division of labour restored – whether that division is socialist or capitalist is an issue for another day. In the second place, the House of Lots should become a Hotel of Lots: Lotreps should be selected for short terms – perhaps a year – in order to prevent them from 'going native'. In the third place, they should be rewarded generously, provided they do not dodge their responsibilities. Only in exceptional cases – serious and chronic illness, a prison sentence, a dying partner – are they allowed to refuse service and stay home. In the fourth place, all the laws they pass can be challenged and corrected or vetoed by another institution – preferably a referendum, possibly a constitutional court or an elected parliament. Under these conditions, Aleatoria might be an attractive place to live for classical democrats, but one where Goodwin's fatalists may not feel at home.

Notes

1 These specific examples are not given by Burnheim, but are based on my interpretation of his work.
2 Discussion on www.equalitybylot.wordpress.com in January 2010.
3 Burnheim, on www.equalitybylot.wordpress.com, 20 January 2010.

Aleatoria: sortitionist democracy 153

4   Gat, on www.equalitybylot.wordpress.com, 23 January 2010.
5   Email from Tomas Mancebo, Partido Azar, 16 December 2011.
6   It is not clear to me whether the assembly could overrule the people's initiative, or vice versa.
7   'El Ejecutivo actual formado mayoritariamente por políticos, se sustituye por profesionales de prestigio en las distintas áreas del conocimento, elegidos por la Asamblea y sometidos a esta' (Partido Azar, 2011).
8   Email from Tomas Mancebo, Partido Azar, 16 December 2011.
9   In 2008 it was republished by Imprint Academic in England; most quotes here will be from the latter edition. Callenbach, who was born 1961 in Wisconsin and died in 2012, worked at the University of California Press and wrote film critiques as well as novels (autobiographical information from his website: www.ernestcallenbach.com, consulted 5 December 2011).
10 First published by Callenbach himself, later by Bantam Books (see his website: www.ernestcallenbach.com, consulted 5 December 2011).
11 The notion of personal knowledge has been developed by Michael Polanyi (1958).
12 In 2009 it was again put to a referendum, but this time supported only by 39 per cent of the voters (Leduc, 2011: 553).
13 Initially, 140 people were selected, but four of them appeared to have withdrawn, so four additional candidates were invited; when three of the four 'missing persons' turned up after all, they were admitted as well, raising the actual number of participants to 143 (Van der Kolk and Brinkman, 2008: 19).

6 Conclusion
Extremist theories and radical practices

Democratic extremism is not an oxymoron or a contradiction in terms – that is the first conclusion of this book. The term 'extremism' has many meanings – though not as many as 'democracy' – and often has negative connotations. A coherent and objective definition has been proposed by Uwe Backes, which has been used (in a slightly amended form) in this book.

Political extremists argue and strive for a pure regime, based on one absolute principle, without compromises, checks and balances. Power should be concentrated in one body, which could be a single person or a small selective group, but also the people as a whole. Autocratic extremists want to allocate sovereignty or supreme power to a single person, either a hereditary monarch, an elected president or a religious leader. Aristocratic extremists would like to lay all power in the hands of 'the best' (*hoi aristoi*), either a hereditary aristocracy or an aristocracy based on political competence, ideological consciousness or popularity and electoral success. Democratic extremists argue that all decisions should be taken by the people, one way or another.

Extremist theories are easy to find; extremist regimes are less common. Yet if we travel a bit in space or time, we will find quite a few examples of extreme autocratic and aristocratic regimes, as Chapter 2 showed: Vichy-France, Fascist Italy, Nazi Germany, Stalinist Russia, the Democratic People's Republic of Korea, the Kingdom of Saudi Arabia and possibly Buddhist Tibet before the Chinese conquest. Most existing regimes, however, can be considered to be mixtures of aristocracy and democracy, often with a few autocratic elements thrown in. In a modern mixed regime, most decisions are taken by an aristocracy of professional politicians, judges and other senior civil servants, yet the politicians are usually elected by the people and may take into account the needs and wants of the people, if only because they would like to be re-elected.

Modern mixed regimes often claim to be representative democracies. Thus they stretch the term 'democracy' beyond its original meaning, which is 'rule by the people' or 'power to the people'. So-called elitist democrats (or democratic elitists) may argue that this original meaning does not make sense and has no empirical reference anywhere in the history of the world. Classical democrats, however, reject this argument and maintain the original meaning, often using it as measuring rod or normative standard to criticise existing regimes. In this book, I have tried to test the elitist argument and the classical counter-arguments by searching for theoretical as well as historical examples of democracy in its pure and classical form – rule by the people.

For analytical purposes, three forms or models of classical democracy can be distinguished, even if they often overlap in practice. In an assembly democracy, practically all decisions are taken by a popular assembly open to all citizens. In a bounded-delegate democracy, decisions are prepared and executed by elected delegates, but approved or vetoed by the people in a plebiscite or in various assemblies or councils. In a sortitionist democracy, decisions are taken by a random sample from the population, which (statistically) reflects all opinions and preferences of the people.

Assembly democracy is no doubt the oldest variety of democracy. It was practiced in ancient Athens, 400 years before our era, but also (possibly considerably earlier) in city-states in Asia, and maybe in tribal societies across the world. Murray Bookchin updated and adapted Athenian democracy to modern society – or rather, his utopian vision of an ecologically sustainable society. This libertarian municipalism, as he describes his theory, is definitely a variety of democratic extremism. All power should be in the hands of a municipal assembly, and these municipalities are completely autonomous, sovereign polities. In fact, the Athenian polity was not quite as extreme, as the assembly's decisions could be reversed by popular courts. Moreover, in the fourth century the assembly's powers were balanced with the powers of the *nomothetai* or lawmakers. The Council of 500 prepared and executed the decisions of the assembly. And the assembly did elect officials with considerable influence, such as the *stratègoi*. Yet the Council of 500, the courts and the law-makers were randomly selected from the people, and in fact functioned like a kind of popular assembly. The *stratègoi* enjoyed rather limited autonomy and could be dismissed quite easily. Therefore, one could still argue that the Athenian people did not have to share power with an aristocracy of professional politicians (let alone an autocrat) as would be the case in a mixed regime.

In this respect Athens differed somewhat from the Swiss cantons that also practiced assembly democracy, but balanced the power of the *Landsgemeinde* with that of the elected parliament and the elected head of the cantonal government, the *Landammann*. Even so, the annual cantonal assembly has to approve of all legislation and all public expenditures over a certain amount. New England Town Meetings exercise similar powers, but enjoy a much more limited autonomy. Critics consider both the *Landsgemeinde* and the Town Meetings rather quaint but outdated institutions. They cannot possibly say this about the participatory budgeting process introduced in Porto Alegre and other Brazilian municipalities at the end of the twentieth century and imitated by hundreds of towns and cities all over the world. However, the role of public assemblies in the participatory budgeting process is rather modest: the final decisions are taken by elected delegates and formally approved by the elected municipal council. Perhaps only the Spanish village of Marinaleda could qualify as an example of extreme assembly democracy that would probably satisfy Bookchin and other libertarian muncipalists. Yet as far as the evidence is reliable, it also shows the dangers of democratic extremism: critics call it a totalitarian system dominated by a strong charismatic leader.

If the citizens of a state are too numerous to take decisions in an assembly, they may elect delegates to act on their behalf. Yet delegates may betray their electorate and serve particular interests. Jean-Jacques Rousseau regarded this as almost inevitable: democracy is something for gods, not men. Yet his disciples in eighteenth century France – Jacobins and *sans-culottes* – tried to behave like gods. They began experimenting with bounded-delegate democracy (though they did not use this term). Delegates were bound by imperative mandates, corrected by referendum and recalled if they displeased their constituents. Between 1792 and 1794 the *sans-culottes* even interfered with the regular meetings of their delegates (in the municipal council and in the national parliament), shouting instructions, and threatening them with pikes or other weapons. This was obviously democratic extremism in action. It was violent, erratic and short-lived: repression and famine destroyed the movement. The *Communards* practiced a less terroristic and more structured form of bounded-delegate democracy in Paris in 1871 – though it ended also in a bloodbath when regular troops invaded the city.

The Commune could be seen as a turning point in the history of bounded-delegate democracy. On the one hand, it served as a model of 'proletarian democracy' for Marx, Lenin and other Marxists. On the other hand, one could argue that it marked the end of the revolutionary Jacobin tradition and its transformation into reformist democratic radicalism in France – and elsewhere. Chapter 4 tells the story of both the Marxist and the Radical traditions.

The proletarian democracy praised by Marx in 1871 and by Lenin in 1917 incorporated the principles of bounded-delegate democracy, i.e. frequent elections of delegates, bound by mandates and revocable at will. Added were three other elements, also implemented by the Paris Commune: delegates received a workman's wage, they combined legislative and executive functions, and workers were armed. These principles were applied by the Soviets in the Russian Revolution of 1917. Workers met in factory assemblies and elected a workers' council or Soviet; soldiers did the same in their barracks. Again, democratic extremism was practiced briefly. Within a few years, however, power had shifted from the Soviets to a new aristocracy of Communist cadres. Yet the Soviet system inspired Pannekoek, Rühle and other theorists of council-democracy. Council-democracy was advocated in the 1960s and 1970s by groups like *Socialisme ou Barbarie*, the Situationist International, the French *Parti Socialiste Unifié* (PSU, United Socialist Party), the *Sozialistische Deutsche Studentenbund* (SDS, Socialist German Student League) and the Dutch Pacifist Socialist Party. It has been practiced very rarely, during revolutionary crises, usually only for a few months or less. In recent years experiments have been set up in Venezuela which have lasted longer, but they are controversial and hard data do not seem to be available yet.

Democratic Radicalism may have been inspired by Rousseau, but has abandoned his dogmatic rigour. Radicals in France, Germany, Switzerland and

Britain agreed that sovereignty should reside with the people and that the people should be able to control their delegates, by frequent (preferably annual) elections, by recall and possibly by binding mandates or 'pledges' (in the British case). Moreover, the people should be able to repeal or veto decisions taken by their delegates and to initiate legislation directly. Similar ideas were advocated in the nineteenth century by the People's Party in the US, and by populists all over the world in the twentieth and twenty-first centuries. Most of these ideas have already been implemented in Switzerland in the 1800s, when Radicals were in power, and in California and other American states in the twentieth century. This populist or plebiscitary democracy rarely qualifies as democratic extremism, as power has to be shared (and balanced) between the people and its elected representatives in parliament or in the Governor's mansion. The two interact: the representatives will anticipate the wishes of the people when they prepare and approve legislation, but they may also influence the outcome of plebiscites by public speeches or spots on radio and television. Thus a plebiscitary democracy may in fact resemble the dialectical ideal advocated by scholars such as Nadia Urbinati, who reject direct democracy in principle. Even so, it should also please radical or classical democrats.

However, one weakness of plebiscitary democracy that often disturbs classical democrats is the lack of serious and thorough public deliberation before the people vote. Debates may be held in the media, but they tend to be monopolised by political and (to a lesser extent) intellectual elites. This seems to happen not only in the press and on television, but also in the new digital media – with a vengeance, if Matthew Hindman is right. Therefore, deliberative democrats such as Peter Dienel, Ned Crosby and James Fishkin have designed new institutions to provide for greater deliberation among the common citizens. Randomly selected citizens are invited to participate in citizen panels, assemblies or deliberative opinion polls to discuss salient problems and elaborate a solution. Sortitionist democrats have generalised this principle of selection by lot (*sortitio* in Latin). They argue that randomly selected citizens might be better legislators than the professional politicians elected to parliament or Congress. The latter are often alienated from the electorate, manipulated – if not corrupted – by particular interests and no longer representative of the average population. Allotted representatives will draw from a much wider variety of experiences and perspectives, coming from groups that are practically always under-represented in elected bodies such as ethnic minorities, immigrants, women or unemployed youth.

Sortition is not a modern invention, of course. In ancient Athens it was practiced to select the Council of 500 as well as the popular courts or juries and the law-makers. It has also been used since medieval times to select criminal and civil juries in the United Kingdom, and later in the US and several other countries. Modern statistics and sampling techniques have given it a new political legitimation, however. Since Gallup developed his sophisticated opinion polls in the US in the 1930s, we have come to identify random samples with the population they are drawn from. If 60 per cent of a sample approves of abortion, we believe that 'the people' approve of abortion. So, decisions taken by a randomly selected citizen assembly are in fact seen as decisions taken by the people.

Very few sortitionists want to replace all elected bodies with randomly selected citizen assemblies. Perhaps the Canadian lawyer Simon Threlkeld and the small Spanish Chance Party (*Partido Azar*) might favour this variety of democratic extremism. I might do them an injustice here, however, as their ideas have not been elaborated in detail. Only John Burnheim designed a complete political system based entirely on sortition, which he baptised 'demarchy'. All political and even administrative decisions are taken by councils consisting of randomly selected citizens. However, the power of each council is far from absolute: it deals only with specific sectors of society such as health care, education or public transport. Hence, the councils may check and balance each other to some extent, as jurisdictions will overlap – a weakness of the system, in the eyes of some critics, but possibly a safeguard against extreme monism. Council members will be selected (at random) from a list of volunteers who will have some affinity with or experience within that sector. The voluntary character of the council membership, however, may detract from the democratic qualities of the system and produce oligarchies of full-time activists – or of Bolsheviks in a new garb, who might even intimidate rivals and try to monopolise the lists of volunteers. So, demarchy need not be extreme democracy; at the end of the day it might not even be very democratic at all.

The other proposals discussed in Chapter 5 are cautious compromises between allotted and electoral representation. Ernest Callenbach and Michael Phillips, Keith Sutherland, Alex Zakaras, Kevin O'Leary and Ethan Leib advocate different combinations of sortition and election, in order to extract the best from both worlds. So far, none of these proposals seem to have been tested in real life.

As a closer look at the historical evidence and theories shows, the first conclusion of this book has to be qualified a little. Indeed, democratic extremism is possible and has existed, in theory and in practice – but it turns out to be a rare and ephemeral phenomenon. During a revolutionary crisis, extreme democratic practices may develop, but within a short time internal strife, apathy, manipulation by a political party or brutal repression by regular troops or foreign armies will nip them in the bud. Moreover, the people who exercised power in revolutionary moments never comprised the entire population – at best the majority, at worst a passionate minority. For brief moments they might articulate the will of the whole people, but inevitably divergent interests will spoil the illusion of unity and homogeneity. As Margaret Canovan points out, the idea of the people as active sovereign is a myth, but in a fleeting moment it may be close to reality (2005: 122–138).

From a normative viewpoint, the rare occurrence of democratic extremism might be a good thing. Though the theories of Bookchin, Pannekoek and Burnheim display an attractive coherence and daring imagination, when practiced democratic extremism shows an uglier face. Like other forms of extremism, it tends to go together with intolerance, conformism and violence. Absolute power corrupts absolutely, not only in the hands of a dictator or oligarchy, but also in the hands of the people. That is the second conclusion of this book.

This is not the whole story, however. If any democratic (or aristocratic) elitists read this book, they might nod gleefully in agreement now – but they might not like the next conclusion. Whereas democratic extremism may work well in theory only and not in practice, democratic radicalism plays in a different league. It does not claim all power for the people, but only a substantial amount. Political elites may be inevitable and useful to a certain degree, but the most important issues should be decided by the people, one way or another. As the preceding chapters have shown, radical democracy has functioned quite well, usually without major upheavals or violent excesses, in ancient Athens and in new social movements, in Swiss cantons such as Appenzell and Glarus, in New England town meetings and Brazilian participatory budgeting processes, in citizen assemblies and citizen juries all over the world, in California and the Swiss Confederation. As a theory, democratic radicalism may lack the creative power or systematic rigour of Bookchin's libertarian municipalism, Pannekoek's council-communism or councilism and Burnheim's demarchy. Rousseau may be seen as the spiritual father of democratic radicalism, even if he would probably refuse to acknowledge it, like he refused to recognise his biological children. The nineteenth-century Radical parties that were often inspired by him also abandoned their radical-democratic tendencies and evolved into more conservative liberal parties (in France and Switzerland) or merged with them (in Britain). So democratic radicalism remains a very thin ideology without major theorists, and an ideology that is rarely propagated explicitly in the twenty-first century. Yet the radical democratic institutions that the Radicals helped to create have survived in Switzerland, and spread to other countries, too. Moreover, new institutions such as participatory budgeting and citizen juries have emerged that also chime in with radical-democratic principles.

The fact that radical democratic practices have existed and are still flourishing in many parts of the world may prove their feasibility, but not their desirability. Do they measure up to democratic standards? Do they allow citizens effective opportunities to take part in decision-making on important issues? Do they also offer opportunities for public deliberation? Are the decisions implemented? Are all citizens included, at least in principle? And can the outcomes be seen as beneficial in terms of democratic values? If the answers to these questions are mostly negative, elitists can still relax and enjoy their triumph. Only if the answers are mainly positive may they have to admit defeat to the classical and radical democrats.

The preceding chapters have presented at least tentative answers to the five main questions – for a schematic summary see Table 6.1. For comparative purposes, dictatorship and the parliamentary or presidential regime prevailing in most parts of the world have been added to the four models of democracy discussed in this book.

Obviously, no system is perfect. Dictatorship naturally scores low on all criteria for democracy. The large majority of the people have hardly any opportunities to

Table 6.1 Evaluation of different regimes

Regime type	Participation in decision-making	Quality of public deliberation	Impact of the people on policy	Inclusiveness	Indirect consequences re democratic values
Dictatorship	Very low	Very low	Very low	Usually limited	Negative
Parliamentary or presidential regime	Low	Low	Low	Usually high	Very mildly positive
Assembly democracy	High in theory, moderate in practice	Moderate (time and size restraints)	High	Usually high (in modern era)	Fairly positive
Council democracy	High initially, later low	High initially, later low	Unclear (co-ordination problem)	Varies	In theory very positive, but in practice often totalitarian
Plebiscitary democracy	High (but frequency may vary)	Low	High	Usually high	Mildly positive
Sortitionist democracy	Limited to random sample(s)	High	Varies	Very high	Mildly positive

participate in decision-making – if elections or plebiscites are held at all, they tend to be acclamation rituals. Public deliberation does not exist; mass media are mainly used by the regime to propagate its ideology and disqualify opposition. Very often the regime targets internal enemies, such as ethnic minorities or the remnants of an old dominant class – land-owning aristocrats, capitalists, wealthy farmers – as scapegoats in case of economic or military adversities and to create a feeling of solidarity between the majority and the regime. And an authoritarian regime will inculcate and promote authoritarian, anti-democratic values, for obvious reasons.

The parliamentary and presidential regimes that we are all familiar with in the US, the UK, France, Germany, the Netherlands, and so on, offer the people at least the opportunity to elect representatives, but only once every two or four years or so. By voting for a particular candidate or party, people can at best exercise some indirect influence on policy-making. If the candidate or party fails to fulfil their election promises, the people cannot recall them or veto their decisions, only 'punish' them by voting for another candidate or party at the next election. The British and the French people have had a direct impact upon policies through a referendum, but only a few times and at the initiative of the government. In several American states the people have substantially more powers, but not at the federal level.

Assembly democracy does much better in practically every respect. Turnout at assemblies is usually lower than at elections, however. Yet the assemblies may be held more frequently, and take direct decisions on a broad range of issues. People can also participate actively in deliberations, whereas they remain passive spectators at most election debates – if they pay any attention to them at all. The decisions of assemblies are usually faithfully implemented by the (local) government. Assembly democracy may also contribute to a sense of efficacy and possibly to solidarity among citizens. It requires at least some decentralisation of political power and a federal type of state.

Council-democracy is more difficult to evaluate, given its ephemeral and fleeting existence in history. In theory, it implies high participation, serious deliberation and a strong impact upon policy-making. Yet the historical evidence suggests that participation in workers' and soldiers' councils declines rapidly after a revolutionary crisis, that deliberation becomes rare and that decisions are not always implemented because of conflicts between authorities, manipulation by external forces (political parties, trade unions) and other problems. Because of their class base, the workers' councils excluded bourgeois and petty-bourgeois groups, but also old-age pensioners and unemployed workers. In New Left theories of council-democracy, however, these groups would be able to participate in neighbourhood councils. Council-democracy has enormous consequences for society, involving a total revolution of the social and economic order and a cultural revolution as well. The revolution did result in a totalitarian system in Russia.

Plebiscitary democracy has a less ambivalent record. Participation can be quite high, depending on the frequency of the plebiscites and the salience of the issues at stake. The impact is usually quite clear: a law is repealed or approved.

162 Conclusion

Public deliberation may be a weak point, as it is in a presidential or parliamentary regime. Plebiscitary democracies tend to go together with high satisfaction among citizens, but the effect on society will probably be quite modest.

Sortitionist democracy seems strong where plebiscitary democracy is weak, and vice versa. Participation is limited to a random sample from the population, which may cause a legitimation problem. There is ample room for deliberation, but the impact is not always clear. Statistical samples tend to be perfectly inclusive, yet if participation is voluntary (as it usually is in citizen juries and similar bodies) self-selection may lead to under-representation of certain groups such as ethnic minorities or people without much formal education. However, weighing procedures or special sub-samples might compensate for this.

The fourth conclusion of this book vindicates classical or radical democracy: all three models investigated here seem not only feasible but also superior (from a democratic point of view) to existing regimes in most (though not all) aspects. This will be even more clear if we confront the status quo with a mixture from the three models which optimises their strongest elements. The models may follow different principles, but that should not prevent us from meshing them, as Michael Saward has argued (2001). Earlier, Benjamin Barber presented a long list of institutional reforms, which includes neighbourhood assemblies, a national referendum and initiative, a universal citizen service and civic education, and election by lot (1984: 261–311). His lotteries are mainly local affairs to select school committees, housing authorities or zoning boards. He might have been more daring in this respect if he had known about the qualities of citizen juries and deliberative opinion polls, but when he wrote his epoch-making essay the former were still in their infancy while the latter were not even born yet.[1] Let us amend his list, starting at the local level.

Imagine a city of about a million inhabitants. Obviously it is too large to assemble all citizens on a square and let them deliberate, so it is divided into 100 municipal districts, each large enough to exercise some autonomy but small enough to convene their inhabitants in a large theatre or stadium in the civic centre. The civic centre also contains a public library, a school for civic education and training, sports facilities and a large green area. It is maintained mainly by volunteers who are rewarded with vouchers or free use of the facilities. The district assemblies decide the district budget and they have to approve all expenditures over a certain amount. They also discuss priorities and proposals for the city budget, as well as problems that should be put on the city council's agenda. Their preferences can be overruled by the city council but only with a qualified majority. The city council is elected by the citizens, who can recall any member who fails to meet their expectations. Moreover, citizens can veto council decisions in a referendum and impose decisions through a popular initiative. And finally, most departments of the city administration as well as corporations which offer a public service, such as public transport, council housing, local radio and television, theatres, parks and schools, will consult a users' council as well as a workers' or employees' council when they take important decisions. The users' councils consist of randomly selected registered users or consumers of the services: regular passengers of buses and subways, tenants, regular listeners of the radio, frequent visitors of the theatre or the park, patients of hospitals and health care centres, pupils of schools (or their parents). The selected candidates will be rewarded for their efforts with vouchers or free services. The councils may have a strong advisory status, meaning that their advice cannot be ignored without arguments. In certain cases, e.g. when privatisation, mergers or other drastic changes to services are considered, the councils might even have veto powers. If participation in the councils or district assemblies should drop below a certain level (say, 10 per cent of the relevant population), Tännsjö's rule should apply and representatives should be elected.

A similar combination could be imagined at the level of a national (or federal) state. Even if we do not want to replace elected legislatures by a House of Lots (as in Aleatoria), we might combine allotted and elected chambers the way Callenbach and Phillips, Sutherland or Zakaras have suggested. Furthermore, Burnheim's randomly selected users' councils could also be tried out at the national level, at least in certain sectors such as public transport, higher education, national parks and museums. The laws passed by allotted and elected legislators could be initiated or repealed by the people in a popular initiative or referendum (respectively).

If we follow Torbjörn Tännsjö, we might even try to design a democratic World Government (1992: 106–122). The World Government should be elected by a World Parliament, in turn elected by the member states. It is clearly a utopian idea. Critics will point out that there is not a global *demos*, as mankind does not constitute one people (see also Canovan, 2005: 57–64). Popular sovereignty at the national level is problematic enough; at the global level it defies the imagination. Even so, a mixed regime might be feasible at some point in the future. Delegates at the World Parliament may be bound by imperative mandates from their national parliament – as they are now, in fact, at the United Nations Assembly.

However, not all nations in the world may want to follow our advice and introduce a (radical) democratic regime. Perhaps the Chinese or the Ethiopian people would prefer a more aristocratic regime, at least for the time being? Democracy is not a regime one should impose upon a reluctant population, even in moderate forms, as recent events in Afghanistan and Iraq have shown. One could imagine that people decide by referendum to install an aristocratic or autocratic regime. Yet even within an aristocratic regime there may be room for democratic experiments, as the success of deliberative opinion polls in China has indicated. The Chinese experience does also suggest that democratic values may be universal after all and not merely a North Atlantic bias.

Two cheers for democracy! That was the conclusion of the British writer E.M. Forster in 1951: 'Two cheers are quite enough: there is no occasion to give three' (Forster, 1951: 79). By democracy he meant the prevailing parliamentary regime of the United Kingdom, in my opinion a mixture of aristocracy and democracy which does not quite meet the requirements of classical or radical democracy. For this type of mixed regime, one cheer might do. Yet two cheers is enough even for the radical democracies investigated and evaluated (quite positively) in this book. Neathena, Jacobinland and Aleatoria may be fascinating places to visit, but none of them seem to be a paradise on earth. In fact, quite a few readers of this book might not even want to live there at all and prefer their own country, with its mixture of aristocracy and democracy. Others might be daring and curious enough to try out one or more of the radical practices described here. Hopefully, this book will have been useful for both types of reader. The former might appreciate more the mixed nature of their favourite regime, whereas the latter may feel stimulated to pursue democratic reforms and experiments.

Note

1 In fact, Barber hardly builds on any empirical or historical evidence when developing his institutional proposals – that seems to me to be one of the few weaknesses of his impressive book.

References

Abers, Rebecca Neaera (2003) 'Reflections on What Makes Empowered Participatory Governance Happen', in: Archon Fung and Erik Olin Wright (eds) *Deepening Democracy. Institutional Innovations in Empowered Participatory Governance*, London: Verso, pp. 200–207.
Abramson, Jeffrey (2000) *We, the Jury*, Cambridge: Harvard University Press (second edition).
Abts, Koen and Stefan Rummens (2007) 'Populism versus Democracy', *Political Studies*, 55: 2, pp. 405–424.
Adolf, Steven (2007) 'Heilstaat van bonen, olijven en paprika', *NRC Handelsblad*, 28 August, p. 20.
Ajzenstat, Janet (1986) 'Is Democracy Possible? The Alternative to Electoral Politics', *Canadian Journal of Political Science*, 19: 3, pp. 637–639.
Akoun, A. et al. (1979) *Dictionnaire de Politique. Le Présent en Question*, Paris: Librairie Larousse.
Alatas, Hussein (1956) *The Democracy of Islam*, The Hague/Bandung: W. van Hoeve.
Almond, Gabriel A. and Sidney Verba (1963) *The Civic Culture. Political Attitudes and Democracy in Five Nations*, Princeton: Princeton University Press.
Aminzade, Ronald (1993) *Ballots and Barricades. Class Formation and Republican Politics in France, 1830–1871*, Princeton: Princeton University Press.
Anonymous (1966) 'Contribution au programme des conseils ouvriers en Espagne', *Internationale Situationniste*, No. 10, pp. 27–32.
Anweiler, Otto (1958) *Die Rätebewegung in Russland 1905–1921*. Leiden: Brill.
Ankersmit, Frank (2010) *De representatieve democratie is een electieve aristocratie*, Groningen: Faculteit der Letteren.
Arblaster, Anthony (1987) *Democracy*, Milton Keynes: Open University Press.
Aristotle [edited and translated by Ernest Barker] (1958) *The Politics*, London/Oxford: Oxford University Press.
Aryan Nations (no date) 'About us', online: www.aryan-nations.org/about.htm (accessed 3 January 2006).
Asamblea Nacional Constituyente (1999) 'Proyecto de Constitución Nacional', online: www.analitica.com/constituyente/nueva/c01_1.asp (accessed 2 February 2005).
Azzellini, Dario (2012) 'Workers' Control under Venezuela's Bolivarian Revolution', in: Immanuel Ness and Dario Azzellini (eds) *Ours to Master and to Own. Workers' Control from the Commune to the Present*, Chicago: Haymarket Books, pp. 382–399.
Backes, Uwe (2000) *Liberalismus und Demokratie – Antinomie und Synthese. Zum Wechselverhältnis zweier politischer Strömungen im Vormärz*, Düsseldorf: Droste Verlag.

Backes, Uwe (2006) *Politische Extreme. Eine Wort- und Begriffsgeschichte von der Antike bis zur Gegenwart*, Göttingen: Vandenhoeck & Ruprecht.

Backes, Uwe and Eckhard Jesse (1985) *Totalitarismus, Extremismus, Terrorismus: Ein Literaturführer und Wegweiser zur Extremismusforschung in der Bundesrepublik Deutschland*, Opladen: Leske+Budrich.

Backes, Uwe and Eckhard Jesse (1987) 'Extremismusforschung – ein Stiefkind der Politikwissenschaft', in: Wolfgang Michalka (ed.) *Extremismus und Streitbare Demokratie*, Stuttgart: Franz Steiner Verlag, pp. 9–28.

Badinter, Elisabeth and Robert Badinter (1988) *Condorcet. Un intellectuel en politique*, Paris: Fayard.

Baiocchi, Gianpaolo (2001) 'Participation, Activism, and Politics: The Porto Alegre Experiment and Deliberative Democratic Theory', *Politics & Society*, 29: 1, pp. 43–72.

Barber, Benjamin (1984) *Strong Democracy: Participatory Politics for a New Age*, Berkeley: University of California Press.

Barr, Robert R. (2009) 'Populists, Outsiders and Anti-Establishment Politics', *Party Politics*, 15: 1, pp. 29–48.

Barry, Norman P. (1986) *On Classical Liberalism and Libertarianism*, Basingstoke: Macmillan.

Beck, Reinhart (1977) *Sachwörterbuch der Politik*, Stuttgart: Alfred Kröner Verlag.

Beer, Samuel H. (1969) *British Politics in the Collectivist Age*, New York: Vintage Books/Random House.

Beetham, David (1994) 'Key Principles and Indices for a Democratic Audit', in: David Beetham (ed.) *Defining and Measuring Democracy*, London: Sage, pp. 25–43.

Beetham, David (2012) 'Evaluating new vs old forms of citizen engagement and participation', in: Brigitte Geissel and Kenneth Newton (eds), *Evaluating Democratic Innovations. Curing the Democratic Malaise?* London/New York: Routledge, pp. 56–67.

Bentley, Michael (1987) *The Climax of Liberal Politics: British Liberalism in Theory and Practice 1868–1918*, London: Edward Arnold.

Bermbach, Udo (1968) 'Ansätze zu einer Kritik des Rätesystems', *Berliner Zeitschrift für Politologie*, 9: 4, pp. 21–31.

Bertonneau, Thomas F. (2004) 'Ayn Rand's Atlas Shrugged: From Romantic Fallacy to Holocaustic Imagination', *Modern Age*, 46: 4, pp. 296–306.

Betz, Hans-Georg and Carol Johnson (2004) 'Against the current – stemming the tide: the nostalgic ideology of the contemporary radical populist right', *Journal of Political Ideologies*, 9: 3, pp. 311–327.

Bezirksamt Lichtenberg von Berlin (2012) 'Rahmenregelung zur Vergabe des Kiezfonds durch eine Bürgerjury ab dem Jahr 2012 ff', online: www.buergerhaushalt-lichtenberg. de (accessed 21 October 2012).

Biehl, Janet (1998) *The Politics of Social Ecology. Libertarian Municipalism*, Montreal: Black Rose Books.

Bishop, George F. (2005) *The Illusion of Public Opinion. Fact and Artifact in American Public Opinion Polls*, Oxford/Lanham (Md): Rowman & Littlefield.

Bispham, Edward (2007) *From Asculum to Actium: the Municipalization of Italy from the Social War to Augustus*, Oxford: Oxford University Press.

Blackburn, Robin (1999) 'The Unexpected Dialectic of Structural Reforms', in: Gilbert Achcar (ed.) *The Legacy of Ernest Mandel*, London/New York: Verso, pp. 16–23.

Blais, André, R. Kenneth Carty and Patrick Fournier (2008), 'Do citizens' assemblies make reasoned choices?', in: Mark E. Warren and Hilary Pearse (eds) *Designing*

Deliberative Democracy. The British Columbia Citizens' Assembly, Cambridge: Cambridge University Press, pp. 127–144.

Blumer, Herbert (1948) 'Public Opinion and Public Opinion Polling', *American Sociological Review*, 13: 5, pp. 542–549.

Bobbio, Norberto (1996) *Left and Right. The Significance of a Political Distinction*, Cambridge: Polity Press (translated from Italian original published in 1994).

Bock, Hans Manfred (1976) *Geschichte des "linken Radikalismus" in Deutschland. Ein Versuch*, Frankfurt on Main: Suhrkamp Verlag.

Bogdanor, Vernon (2008) 'Pick any card', *Times Literary Supplement*, No. 5511, 14 November 2008, p. 28.

Bonnet, Alberto R. (2011) 'The Political Form at Last Discovered: Workers' Councils against the Capitalist State', in: Immanuel Ness and Dario Azzellini (eds) *Ours to Master and to Own. Workers' Control from the Commune to the Present*, Chicago: Haymarket Books, pp. 66–81.

Bookchin, Murray (1971) 'Post-Scarcity Anarchy', in: Arthur Lothstein (ed.) *"All we are saying...": The Philosophy of the New Left*, New York: Capricorn, pp. 343–364.

Bookchin, Murray (1980) *Toward an Ecological Society*, Montreal/Buffalo: Black Rose Books.

Bookchin, Murray (1990a) *Remaking Society. Pathways to a Green Future*, Boston: South End Press.

Bookchin, Murray (1990b) *The Philosophy of Social Ecology. Essays on Dialectical Naturalism*, Montreal/New York: Black Rose Books.

Bookchin, Murray (1991) 'Libertarian Municipalism: An Overview', *Green Perspectives*, 24, online: www.democracynature.org/dn/vol. 1/bookchin_libertarian.htm (accessed 14 March 2005).

Bookchin, Murray (1995) 'Libertarian Municipalism: The New Municipal Agenda', online: http://dwardmac.pitzer.edu/Anarchist_Archives/bookchin/libmuni.html (accessed 14 March 2005).

Bouloiseau, Marc and Albert Soboul (eds) (1967) *Oeuvres de Maximilien Robespierre. Tome X. Discours (5e partie) 27 Juillet 1793–27 Juillet 1794*, Paris: Presses Universitaires de France.

Bowler, Shaun and Todd Donovan (2000) 'California's Experience with Direct Democracy', *Parliamentary Affairs*, 53: 4, pp. 644–656.

Bowler, Shaun and Todd Donovan (2006) 'Direct Democracy and Political Parties in America', *Party Politics*, 12: 5, pp. 649–669.

Brown, Mark B. (2006) 'Survey Article: Citizen Panels and the Concept of Representation', *Journal of Political Philosophy*, 14: 2, pp. 203–225.

Bruce, Iain (2004a) 'Participatory Democracy – The Debate', in: Iain Bruce (ed.) *The Porto Alegre Alternative. Direct Democracy in Action*, London: Pluto Press, pp. 23–37.

Bruce, Iain (2004b) 'From First Steps to Final Strategies', in: Iain Bruce (ed.) *The Porto Alegre Alternative. Direct Democracy in Action*, London: Pluto Press, pp. 38–53.

Bruhat, Jean (1972) 'Le socialisme français de 1815 à 1848', in: Jean Droz (ed.), *Histoire Générale du Socialisme I. Des origines à 1875*, Paris: Presses Universitaires de France, pp. 331–406.

Bryan, Frank M. (2004) *Real Democracy. The New England Town Meeting and How It Works*, Chicago: University of Chicago Press.

Buchstein, Hubertus (2009) *Demokratie und Lotterie. Das Los als politisches Entscheidungsinstrument von der Antike bis zur EU*, Frankfurt on Main/New York: Campus Verlag.

Buddingh', Hans (2008) 'Hoogeveen Vindt de Democratie Opnieuw Uit', *NRC Handelsblad*, 7 June, pp. 14–17.
Budge, Ian (1996) *The New Challenge of Direct Democracy*, Cambridge: Polity Press.
Budge, Ian (2012) 'Implementing popular preferences. Is direct democracy the answer?' in: Brigitte Geissel and Kenneth Newton (eds), *Evaluating Democratic Innovations. Curing the Democratic Malaise?* London/New York: Routledge, pp. 23–38.
Bundesverfassung der Schweizerischen Eidgenossenschaft ([1999] 2005), online: www.verfassungen.de/ch/verf99-i.htm (accessed 29 March 2013).
Bündnis 90/Die Grünen (2002) 'Grundsatzprogramm von Bündnis90/Die Grünen. Die Zukunft ist grün', online: www.gruene-partei.de/cms/files/dokbin/68/68245.grundsatzprogramm_die_zukunft_ist_gruen.pdf (accessed 2 March 2013).
Burdeau, Georges (1980) *Traité de science politique. Tome I, Volume I*, Paris: Librairie Générale de Droit et Jurisprudence (third edition).
Burgerforum Kiesstelsel (2006) 'Het Burgerforum', online: www.burgerforumkiesstelsel.nl/hetburger.php (accessed 8 March 2007).
Burgers, Jan Willem (2013) *Choice by Chance*, Canberra: Australian National University, PhD Thesis.
Burgers, Jan Willem (forthcoming) 'Are Citizens Capable of Representing Themselves?', *Constellations*.
Burnheim, John (2006) *Is Democracy Possible? The Alternative to Electoral Democracy*, Sydney: Sydney University Press [first edition published in 1985].
Burnheim, John (1990) 'Democracy by Statistical Representation', *Social Alternatives*, 8: 4, pp. 25–28.
Burnheim, John (1995) 'Power-Trading and the Environment', *Environmental Politics*, 4: 4, pp. 49–65.
Burns, James MacGregor and Jack Walter Peltason (1955) *Government by the People. Dynamics of American National, State and Local Government*, Englewood Cliffs NJ: Prentice Hall (second edition).
Butler, David and Austin Ranney (1994) 'Practice', in: David Butler and Austin Ranney (eds) *Referendums around the World. The Growing Use of Direct Democracy*, London/Basingstoke: Macmillan, pp. 1–10.
Caciagli, Mario (1988) 'The Movimento Sociale Italiano-Destra Nazionale and Neo-Fascism in Italy', *West European Politics*, 11: 2, pp. 19–33.
Callenbach, Ernest and Michael Phillips (2008) *A Citizen Legislature*, Exeter: Imprint Academic [originally published by Banyan Tree Books (Berkeley) and Clear Glass (Bodega) in 1985].
Calman, Alvin R. (1921), *Ledru-Rollin après 1848 et les Proscrits Français en Angleterre*. Paris: F. Rieder.
Canetti-Nisim, Daphna (2004) 'Two Religious Meaning Systems, One Political Belief System: Religiosity, Alternative Religiosity and Political Extremism', in: Leonard Weinberg and Ami Pedahzur (eds) *Religious Fundamentalism and Political Extremism*, London/Portland: Frank Cass, pp. 35–54.
Canfora, Luciano (2006) *Democracy in Europe. A History of an Ideology* [translated by Simon Jones], Oxford: Blackwell.
Canovan, Margaret (2005) *The People*, Cambridge: Polity Press.
Carlen, L. (1976) *Die Landsgemeinde in der Schweiz. Schule der Demokratie*. Sigmaringen: Jan Thorbecke Verlag.
'Carolina' (2011) 'Quick guide on group dynamics in people's assemblies', online:

http://takethesquare.net/2011/07/31/quick-guide-on-group-dynamics-in-peoples-assemblies/ (accessed 31 July 2012).

Carr, E.H. (1966) *The Bolshevik Revolution, 1917–1923*, Harmondsworth: Penguin (two volumes).

Carson, Lyn and Janette Hartz-Karp (2005) 'Adapting and Combining Deliberative Designs. Juries, Polls and Forums', in: John Gastil and Peter Levine (eds) *The Deliberative Handbook. Strategies for Effective Civic Engagement in the 21st Century*, San Francisco: Jossey Bass/ Wiley , pp. 120–138.

Carson, Lyn and Brian Martin (1999) *Random Selection in Politics*. Westport (CT): Praeger.

Carsten, F.L. (1977) *Fascist Movements in Austria. From Schönerer to Hitler*, London/ Beverly Hills: Sage.

Carter, April (1971) *The Political Theory of Anarchism*, London: Routledge & Kegan Paul.

Cassinelli, C.W. (1976) *Total Revolution. A Comparative Study of Germany under Hitler, the Soviet Union under Stalin, and China under Mao*, Santa Barbara: Clio Press.

Castells, Manuel (1983) *The City and the Grassroots. A Cross-Cultural Theory of Urban Social Movements*, London: Edward Arnold.

Cayrol, Roland (1969) 'Histoire et sociologie d'un parti', in: Michel Rocard, *Le P.S.U. et l'avenir socialiste de la France*, Paris: Seuil, pp. 5–44.

Cayrol, Roland (1975) 'Le PS et l'autogestion: un beau texte ou un choix politique?', *Projet*, No. 88, pp. 969–974.

Chabrun, Laurent and Franck Hériot (1999) *Jean-Pierre Chevènement. Biographie*, Paris: Le cherche midi.

Charzat, Michel, Jean-Pierre Chevènement and Ghislaine Toutain (1975) *Le CERES: un Combat pour le Socialisme*, Paris: Calmann-Levy.

Chaulieu, Pierre [=Castoriadis, Cornelius] (1957) 'Sur le contenu du socialisme', *Socialisme ou Barbarie*, No. 22, pp. 1–75.

Chouard, Étienne (2011) 'Centralité du tirage au sort en démocratie', online: http://etienne.chouard.free.fr/Europe/centralite_du_tirage_au_sort_en_democratie.pdf (accessed 16 March 2012).

Choueiri, Youssef M. (1997) *Islamic Fundamentalism*, London/Washington: Pinter.

Christophersen, Jens A. (1968) *The Meaning of "Democracy" as used in European Ideologies from the French to the Russian Revolution. An Historical Study in Political Language*, Oslo: Universitetsforlaget

Christos, George A. (2011) 'Democracy by random selection', online: http://danchristos.com.au/Random_Parliament/Democracy_By_Random_Selection.pdf (accessed 9 January 2012).

Citrin, Jack (2009) 'Proposition 13 and the Transformation of California Government', *The California Journal of Politics and Policy*, 1: 1, online: www.bepress.com/cjpp/vol.1/iss1/16 (accessed 14 December 2010); also published in: Jack Citrin and Isaac William Martin (eds) *After the Tax Revolt: California's Proposition 13 Turns Thirty*, Berkeley: Berkeley Public Policy Press, 2009.

Clark, John (1998) 'Municipal Dreams. A Social Ecological Critique of Bookchin's Politics', in Andrew Light (ed.) *Social Ecology after Bookchin*, New York/London: Guilford Press, pp. 137–191.

Clark, Sherman J. (1998) 'A Populist Critique of Direct Democracy', *Harvard Law Review*, 112: 2, 434–482.

Cochran, Clarke E. (1994) 'The Dialogue of Justice: Towards a Self-Reflective Society.

By James A. Fishkin; Justice by Lottery. By Barbara Goodwin. Review', *The Journal of Politics*, 56: 3, pp. 847–850.

Cohen, Joshua and Joel Rogers (2003) 'Power and Reason', in: Archon Fung and Erik Olin Wright (eds) *Deepening Democracy. Institutional Innovations in Empowered Participatory Governance*, London: Verso, pp. 237–255.

Collard, Pierre (1910) *Victor Considérant (1808–1893). Sa Vie – Ses Ideés*, Dijon: Barbier.

Conze, Werner (1972) 'Demokratie in der modernen Bewegung', in: Otto Brunner, Werner Conze and Reinhart Koselleck (eds), *Geschichtliche Grundbegriffe. Historisches Lexikon zur politisch-sozialen Sprache in Deutschland, I*, Stuttgart: Ernst Klett Verlag, pp. 873–898.

Corrales, Javier (2010) 'The Repeating Revolution: Chávez's New Politics and Old Economics', in: Kurt Weyland, Raúl L. Madrid and Wendy Hunter (eds), *Leftist Governments in Latin America. Successes and Shortcomings*, Cambridge: Cambridge University Press, pp. 28–56.

Cronin, Thomas E. (1989) *Direct Democracy: The Politics of Initiative, Referendum and Recall*, Cambridge (Mass.): Harvard University Press.

Crosby, Ned and Doug Nethercut (2005) 'Citizens Juries: Creating a Trustworthy Voice of the People', in: John Gastil and Peter Levine (eds) *The Deliberative Democracy Handbook. Strategies for Effective Civic Engagement in the 21st Century*, San Francisco: Jossey Bass/Wiley, pp. 111–119.

Crouch, Colin (2004) *Post-Democracy*, Cambridge: Polity Press.

Curti, Theodor (1882) *Geschichte der Schweizerischen Volksgesetzgebung (Zugleich eine Geschichte der Schweizerischen Demokratie)*, Bern: Dalpsche Buchhandlung.

Cutler, Fred, Richard Johnston, R. Kenneth Carty, André Blais and Patrick Fournier (2008) 'Deliberation, information, and trust: the British Columbian Citizens' Assembly as agenda-setter', in: Mark E. Warren and Hilary Pearse (eds) *Designing Deliberative Democracy. The British Columbia Citizens' Assembly*, Cambridge: Cambridge University Press, pp. 166–191.

Dahl, Robert A. (1956) *A Preface To Democratic Theory*, Chicago/London: The University of Chicago Press.

Dahl, Robert A. (1970) *After the Revolution? Authority in a Good Society*, New Haven: Yale University Press.

Dahl, Robert A. (1989) *Democracy and its Critics*, New Haven/London: Yale University Press.

Daniels, Bruce C. (1993) 'Local Government', in: Jacob Ernest Cooke (ed.), *Encyclopaedia of the North American Colonies*, I, New York: Charles Scribner's Sons, pp. 341–362.

Davies, Nancy (2007) 'Popular Assemblies and the Growing Popular Assembly Movement', online: http://www.umn.edu/faculty/salzman_g/Strate/2007-01-04.htm (accessed 15 August 2011).

De Geus, Marius (1999) *Ecological Utopias. Envisioning the Sustainable Society*, Utrecht: International Books (translated from Dutch by Paul Schwartzman).

De Jong, Rudolf (1972) 'Provos and Kabouters' in: David E. Apter and James Joll (eds) *Anarchism Today*, Garden City NY: Anchor Books Doubleday, pp. 191–209.

De Jonge, A.A. (1968) *Crisis en critiek der democratie. Anti-democratische stromingen en de daarin levende denkbeelden over de staat in Nederland*, Assen: Van Gorcum.

De Maistre, Joseph ([1821] 1960) *Les soirées de Saint-Pétersbourg*, Paris: La Colombe.

De Souza, Ubiratan (2004) 'On a Bigger Scale: Rio Grande do Sul and Nationwide', in:

Iain Bruce (ed.) *The Porto Alegre Alternative. Direct Democracy in Action*, London: Pluto Press, pp. 100–107 (translated by Iain Bruce).
Debord, Guy (1958) 'Théorie de la dérive', *Internationale Situationniste*, No. 2, pp. 19–23.
Debord, Guy (1967) *La Société du Spectacle*, Paris: Buchet-Chastel.
Decker, Frank (2006) 'Die populistische Herausforderung. Theoretische und ländervergleichende Perspektiven', in: Frank Decker (ed.) *Populismus. Gefahr für die Demokratie oder nützliches Korrektiv?* Wiesbaden: VS Verlag für Sozialwissenschaften, pp. 9–32.
Delannoi, Gil (2010) *Le retour du tirage au sort en politique*, Paris: Fondapol (Fondation pour l'innovation politique).
Demirovic, Alex (1998) 'Grassroots Democracy: Contradictions and Implications', in: Margit Mayer and John Ely (eds), *The German Greens: Paradox between Movement and Party*, Philadelphia: Temple University Press, pp. 141–161.
Dermott, Kevin and Jeremy Agnew (1996) *The Comintern. A History of International Communism from Lenin to Stalin*, Basingstoke: Macmillan.
Die Grünen (1980) 'Das Saarbrückener Bundesprogramm – Kurzfassung', in: Hans-Werner Lüdke and Olaf Dinné (eds), *Die Grünen: Personen, Projekte, Programme*. Stuttgart-Degerloch: Seewald, pp. 211–244.
Dieterich, Heinz (2005) *Hugo Chávez y el Socialismo del Siglo XXI*, Buenos Aires: Editorial Nuestra América.
Dieterich, Heinz (2009) 'Asesinato politico en Venezuela', online: www.rebelion.org/noticia.php?id=96407 (accessed 5 March 2013).
Dieterich, Heinz (2011) 'Ruptura con Chávez', online: www.old.kaosenlared.net/noticia/dia-de-ruptura-con-hugo-chavez (accessed 5 March 2013).
Domes, Jürgen (1990) 'Ideology and Politics', in: Franz Michael, Carl Linden, Jan Prybyla, and Jürgen Domes, *China and the Crisis of Marxism–Leninism*, Boulder: Westview Press, 174-203.
Dörig, Toni (2008) '"Mit vier Jahren noch zu jung für die Schule": die Innerrhoder Stimmberechtigten lehnen die Revision des Schulgesetzes mit deutlichem Mehr ab', *Appenzeller Volksfreund*, 28 April, p. 5.
Dowlen, Oliver (2008) *The Political Potential of Sortition. A Study of the Random Selection of Citizens for Public Office*, Exeter: Imprint Academic.
Dryzek, John S. (2002) *Deliberative Democracy and Beyond. Liberals, Critics, Contestations*, Oxford: Oxford University Press.
Dürrenmatt, P. (1976) *Schweizer Geschichte, 3: Die Schweiz im 19. Jahrhundert*, Zürich: Schweizer Verlagshaus.
Dutschke, Gretchen (1996) *Wir hatten ein barbarisches, schönes leben: Rudi Dutschke. Eine Biographie*, Cologne: Kiepenheuer & Witsch.
Dutschke, Rudi (1976[1964]) 'Diskussion: Das Verhältnis von Theorie und Praxis', in: Frank Böckelmann and Herbert Nagel (eds) *Subversive Aktion. Der Sinn der Organisation ist ihr Scheitern*, Frankfurt on Main: Neue Kritik, 190–195 (originally published in *Anschlag*, No. 1).
Duverger, Maurice (1964) *Political Parties: Their Organization and Activity in the Modern State*, London: Methuen [translated by Barbara and Robert North; first edition in 1951].
Eatwell, Roger (1995) *Fascism: A History*. New York/London: Penguin Books.
Edwards, Stewart (1971) *The Paris Commune 1871*. London: Eyre & Spottiswoode.
Ellner, Steve (2005) 'Revolutionary and Non-Revolutionary Paths of Radical Populism:

Directions of the *Chavista* Movement in Venezuela', *Science & Society*, 69: 2, pp. 160–190.

Ellner, Steve and Daniel Hellinger (2003) 'Conclusion: The Democratic and Authoritarian Directions of the *Chavista* Movement', in: Steve Ellner and Daniel Hellinger (eds) *Venezuelan Politics in the Chávez Era. Class, Polarization, and Conflict*, Boulder/London: Lynne Rienner, pp. 215–226.

Engels, Friedrich ([1891] 2001) 'Introduction' in: Karl Marx, *The Civil War in France*, London: Electric Book Company, pp. 4–23.

Felicetti, Andrea, John Gastil, Janette Hartz-Karp and Lyn Carson (2012) 'Collective Identity and Voice at the Australian Citizens' Parliament', *Journal of Public Deliberation*, 8: 1, Article 5, online: www.publicdeliberation.net/cgi/viewcontent.cgi?article=1169&context=jpd (accessed 27 April 2013).

Ferguson, William Scott ([1913] 1967) 'Athens: An Imperial Democracy', in: Jill N. Claster (ed.) *Athenian Democracy: Triumph or Travesty?* New York: Holt, Rinehart and Winston, pp. 11–19.

Ferraresi, Franco (1996) *Threats to Democracy. The Radical Right in Italy after the War*, Princeton: Princeton University Press.

Ferrer i Panadès, Carles (2011) 'La democracia en sus orígines. Los indignados recuperan ahora el afán de los griegos en la vieja Atenas por debatir', *El País*, 11 August, online: www.politica.elpais.com (accessed 16 August 2011).

Fichter, Tilman and Siegward Lönnendonker (1977) *Kleine Geschichte des SDS. Der Sozialistische Deutsche Studentenbund von 1946 bis zur Selbstauflösung*, Berlin: Rotbuch Verlag.

Finley, M.I. (1973) *Democracy, Ancient and Modern*, London: Chatto & Windus.

Fishkin, James S. (1991) *Democracy and Deliberation. New Directions for Democratic Reform*, New Haven/London: Yale University Press.

Fishkin, James S. (1995) *The Voice of the People. Public Opinion and Democracy*, New Haven/London: Yale University Press.

Fishkin, James S. and Cynthia Farrar (2005) 'Deliberative Polling: From Experiment to Community Resource', in: John Gastil and Peter Levine (eds) *The Deliberative Democracy Handbook. Strategies for Effective Civic Engagement in the 21st Century*, San Francisco: Jossey Bass/Wiley, pp. 68–79.

Fishkin, James S., Baogang He, Robert C. Luskin and Alice Siu (2010) 'Deliberative Democracy in an Unlikely Place: Deliberative Polling in China', *British Journal of Political Science*, 40: 2, pp. 435–448.

Font, Joan and Ismael Blanco (2007) 'Procedural legitimacy and political trust: The case of the citizen juries in Spain', *European Journal of Political Research*, 46: 4, pp. 557–589.

Fontana, Biancamaria (1993) 'Democracy and the French Revolution', in John Dunn (ed.) *Democracy: The Unfinished Journey, 508 BC to AD 1993*, Oxford: Oxford University Press, pp. 107–124.

Forster, E.M. (1951) *Two Cheers for Democracy*, London: Edward Arnold.

Fossedal, Gregory A. (2002) *Direct Democracy in Switzerland*, New Brunswick/London: Transaction Publishers.

Frank, Pierre (1973) *La Quatrième Internationale. Contribution à l'histoire du mouvement trotskyste*, Paris: Maspero.

Franklin, James (1999) 'The Sydney Philosophy Disturbances', *Quadrant*, 43: 4, 16–21; also online: www.web.maths.unsw.edu.au/~jim/sydq.html (accessed 14 December 2011).

Franks, Benjamin (2012) 'Between Anarchism and Marxism: The Beginnings and Ends of the Schism', *Journal of Political Ideologies*, 17: 2, 207–227.

Franz, Günther (ed.) (1964) *Staatsverfassungen. Eine Sammlung wichtiger Verfassungen der Vergangenheit und Gegenwart in Urtext und Übersetzung*, München: Oldenbourg.
Freeden, Michael (1998a) *Ideologies and Political Theory: A Conceptual Approach*, Oxford: Clarendon Press.
Freeden, Michael (1998b) 'Is Nationalism a Distinct Ideology?', *Political Studies*, 46: 4, pp. 748–765.
Fuller, Graham (2003) *The Future of Political Islam*, New York/Basingstoke: Palgrave Macmillan.
Furet, François (1988) 'Révolution française et tradition jacobine', in: Colin Lucas (ed.), *The French Revolution and the Creation of Modern Political Culture*, Vol. 2, Oxford: Pergamon Press, pp. 329–339.
Furet, François and David Richler (1973) *La Révolution Française*, Paris: Fayard.
Galeotti, Gianluigi (2002) 'At the outskirts of the Constitution', in: Albert Breton, Gianluigi Galeotti, Pierre Salmon, and Ronald Wintrobe (eds) *Political Extremism and Rationality*, Cambridge: Cambridge University Press, pp. 122–138.
Gallup, George and Saul Forbes Rae ([1940] 1968) *The Pulse of Democracy. The Public Opinion Poll and How It Works*, Westport (CT): Greenwood Press.
Gastil, John (2000) *By Popular Demand: Revitalizing Representative Democracy through Deliberative Elections*, London: University of California Press.
Gastil, John and William Keith (2005) 'A Nation That (Sometimes) Likes to Talk: A Brief History of Public Deliberation in the United States', in: John Gastil and Peter Levine (eds) *The Deliberative Democracy Handbook. Strategies for Effective Civic Engagement in the 21st Century*, San Francisco: Jossey Bass/Wiley, pp. 3–19.
Gerstein, Dietmar (1969) *Das Funktionieren der unmittelbaren Demokratie in rechtsvergleichender Sicht*, Munich: Dissertationsdruck Zielezinski (PhD Thesis).
Gilcher-Holtey, Ingrid (2008) 'France', in: Martin Klimke and Joachim Scharloth (eds), *1968 in Europe. A History of Protest and Activism, 1956–1977*, Basingstoke: Palgrave Macmillan, pp. 111–124.
Gilley, Bruce (2009) 'Is Democracy Possible?', *Journal of Democracy*, 20: 1, 113–127.
Ginzel, Günther Bernd (1981) *Hitlers (Ur)Enkel. Neonazi's: ihre Ideologien und Aktionen*, Düsseldorf: Droste Verlag.
Glarner Kantonalbank (2006) *Der Kanton Glarus in Zahlen. Ausgabe 2006*, Glarus: Glarner Kantonalbank.
Gluckstein, Donny (2011) 'Workers' Councils in Europe: A Century of Experience', in: Immanuel Ness and Dario Azzellini (eds) *Ours to Master and to Own. Workers' Control from the Commune to the Present*, Chicago: Haymarket Books, pp. 32–47.
Gobierno Bolivariano de Venezuela ([1999] 2006) *Constitution of the Bolivarian Republic of Venezuela*, Caracas: Ministerio de Comunicación e Información (translated from Spanish).
Godwin, William ([1798] 1971) *Enquiry Concerning Political Justice*, (abridged and edited by K. Codell Carter) London: Oxford University Press.
Goldstein, Melvyn C. (1989) *A History of Modern Tibet, 1913–1951. I. The Demise of the Lamaist State*, Berkeley: University of California Press.
Goldwater, Barry (1964) 'Acceptance Speech', online: www.washingtonpost.com/up-srv/politics/daily/may98/goldwaterspeech.htm (accessed 13 August 2013).
Golliet, M. (1903) *Louis Blanc – Sa Doctrine, Son Action*, Paris: A. Pedone.
Gombin, Richard (1969) *Le Projet révolutionnaire. Éléments d'une sociologie des événements de mai-juin 1968*. Paris/The Hague: Mouton.
Gombin, Richard (1971) *Les origines du gauchisme*, Paris: Seuil.

Goodwin, Barbara (1992) *Justice by Lottery*, Chicago: University of Chicago Press.
Gott, Richard (2000) *In the Shadow of the Liberator. Hugo Chavez and the Transformation of Venezuela*, London/New York: Verso.
Gottfried, Paul (1996) 'Liberalism vs Democracy', *The Journal of Libertarian Studies*, 12: 2, pp. 231–251.
Gottschalch, Wilfried (1968) *Parlamentarismus und Rätedemokratie*, Berlin: Wagenbach.
Government of California (no date) 'California Constitution', online: www.leginfo.ca.gov/.const (accessed 14 December 2010).
Government of California (2013) 'California Recall History', online: www.sos.ca/gov/elections/recalls/california-recall-history.htm (accessed 28 March 2013).
GroenLinks (1994) *GroenLinks of laten we het zo?* Amsterdam: GroenLinks.
Griffin, Roger (1993) *The Nature of Fascism*. London/New York: Routledge.
Guillerm, Alain (1973) 'Autogestion et démocratie directe', *Critique Socialiste*, No. 13–14, pp. 82–91.
Gundersen, Adolf G. (1998) 'Bookchin's Ecocommunity as Ecotopia. A Constructive Critique', in Andrew Light (ed.) *Social Ecology after Bookchin*, New York/London: Guilford Press, pp. 192–210.
Gurvitch, Georges (1965) *Proudhon. Sa vie, son oeuvre, avec un exposé de sa philosophie*, Paris: Presses Universitaires de France.
Habermas, Jürgen ([1962] 1968) *Strukturwandel der Öffentlichkeit. Untersuchungen zu einer Kategorie der bürgerlichen Gesellschaft*, Neuwied am Rhein: Luchterhand (third edition).
Hamilton, Douglas (2010) 'A Town Called Marinaleda', online: www.counterpunch.org/hamilton04302010.html (accessed 17 May 2011).
Hanley, David (1988) *Keeping Left: Ceres and the French Socialist Party*, Manchester: Manchester University Press.
Hansen, Mogens Herman (1984) *Die athenische Volksversammlung im Zeitalter des Demosthenes*, Konstanz: Universitätsverlag Konstanz.
Hansen, Mogens Herman (1991) *The Athenian Democracy in the Age of Demosthenes. Structure, Principles and Ideology*, Oxford: Blackwell (translated from Danish by J.A. Crook).
Harding, Neil (1993) 'The Marxist-Leninist Detour', in: John Dunn (ed.) *Democracy: The Unfinished Journey, 508 BC to AD 1993*, Oxford: Oxford University Press, 155-187.
Hauss, Charles (1978) *The New Left in France*, Westport (CT): Greenwood Press.
Hawkins, Kirk (2009) 'Is Chávex Populist? Measuring Populist Discourse in Comparative Perspective', *Comparative Political Studies*, 42: 8, pp. 1040–1067.
Hawkins, Kirk A. (2010) *Venezuela's Chavismo and Populism in Comparative Perspective*, Cambridge/ New York: Cambridge University Press.
Hecken, Thomas and Agatha Grzenia (2008) 'Situationism', in: Martin Klimke and Joachim Scharloth (eds), *1968 in Europe. A History of Protest and Activism, 1956–1977*, Basingstoke: Palgrave Macmillan, pp. 23–32.
Heller, Agnes (1986) 'John Burnheim, Is Democracy Possible?', *Thesis Eleven*, 14, pp. 129–132.
Hendriks, Carolyn M. (2005) 'Consensus Conferences and Planning Cells: Lay Citizen Deliberations', in: John Gastil and Peter Levine (eds) *The Deliberative Democracy Handbook. Strategies for Effective Civic Engagement in the 21st Century*, San Francisco: Jossey Bass/Wiley, pp. 80–110.

Hicks, John D. ([1931] 1961) *The Populist Revolt. A History of the Farmers' Alliance and the People's Party*, Lincoln: University of Nebraska Press.
Higonnet, Patrice (1998) *Goodness beyond Virtue. Jacobins during the French Revolution*, Cambridge (Mass)/London: Harvard University Press.
Hildebrandt, Günther (1975) *Parlamentsopposition auf Linkskurs. Die kleinbürgerlich-demokratische Fraktion Donnersberg in der Frankfurter Nationalversamlung 1848/49*, Berlin: Akademie Verlag.
Hindman, Matthew (2009) *The Myth of Digital Democracy*, Princeton/Oxford: Princeton University Press.
Hirschman, Albert O. (1982) *Shifting Involvements. Private Interest and Public Action*, Oxford: Martin Robertson.
Hirst, Paul (1986) 'Is Democracy Possible?', *The Sociological Review*, 34: 3, pp. 669–673.
Hitler, Adolf ([1925] 1941) *Mein Kampf*, Munich: Zentralverlag der NSDAP [original edition: Franz Eher Nachfolger].
Hobson, Christopher (2008) 'Revolution, Representation and the Foundations of Modern Democracy', *European Journal of Political Theory*, 7: 4, pp. 449–471.
Hoffrogge, Ralf (2011) 'From Unionism to Workers' Councils: The Revolutionary Shop Stewards in Germany, 1914–1918', in: Immanuel Ness and Dario Azzellini (eds) *Ours to Master and to Own. Workers' Control from the Commune to the Present*, Chicago: Haymarket Books, pp. 84–103.
Hofman, Joop and Eisse Kalk (2007) *Vuurdoop. Wijk- en dorpsgericht werken in Hoogeveen*, Hoogeveen: Gemeente Hoogeveen.
Hoogeveen (2008) 'De smederijen van Hoogeveen: zo werken ze!', online: www.desmederijenvanhoogeveen.nl (accessed 3 August 2008).
Hornblower, Simon (1993) 'Creation and Development of Democratic Institutions in Ancient Greece', in: John Dunn (ed.) *Democracy: The Unfinished Journey, 508 BC to AD 1993*, Oxford: Oxford University Press, pp. 1–16.
Hospers, John (1974) 'What Libertarianism Is', in: Tibor Machan (ed.) *The Libertarian Alternative: Essays in Social and Political Philosophy*. Chicago: Nelson-Hall, pp. 3–20.
Houwen, Tim (2013) *Reclaiming Power for the People. Populism in Democracy*, Nijmegen: Radboud University, PhD Thesis.
Howard, Dick (1977) *The Marxian Legacy*, New York: Urizen Books.
Huitema, Dave, Marleen van de Kerkhof and Udo Pesch (2007) 'The Nature of the Beast: Are Citizens' Juries Deliberative or Pluralist?', *Policy Science*, 40: 4, pp. 287–311.
Humilière, Jean Michel (1982), *Louis Blanc (1811–1882)*, Paris: Les éditions ouvrières.
Humphrys, John (2004) *Lost for Words. The Mangling and Manipulating of the English Language*, London: Hodder & Stoughton.
Ignazi, Piero (2003) *Extreme Right Parties in Western Europe*, Oxford: Oxford University Press.
Institute for Social Ecology (2012) 'History', online: www.social-ecology.org (accessed 5 July 2012).
Iyengar, Shanto and Donald R. Kinder (1987) *News that Matters: Television and American Opinion*, Chicago: The University of Chicago Press.
James, Michael Rabinder (2008) 'Descriptive Representation in the British Columbia Citizens' Assembly', in: Mark E. Warren and Hilary Pearse (eds) *Designing Deliberative Democracy. The British Columbia Citizens' Assembly*, Cambridge: Cambridge Universitry Press, pp. 106–126.

Jansen, Robert S. (2011) 'Populist Mobilization: A New Theoretical Approach to Populism', *Sociological Theory*, 29: 2, 75-96.
Jardin, André (1985) *Histoire du libéralisme politique de la crise de l'absolutisme à la constitution de 1875*, Paris: Hachette.
Johnson, Claudia Durst (2002) *Daily Life in Colonial New England*, Westport (CT): Greenwood Press.
Jones, A.H.M. ([1957] 1977) *Athenian Democracy*, Oxford: Basil Blackwell.
Jones, Nicholas F. (1999) *The Associations of Classical Athens. The Response to Democracy*, New York/Oxford: Oxford University Press.
Kadlec, Alison and Will Friedman (2007) 'Deliberative Democracy and the Problem of Power', *Journal of Public Deliberation*, 3: 1, Article 8, online: http://www.public deliberation.net/cgi/viewcontent.cgi?article=1035&context=jpd (accessed 16 April 2013).
Kaldor, Mary and Diego Muro (2003) 'Religious and Nationalist Militant Groups', in: Mary Kaldor, Helmut Anheier and Marlies Glasius (eds), *Global Civil Society 2003*, Oxford: Oxford University Press, pp. 151–184.
Kamrava, Mehran (1992) *The Political History of Modern Iran: From Tribalism to Theocracy*, Westport (CT)/London: Praeger.
Kanton Appenzell Innerrhoden (2008) 'Grosser Rat', www.ai.ch/de/politik/grosserat/ grosseratmain (accessed 21 July 2008).
Kanton Appenzell Innerrhoden (2013) *Verfassung für den Eidgenössischen Stand Appenzell I. Rh.*, online: http://www.admin.ch/opc/de/classified-compilation/18720003/20130 3110000/131.224.2.pdf (accessed 28 April 2013).
Kapstein, Matthew (2006) *The Tibetans*. Oxford: Blackwell.
Karpowitz, Christopher F., Chad Raphael and Allen S. Hammond, IV (2009) 'Deliberative Democracy and Inequality: Two Cheers for Enclave Deliberation among the Disempowered', *Politics & Society*, 37: 4, pp. 576–615.
Katz, Richard S. and Peter Mair (1995) 'Changing Models of Party Organization and Party Democracy', *Party Politics*, 1: 1, pp. 5–28.
Kazin, Michael (1995) *The Populist Persuasion. An American History*, New York: Basic Books.
Keane, John (2009) *The Life and Death of Democracy*, London: Simon & Schuster/ Pocket Books.
Kergoat, Jacques (1997) *Histoire du Parti Socialiste*, Paris: La Découverte.
Khasnabish, Alex (2010) *Zapatistas. Rebellion from the Grassroots to the Global*, Black Point NS/London: Fernwood/Zed Books.
Khomeyni, Ayatollah Seyyed Ruhollah (1979) *Pour un Gouvernement Islamique*, Paris: Fayolle [translated by M. Kotobi and B. Simon].
King, Nancy Jean (2000) 'The American Criminal Jury', in: Neil Vidmar (ed.), *World Jury Systems*, Oxford: Oxford University Press, pp. 93–124.
Kleroterians (no date) website: www.equalitybylot.wordpress.com (accessed 10 October 2011).
Klimke, Martin (2008) 'West Germany', in: Martin Klimke and Joachim Scharloth (eds), *1968 in Europe. A History of Protest and Activism, 1956–1977*, Basingstoke: Palgrave Macmillan, pp. 97–110.
Kloosterman, Jaap (1972) 'Nawoord (Thesen *ad* Pannekoek)', in: Jaap Kloosterman (ed.) *Anton Pannekoek: Partij, Raden, Revolutie*, Amsterdam: Van Gennep, pp. 227–233.
Kobach, Kris W. (1994) 'Switzerland', in: David Butler and Austin Ranney (eds) *Referendums around the World*, Basingstoke/London: Macmillan, pp. 98–153.

Kock Marti, Claudia (2008) '20 Landräte erhalten die Kündigung', *Die Südostschweiz*, 5 May, p. 3.
Kolb, Eberhard ([1962] 1978) *Die Arbeiterräte in der deutschen Innenpolitik 1918–1919*, Frankfurt on Main: Ullstein.
König, Christine (2008) 'Etwas überraschend zum Präsidenten gewählt', *Appenzeller Zeitung*, 28 April, p. 41.
Kraushaar, Wolfgang (1976) 'Vorwort. Kinder einer abenteuerlichen Dialektik', in: Frank Böckelmann and Herbert Nagel (eds) *Subversive Aktion. Der Sinn der Organisation ist ihr Scheitern*, Frankfurt on Main: Neue Kritik, pp. 8–32.
Kriesi, Hanspeter (1995) *Le système politique suisse*, Paris: Economica.
Kriesi, Hanspeter (2012) 'Direct democracy. The Swiss experience', in: Brigitte Geissel and Kenneth Newton (eds), *Evaluating Democratic Innovations. Curing the Democratic Malaise?* London/New York: Routledge, pp. 39–55.
Kurrild-Klitgaard, Peter (2001) 'An empirical example of the Condorcet paradox of voting in a large electorate', *Public Choice*, 107, pp. 135–145.
La CFDT (1971) *La C.F.D.T.* Paris: Seuil.
Laclau, Ernesto (2005) *On Populist Reason*, London/New York: Verso.
Laffont, Jean-Jacques and David Martimort (2002) *The Theory of Incentives. The Principal-Agent Model*, Princeton: Princeton University Press.
Landemore, Hélène (2007) 'Is Representative Democracy Really Democratic?', *Books and Ideas*, online: www.booksandideas.net/Is-representative-democracy-really.html (accessed 20 June 2012).
Lang, Amy (2008) 'Agenda-setting in deliberative forums: expert influence and citizen autonomy in the British Columbia Citizens' Assembly', in: Mark E. Warren and Hilary Pearse (eds) *Designing Deliberative Democracy. The British Columbia Citizens' Assembly*, Cambridge: Cambridge University Press, pp. 85–105.
Lang, Amy (2007) 'But Is It for Real? The British Columbia Citizens'Assembly as a Model of State-Sponsored Citizen Empowerment', *Politics & Society*, 35: 1, pp. 35–69.
Laponce, Jean A. (1981) *Left and Right: The Topography of Political Perceptions*, Toronto: University of Toronto Press.
Lasswell, Harold D. (1950) *Who Gets What, When, How*, New York: Peter Smith.
Lawrence, Eric, Todd Donovan and Shaun Bowler (2011) 'The Adoption of Direct Primaries in the United States', *Party Politics*, 19: 1, pp. 3–18.
Le Goff, Jean-Pierre (1998) *Mai 68, L'héritage impossible*, Paris: La Découverte.
Le Pen, Jean-Marie (1984) *Les Français d'abord*, Paris: Editions Carrere-Michel Lafon.
Leduc, Lawrence (2003) *The Politics of Direct Democracy. Referendums in Global Perspective*, Peterborough: Broadview Press.
Leduc, Lawrence (2011) 'Electoral Reform and Direct Democracy in Canada: When Citizens Become Involved', *West European Politics*, 34: 3, 551–567.
Leib, Ethan J. (2004) *Deliberative Democracy in America. A Proposal for a Popular Branch of Government*, University Park (PA): The Pennsylvania State University Press.
Lemire, Laurent (1998), *Cohn Bendit*, Paris: Liana Levi.
Lenin, V.I. ([1917] 1964) 'The State and Revolution. The Marxist Theory of the State and the Tactics of the Proletariat in the Revolution', in: *Collected Works*, 25, Moscow: Progress Publishers [translated from Russian], pp. 385–497.
Lenin, V.I. ([1920] 1970) *'Left-wing' Communism, An Infantile Disorder*, Moscow: Novosti Publishing House [translated from Russian].

Les Verts (1999) *Le nouveau Livre des Verts. Et si le vert était la couleur du XXIe siècle?* Paris: Éditions du Félin.
Leval, Gaston (1974) 'The Characteristics of the Libertarian Collectives', in: Sam Dolgoff (ed.), *The Anarchist Collectives. Workers' Self-Management in the Spanish Revolution 1936–1939*, Montreal: Black Rose Books, pp. 166–170.
Levin, Martin (1970) *Fission and Fusion on the French Left*, Ithaca (NY): Cornell University PhD Thesis.
Leyenaar, Monique (2009) *De burger aan zet. Burgerforum: theorie en praktijk*, The Hague: Ministerie van Binnenlandse Zaken en Koninkrijksrelaties.
Levine, Peter, Archon Fung and John Gastil (2005) 'Future Directions for Public Deliberation', in: John Gastil and Peter Levine (eds) *The Deliberative Handbook. Strategies for Effective Civic Engagement in the 21st Century*, San Francisco: Jossey Bass/ Wiley, 271-288.
Levy, Andrea (2007) 'Progeny and Progress', in: Dimitrios Roussopoulos (ed.) *The New Left. Legacy and Continuity*, Montreal: Black Rose Books, pp. 15–48.
Libertarian Party (2005) 'Our History', on line: www.lp.org/organization/printer_history.shtml (accessed 30 December 2005).
Lichtheim, George (1967) *Marxism*, London: Routledge & Kegan Paul.
Linden, Carl (1990) 'Marxism-Leninism in the Soviet Union and the PRC: Utopia in Crisis', in: Franz Michael, Carl Linden, Jan Prybyla, and Jürgen Domes, *China and the Crisis of Marxism-Leninism*, Boulder: Westview Press, 6-23.
Lipset, Seymour Martin (1963) *Political Man. The Social Bases of Politics*, Garden City NY: Anchor Books/Doubleday.
Lipset, Seymour M. and Earl Raab (1971) *The Politics of Unreason. Right Wing Extremism in America, 1790–1970*, London: Heinemann.
Lloyd-Bostock, Sally and Cheryl Thomas (2000) 'The Continuing Decline of the English Jury', in: Neil Vidmar (ed.), *World Jury Systems*, Oxford: Oxford University Press, pp. 53–91.
Lucardie, Anthonie Paul Marius (1980) *The New Left in the Netherlands, 1960–1977. A Critical Study of New Political Ideas and Groups on the Left in the Netherlands with Comparative References to France and Germany*, Kingston: Queen's University, PhD Thesis, online: http://irs.ub.rug.nl/dbi/4e1ee3f559555 (accessed 16 April 2013).
Lucardie, A.P.M. (1994) 'Op zoek naar zusterpartijen. D66 en het democratisch radicalisme in West-Europa', *Jaarboek 1993 DNPP*, Groningen: Documentatiecentrum Nederlandse Politieke Partijen, pp. 200–228.
Lucardie, Paul and Paul Pennings (2010) 'Van groen en rood naar groen en paars? De programmatische ontwikkeling van GroenLinks', in: Paul Lucardie and Gerrit Voerman (eds) *Van de straat naar de staat? GroenLinks 1990–2010*, Amsterdam: Boom, pp. 149–162.
Lupia, Arthur and John G. Matsusaka (2004) 'Direct Democracy: New Approaches to Old Questions', *Annual Review of Political Science*, 7: pp. 463–482.
Lynch, Tony (1989) 'Debating Democracy', *Economy and Society*, 18: 1, pp. 110–124.
Macdonald, Joan (1965) *Rousseau and the French Revolution 1762–1791*, London: Athlone Press.
MacRae, Donald (1969) 'Populism as an ideology', in: Ghita Ionescu en Ernest Gellner (eds) *Populism. Its Meanings and National Characteristics*, London: Weifenfeld & Nicolson, pp. 153–165.
Magleby, David B. (1994) 'Direct legislation in the American States', in: David Butler and Austin Ranney (eds) *Referendums around the World. The Growing Use of Direct Democracy*, London/Basingstoke: MacMillan, pp. 218–257.

Maier, Charles S. (1993) 'Democracy since the French Revolution', in: John Dunn (ed.) *Democracy: The Unfinished Journey, 508 BC to AD 1993*, Oxford: Oxford University Press, pp. 125–154.
Maier, Hans (1972) 'Die Demokratie als Indikator geschichtlicher Bewegung (19. Jahrhundert)', in: Otto Brunner, Werner Conze and Reinhart Koselleck (eds), *Geschichtliche Grundbegriffe. Historisches Lexikon zur politisch-sozialen Sprache in Deutschland, I*, Stuttgart: Ernst Klett Verlag, pp. 861–873.
Maintenant, Gérard (1984) *Les Jacobins*, Paris: Presses Universitaires de France.
Mair, Peter (2002) 'Populist Democracy versus Party Democracy', in: Yves Mény and Yves Surel (eds) *Democracies and the Populist Challenge*, Basingstoke: Palgrave, pp. 81–98.
Maire, Edmond and Jacques Julliard (1975) *La CFDT d'aujourd'hui*, Paris: Seuil.
Maley, William (2001) 'Introduction: Interpreting the Taliban', in: William Maley (ed.) *Afghanistan and the Taliban. The Rebirth of Fundamentalism?* New Delhi: Penguin Books, pp. 1–26.
Mandel, David (2011) 'The Factory Committee Movement in the Russian Revolution', in: Immanuel Ness and Dario Azzellini (eds) *Ours to Master and to Own. Workers' Control from the Commune to the Present*, Chicago: Haymarket Books, pp. 104–129.
Mandel, Ernest (1973) *Vervreemding en revolutionaire perspectieven. Zes Essays*, Amsterdam: Van Gennep.
Mandel, Ernest (1977) *From Class Society to Communism. An Introduction to Marxism*, London: Ink Links (translated by Louisa Sadler).
Manin, Bernard (1997) *The Principles of Representative Government*, Cambridge: Cambridge University Press.
Mansbridge, Jane (1983) *Beyond Adversary Democracy*, Chicago: University of Chicago Press.
Mansbridge, Jane (1999) 'Should Blacks Represent Blacks and Women Represent Women? A Contingent "Yes"', *The Journal of Politics*, 61: 3, pp. 628–657.
Marcano, Cristina and Alberto Barrera Tyszka ([2004] 2006) *Hugo Chávez. The Definitive Biography of Venezuela's Controversial President*, New York: Random House (translated by Kristina Cordero).
Marinaleda (2007) 'Politica Interna', online: www.marinaleda.com/asambleageneral.htm (accessed 5 September 2007).
Marsella, Mauro (2004) 'Enrico Corradini's Italian nationalism: the 'right wing' of the fascist synthesis', *Journal of Political Ideologies*, 9: 2, pp. 203–224.
Marshall, Peter (1992) *Demanding the Impossible: A History of Anarchism*, London: Harper Collins.
Martos, Jean-François (1989) *Histoire de l'Internationale Situationniste*, Paris: Gérard Lebovici.
Marx, Karl ([1852] 1973) 'The Chartists', in: David Fernbach (ed.) *Surveys from Exile. Political Writings. Volume 2*, Harmondsworth: Penguin/NLR, pp. 262–271.
Marx, Karl ([1859] 1971) *Zur Kritik der politischen Ökonomie*, Berlin: Dietz Verlag.
Marx, Karl ([1871] 2001) *The Civil War in France*, London: Electric Book Company.
Marx, Karl (1891) *Der Bürgerkrieg in Frankreich*, with a preface by Friedrich Engels, Berlin: Vorwärts.
Marx, Karl (1972) *Kritik des Gothaer Programms*, Berlin: Dietz Verlag.
Marx, Karl and Friedrich Engels ([1848] 1995) *Das Kommunistische Manifest (Manifest der Kommunistischen Partei)*, Trier: Karl-Marx-Haus (re-edited by Thomas Kuczynski).

Massink, H.F. *et al.* (1994) *Theocratische Politiek. Principes, Geschiedenis en Praktijk*, Houten: Den Hertog.
Maung Maung Than, Tin (2001) 'Myanmar: Military in Charge', in: John Funston (ed.) *Government and Politics in Southeast Asia*, Singapore: Institute of Southeast Asian Studies, pp. 203–251.
Mayer, Gustav (1969) *Radikalismus, Sozialismus und bürgerliche Demokratie*, Frankfurt on Main: Suhrkamp Verlag.
Mény, Yves and Yves Surel (2002) 'The Constitutive Ambiguity of Populism', in: Yves Mény and Yves Surel (eds) *Democracies and the Populist Challenge*, Basingstoke: Palgrave, pp. 1–21.
Michael, Franz (1990) 'The PRC in Crisis', in: Franz Michael, Carl Linden, Jan Prybyla, and Jürgen Domes, *China and the Crisis of Marxism-Leninism*, Boulder: Westview Press, pp. 204–209.
Miliband, Ralph (1969) *The State in Capitalist Society*, London: Weidenfeld and Nicholson.
Mill, John Stuart ([1861] 1948), *On Liberty and Considerations on Representative Government*, Oxford: Basil Blackwell.
Mitchell, Allan (1967) *Revolution in Bayern 1918/1919. Die Eisner-Regierung und die Räterepublik*, Munich: C.H. Beck.
Möckli, Silvano (1987) *Die Schweizerischen Landsgemeinde Demokratien*, Bern: Haupt.
Moslem, Mehdi (2002) 'The State and Factional Politics in the Islamic Republic of Iran', in: Eric Hooglund (ed.) *Twenty Years of Islamic Revolution*, Syracuse: Syracuse University Press, pp. 19–35.
Motta, Sara C. (2011) 'Populism's Achilles' Heel. Popular Democracy beyond the Liberal State and the Market Economy in Venezuela', *Latin American Perspectives*, 38: 1, pp. 28–46.
Moussalli, Ahmed S. (1992) *Radical Islamic Fundamentalism*, Beirut: American University of Beirut [PhD Thesis].
Mudde, Cas (2002) 'Extremist Movements', in: Paul Heywood, Erik Jones and Martin Rhodes (eds), *Developments in West European Politics*, Basingstoke: Palgrave, pp. 135–148.
Mudde, Cas (2004) 'The Populist Zeitgeist', *Government and Opposition*, 39: 4, pp. 541–563.
Mueller, Dennis C., Robert D. Tollison and Thomas D. Willett (1972) 'Representative Democracy via Random Selection', *Public Choice*, 12, pp. 57–68.
Mulholland, Maureen (2002) 'The Jury in English Manorial Courts', in: John W. Cairns and Grant McLeod (eds) *'The Dearest Birth Right of the People of England': The Jury in the History of the Common Law*, Oxford: Hart, pp. 63–73.
Mussolini, Benito ([1932] 1961) *La Dottrina del Fascismo*, in: Edoardo and Duilio Susmel (eds) *Opera Omnia di Benito Mussolini*, Florence: La Fenice, 116–138.
Mussolini, Benito (1934) *Le Fascisme. Doctrine, Institutions*. Paris: Denoël & Steele [translation authorised by the author].
Nania, Guy (1973) *Le PSU avant Rocard*, Paris: Roblot.
Narveson, Jan (2002) *Respecting Persons in Theory and Practice. Essays on Moral and Political Philosophy*, Lanham: Rowman & Littlefield.
Nasr, Seyyed Vali Reza (1996) *Mawdudi and the Making of Islamic Revivalism*, New York: Oxford University Press.
Näsström, Sofia (2011) 'Where is the representative turn going?', *European Journal of Political Theory*, 10: 4, pp. 501–510.

National Front (2004) 'Statement of Policy', online: www.natfront.com/nfsop.html (accessed 11 May 2005).
Nehme, Michel G. (1998) 'The Islamic-Capitalist State of Saudi Arabia: The Surfacing of Fundamentalism', in: Ahmad S. Moussalli (ed.) *Islamic Fundamentalism: Myths and Realities*, Reading: Garnet/Ithaca Press, pp. 275–302.
Neubauer, Helmut (1966) 'München 1918/19', in: Tankred Dorst and Helmut Neubauer (eds) *Die Münchener Räterepublik. Zeugnisse und Kommentar*, Frankfurt on Main: Suhrkamp Verlag, pp. 171–188.
Newman, Bruce I. (1999) *The Mass Marketing of Politics. Democracy in an Age of Manufactured Images*, London: Sage.
Nickson, R. Andrew (1995) *Local Government in Latin America*, Boulder: Lynne Riener.
Nicolet, Claude (1961) *Le Radicalisme*, Paris: Presses Universitaires de France.
Niemeyer, Simon (2011) 'The Emancipatory Effect of Deliberation: Empirical Lessons from Mini-Publics', *Politics & Society*, 39: 1, pp. 103–140.
Nojumi, Neamatollah (2002) *The Rise of the Taliban in Afghanistan. Mass Mobilization, Civil War, and the Future of the Region*, New York/Basingstoke: Palgrave.
Nolte, Ernst ([1963] 1971) *Der Faschismus in seiner Epoche*, Munich: Piper Verlag.
Nouveau Parti Anticapitaliste (2009) 'Principes fondateurs du Nouveau Parti Anticapitaliste', online: www.npa2009.org/sites/default/files/principesfondateurs.doc (accessed 16 March 2009).
Nordmann, J.T. (1974) *Histoire des Radicaux 1820–1973*, Paris: Table Ronde.
Nozick, Robert (1997) *Socratic Puzzles*, Cambridge/London: Harvard University Press.
OBM Network [Omar Bakri Mohammed] (no date) 'Ruling System in Islam', online: www.obm.clara.net/Pages/IslamicSystems/ruling1.html (accessed 2 December 1999).
Ó Broin, Eoin (2013) 'In defence of populism – Eoin Ó Broin answers "Sunday Business Post"', *Anphoblacht*, 3 January 2013, online: www.anphoblacht.com/contents/22613 (accessed 18 January 2013).
Ó Corráin, Donncha (1972) *Ireland before the Normans*, Dublin: Gill and Macmillan.
OccupyWallStreet (2012) 'About', online: http://occupywallst.org/about (accessed 31 July 2012).
O'Leary, Kevin (2006) *Saving Democracy. A Plan for Real Representation in America*, Stanford: Stanford University Press.
O'Sullivan, Noël (1976) *Conservatism*, London: Dent & Sons.
Otto, Karl A. (1977) *Vom Ostermarsch zur APO. Geschichte der ausserparlamentarischen Opposition in der Bundesrepublik 1960–70*, Frankfurt on Main/New York: Campus Verlag.
Otway-Ruthven, A.J. (1968) *A History of Medieval Ireland*, London: Ernest Benn.
Pabst, Angela (2003) *Die Athenische Demokratie*, Munich: C.H. Beck.
Pacifistisch Socialistische Partij (1957) *Beginselprogram*, Amsterdam: Pacifistisch Socialistische Partij.
Pacifistisch Socialistische Partij (1977) *Aktieprogramma PSP 1977–1981. Voor een Werkelijk Socialistische Politiek*, Amsterdam: Pacifistisch Socialistische Partij.
Paine, Thomas ([1792] 1989) *The Rights of Man*, Part II, in *Political Writings*, edited by Bruce Kuklick, Cambridge: Cambridge University Press, pp. 145–203.
Palmer, R.R. (1953) 'Notes on the use of the word "democracy" 1789–1799', *Political Science Quarterly*, 68: 2, pp. 203–226.
Palmer, R.R. (1959) *The Age of the Democratic Revolution. A Political History of Europe and America, 1760–1800. I. The Challenge*, Princeton: Princeton University Press.

Palmer, R.R. (1964) *The Age of the Democratic Revolution. A Political History of Europe and America, 1760–1800. II. The Struggle*, Princeton: Princeton University Press.

Pannekoek, Anton ([1919] 1972) 'Het historisch materialisme', in: Jaap Kloosterman (ed.) *Anton Pannekoek: Partij, Raden, Revolutie*, Amsterdam: Van Gennep, pp. 7–21.

Pannekoek, Anton ([1927] 1972) 'Beginsel en tactiek', in: Jaap Kloosterman (ed.) *Anton Pannekoek: Partij, Raden, Revolutie*, Amsterdam: Van Gennep, pp. 22–50.

Pannekoek, Anton ([1932] 1972) 'Over het vraagstuk van de partijen', in: Jaap Kloosterman (ed.) *Anton Pannekoek: Partij, Raden, Revolutie*, Amsterdam: Van Gennep, pp. 51–62.

Pannekoek, Anton ([1933] 1972) 'De arbeiders, het parlement en het communisme', in: Jaap Kloosterman (ed.) *Anton Pannekoek: Partij, Raden, Revolutie*, Amsterdam: Van Gennep, pp. 63–80.

Pannekoek, Anton ([1936a] 1972) 'Over de vakbonden', in: Jaap Kloosterman (ed.) *Anton Pannekoek: Partij, Raden, Revolutie*, Amsterdam: Van Gennep, pp. 97–110.

Pannekoek, Anton ([1936b] 1972) 'Partij en arbeidersklasse', in: Jaap Kloosterman (ed.) *Anton Pannekoek: Partij, Raden, Revolutie*, Amsterdam: Van Gennep, pp. 111–117.

Pannekoek, Anton ([1936c] 1972) 'De arbeidersraden', in: Jaap Kloosterman (ed.) *Anton Pannekoek: Partij, Raden, Revolutie*, Amsterdam: Van Gennep, pp. 118–127.

Pannekoek, Anton ([1936d] 1972) 'Communisme en godsdienst', in: Jaap Kloosterman (ed.) *Anton Pannekoek: Partij, Raden, Revolutie*, Amsterdam: Van Gennep, pp. 128–142.

Pannekoek, Anton ([1938] 1973) *Lenin als filosoof: een kritische beschouwing over de filosofische grondslagen van het Leninisme*, Amsterdam: De Vlam/Van Gennep.

Pannekoek, Anton ([1946] 1971) *De Arbeidersraden*, Amsterdam: Van Gennep/De Vlam (first edition was published under the pseudonym P. Aartsz).

Parti Socialiste (1975) *Quinze Thèses sur l'autogestion*, Paris: Parti Socialiste/Le Poing et la Rose.

Parti Socialiste Unifié (1969) 'Les 17 thèses du P.S.U.', in: Michel Rocard, *Le P.S.U. et l'avenir socialiste de la France*, Paris: Seuil, pp. 123–183.

Parti Socialiste Unifié (1972) *Manifeste du parti socialiste unifié: contrôler aujourd'hui pour décider demain*, Paris: Tema.

Pasquino, Gianfranco (2008) 'Populism and Democracy', in: Daniele Albertazzi and Duncan McDonnell (eds) *Twenty-First Century Populism. The Spectre of Western European Democracy*, Basingstoke: Palgrave Macmillan, pp. 15–29.

Passos Cordeiro, André (2004) 'Porto Alegre: The City Budget', in: Iain Bruce (ed.) *The Porto Alegre Alternative. Direct Democracy in Action*, London: Pluto Press, pp. 63–84 (translated by Iain Bruce).

Pateman, Carole (1970) *Participation and Democratic Theory*, Cambridge: Cambridge University Press.

Paxton, Robert (1972) *Vichy France. Old Guard and New Order, 1940–1944*, New York: Alfred Knopf.

People's Party ([1892] 1961) 'Omaha Platform', Appendix in: John D. Hicks, *The Populist Revolt. A History of the Farmers' Alliance and the People's Party*, Lincoln: University of Nebraska Press, pp. 439–444.

Perkins, Richard and Ernestine Perkins (1971) *Precondition for Peace and Prosperity: Rational Anarchy*, St. Thomas (Ontario), Phibbs Printing World.

Perlstein, Rick (2001) *Before the Storm. Barry Goldwater and the Unmaking of the American Consensus*, New York: Hill and Wang.

Pina, Christine (2005) *L'extrême gauche en Europe*, Paris: La documentation Française.

Pitkin, Hanna F. (1967) *The Concept of Representation*, Berkeley: University of California Press.
Plato [translated and edited by H.D.P. Lee] (1955) *The Republic*, Harmondsworth: Penguin.
Polanyi, Michael (1958) *Personal Knowledge: Towards a Post-Critical Philosophy*, London: Routledge & Kegan Paul.
Pole, J.R. (2002) '"A Quest of Thoughts": Representation and Moral Agency in the Early Anglo-American Jury', in: John W. Cairns and Grant McLeod (eds) *'The Dearest Birth Right of the People of England': The Jury in the History of the Common Law*, Oxford: Hart, pp. 101–130.
Pont, Raoul (2004) 'Participatory Democracy and Local Power: The Experience of Porto Alegre', in: Iain Bruce (ed.) *The Porto Alegre Alternative. Direct Democracy in Action*, London: Pluto Press, pp. 111–119 (translated by Iain Bruce).
Portelli, Hugues (1992) *Le Parti Socialiste*, Paris: Montchrestien.
Porto Alegre (2008) 'Orçamento Participativo: Funcionamento Geral', online: www2.portoalegre.rs.gov.br/op/default.php?p_secao=15 (accessed 31 July 2008).
Porto Alegre (2012) 'Orçamento Participativo: Funcionamento Geral', online: www2.portoalegre.rs.gov.br/op/default.php? (accessed 27 August 2012).
Poulat, Emile (1981) 'La monarchie pontificale et le pouvoir du pape', *Pouvoirs*, 17, pp. 37–50.
Priester, Karin (2012) *Rechter und Linker Populismus. Annäherung an ein Chamäleon*, Frankfurt on Main/New York: Campus Verlag.
Qvortrup, Mads (2000) 'Are Referendums Controlled and Pro-hegemonic?', *Political Studies*, 48: 4, pp. 821–826.
Radcliff, Benjamin and Ed Wingenbach (2000) 'Preference Aggregation, Functional Pathologies, and Democracy. A Social Choice Defense of Participatory Democracy', *The Journal of Politics*, 62: 4, pp. 977–998.
Rand, Ayn (1957) *Atlas Shrugged*, New York: Signet Books/Random House.
Ratner, R.S. (2008) 'Communicative rationality in the Citizens' Assembly and the referendum process', in: Mark E. Warren and Hilary Pearse (eds) *Designing Deliberative Democracy. The British Columbia Citizens' Assembly*, Cambridge: Cambridge University Press, pp. 145–165.
Raymond, Catherine Zara (2010) 'Al Muhajiroun and Islam4UK: the group behind the ban', published by The International Centre for the Study of Radicalisation and Political Violence in London, online: http://icsr.info/wp-content/uploads/2012/10/1276697989CatherineZaraRaymondICSRPaper.pdf, accessed 7 June 2013.
Rémond, René (1982) *Les Droites en France*, Paris: Aubier Montaigne.
Rensenbrink, John (1992) *The Greens and the Politics of Transformation*, San Pedro: R. & E. Miles.
Richard, Alain (1974) 'Remarques sur l'article "Autogestion et démocratie directe" d'Alain Guillerm', *Critique Socialiste*, No. 18, pp. 61–83.
Riesel, René (1969) 'Préliminaires sur les Conseils et l'organisation conseilliste', *Internationale Situationniste*, No. 12, pp. 64–73.
Rihs, Charles (1973) *La Commune de Paris, 1871: Sa Structure et ses Doctrines*, Paris: Seuil.
Riker, William H. (1982) *Liberalism Against Populism. A Confrontation Between the Theory of Democracy and the Theory of Social Choice*, San Francisco: W.H. Freeman.
Riklin, Alois (2006) *Machtteilung: Geschichte der Mischverfassung*. Darmstadt: Wissenschaftliche Buchgesellschaft.

Riklin, Alois and Silvano Möckli (1983) 'Werden und Wandel der schweizerischen Staatsidee', in: Alois Riklin (ed.) *Handbuch Politisches System der Schweiz. I. Grundlagen*, Bern/Stuttgart: Paul Haupt.

Roberts, Kenneth M. (2012) 'Populism and democracy in Venezuela under Hugo Chávez', in: Cas Mudde and Cristóbal Rovira Kaltwasser (eds) *Populism in Europe and the Americas. Threat or Corrective for Democracy?* Cambridge: Cambridge University Press, pp. 136–159.

Robespierre, Maximilien (1967) 'Sur les principes de morale politique qui doivent guider la Convention Nationale dans l'administration intérieure de la République', Séance du 17 Pluviose An II (5 Février 1794), in: Marc Bouloiseau and Albert Soboul (eds) *Oeuvres de Maximilien Robespierre. Tome X. Discours (5e partie) 27 Juillet 1793–27 Juillet 1794*, Paris: Presses Universitaires de France, pp. 350–367.

Robinson, Peter (2011) 'Workers' Councils in Portugal, 1974–1975', in: Immanuel Ness and Dario Azzellini (eds) *Ours to Master and to Own. Workers' Control from the Commune to the Present*, Chicago: Haymarket Books, pp. 263–281.

Rocard, Michel (1969) *Le P.S.U. et l'avenir socialiste de la France*, Paris: Seuil.

Röcke, Anja (2005) *Losverfahren und Demokratie. Historische und demokratietheoretische Perspektiven*, Munster: LIT Verlag.

Roett, Riordan (1997) 'Brazilian Politics at Century's End', in: Susan Kaufman Purcell and Riordan Roett (eds) *Brazil under Cardoso*, Boulder: Lynn Riener, pp. 19–41.

Rosanvallon, Pierre (2000) *La démocratie inachevée. Histoire de la souveraineté du peuple en France*. Paris: Gallimard.

Rose, R.B. (1972) 'The Paris Commune: the last episode of the French Revolution or the first dictatorship of the proletariat?' in: Eugene Kamenka (ed.) *Paradigm for Revolution? The Paris Commune 1871–1971*, Canberra: Australian National University Press, pp. 12–29.

Rose, Jonathan (2009) 'Institutionalizing Participation through Citizens' Assemblies', in: Joan DeBardeleben and Jon H. Pammett (eds) *Activating the Citizen: Dilemmas of Participation in Europe and Canada*, London: Palgrave, pp. 214–232.

Rosenberg, A. (1938) *Demokratie und Sozialismus. Zur politischen Geschichte der letzten 150 Jahre*, Amsterdam: Allert de Lange.

Ross, George (1987) 'Labor and the Left in Power', in: Patrick McCarthy (ed.), *The French Socialists in Power 1981–1986*, New York: Greenwood Press, pp. 107–128.

Rothbard, Murray N. (1974a) 'The Anatomy of the State', in: Tibor Machan (ed.) *The Libertarian Alternative: Essays in Social and Political Philosophy*. Chicago: Nelson-Hall, pp. 69–93.

Rothbard, Murray N. (1974b) 'Left and Right: The Prospects for Liberty', in: Tibor Machan (ed.) *The Libertarian Alternative: Essays in Social and Political Philosophy*. Chicago: Nelson-Hall, pp. 525–549.

Rothbard, Murray N. (1978) *For a New Liberty. The Libertarian Manifesto*, New York: Libertarian Review Foundation.

Rougerie, Jacques (1973) 'L'A.I.T. et le mouvement ouvrier à Paris pendant les évènements de 1870–1871', in: Jacques Rougerie (ed.) *1871. Jalons pour une histoire de la Commune de Paris*, Assen: Van Gorcum, pp. 3–102.

Rousseau, Jean-Jacques ([1762] 1971) *Emile ou De l'éducation*, in: *Oeuvres complètes. 3. Oeuvres philosophiques et politiques: de l'Emile aux derniers écrits politiques 1762–1772*, Paris: Seuil, pp. 7–325.

Rousseau, Jean-Jacques ([1762] 2001) *Du contrat social*, Paris: Flammarion, (edited by Bruno Bernardi).

Rousseau, Jean-Jacques (1971a) 'Considérations sur le gouvernement de la Pologne et sur sa reformation projetée', in: *Oeuvres complètes. 3. Oeuvres philosophiques et politiques: de l'Emile aux derniers écrits politiques 1762–1772*, Paris: Seuil, pp. 527–569.
Rousseau, Jean-Jacques (1971b) 'Projet de Constitution pour la Corse', in: *Oeuvres Completes. 3. Oeuvres philosophiques et politiques: de l'Emile aux derniers écrits politiques 1762–1772*, Paris: Seuil, pp. 492–515.
Rovira Kaltwasser, Cristóbal (2012) 'The ambivalence of populism: threat and corrective for democracy', *Democratization*, 19: 2, pp. 184–208.
Roy, Olivier (1994) *The Failure of Political Islam*, London: I.B. Tauris (translated from French by Carol Volk).
Royle, E. and J. Walvin (1982) *English radicals and reformers 1760–1848*, Brighton: Harvester Press.
Rubel, Maximilien (1972) 'Socialism and the Commune', in: Eugene Kamenka (ed.) *Paradigm for Revolution? The Paris Commune 1871–1971*, Canberra: Australian National University Press, pp. 30–48.
Rucht, Dieter (2012) 'Deliberation as an ideal and practice in progressive social movements', in: Brigitte Geissel and Kenneth Newton (eds) *Evaluating Democratic Innovations. Curing the Democratic Malaise?* London/New York: Routledge, 112-134.
Rudé, George (1975) *Robespierre. Portrait of a Revolutionary Democrat*, London: Collins.
Rühle, Otto ([1924] 1972) *Von der bürgerlichen zur proletarischen Revolution*, Berlin: Blankertz.
Sabine, George H. and Thomas L. Thorson (1973) *A History of Political Theory*, Hinsdale: Dryden Press (fourth edition).
Sadiki, Larbi (2004) *The Search for Arab Democracy. Discourses and Counter-Discourses*, New York: Columbia University Press.
Sainteny, Guillaume (1992) *Les Verts*, Paris: Presses Universitaires de France.
Samary, Catherine (1999) 'Mandel's Views on the Transition to Socialism', in: Gilbert Achcar (ed.) *The Legacy of Ernest Mandel*, London/New York: Verso, pp. 152–190.
Sanders, R.J. (1989) *Beweging tegen de schijn. De situationisten, een avant-garde*, Amsterdam: Huis aan de Drie Grachten.
Saward, Michael (2001) 'Making Democratic Connections: Political Equality, Deliberation and Direct Democracy', *Acta Politica*, 36: 4, pp. 361–379.
Saward, Michael (2010) *The Representative Claim*, Oxford/New York: Oxford University Press.
Saward, Michael (2012) 'Claims and Constructions', *Contemporary Political Theory*, 11: 1, pp. 123–127.
Schneider, Dieter and Rudolf Kuda (1968) *Arbeiterräte in der Novemberrevolution. Ideen, Wirkungen, Dokumente*, Frankfurt on Main: Suhrkamp Verlag.
Schneller, Martin (1970) *Zwischen Romantik und Faschismus. Der Beitrag Othmar Spanns zum Konservativismus der Weimarer Republik*, Stuttgart: Ernst Klett Verlag.
Schumpeter, Joseph A. (1976) *Capitalism, Socialism and Democracy*, London: Allen & Unwin (fifth edition; first edition published in 1942).
Schweizerische Bundeskanzlei (2010) 'Chronologie Volksabstimmungen', online: www.admin.ch/ch/d/pore/va/vab_2_2_4_1.html (accessed 3 August 2010).
Schweizerische Bundeskanzlei (2013) 'Volksabstimmung "gegen die Abzockerei". Vorläufige amtliche Endergebnisse', online: www.bk.admin.ch/ch/d/pore/va/20130303/det568.html (accessed 3 April 2013).
Sealey, Raphael (1987) *The Athenian Republic. Democracy or the Rule of Law?* University Park: The Pennsylvania State University Press.

Sen, Amartya (2006) *Identity and Violence. The Illusion of Destiny*, New York/London: W.W. Norton.
Shantz, Jeff (2002) 'Green Syndicalism: An Alternative Red-Green Vision', *Environmental Politics*, 11: 4, pp. 21–41.
Sheehan, Séan M. (2003) *Anarchism*, London: Reaktion Books.
Shirinia, Kirill (1996) 'The Comintern: A World Party and Its National Sections', in: Mikhail Narinsky and Jürgen Rojahn (eds) *Centre and Periphery: the History of the Comintern in the Light of New Documents*, Amsterdam: International Institute of Social History, pp. 169–177.
Simon, Rita (1980) *The Jury: Its Role in American Society*, Lexington (Mass.): D.C. Heath.
Sinclair, R.K. (1988) *Democracy and Participation in Athens*, Cambridge: Cambridge University Press.
Sinn Féin (no date) 'Towards a New Republic', online: www.sinnfein.ie/towards-a-new-republic (accessed 24 January 2013).
Sintomer, Yves (2007) *Le pouvoir au peuple. Jurys citoyens, tirage au sort et démocratie participative*, Paris: La Découverte.
Sintomer, Yves, Carsten Herzberg, Anja Röcke and Giovanni Allegretti (2012) 'Transnational Models of Citizen Participation: The Case of Participatory Budgeting', *Journal of Public Deliberation*, 8: 2, Article 9, online: www.publicdeliberation.net/jpd/vol. 8/iss2/art9 (accessed 17 April 2013).
Sirianni, Carmen (1980) 'Workers' Control in the Era of World War I. A Comparative Analysis of the European Experience', *Theory and Society*, 9: 1, pp. 29–88.
Sirianni, Carmen (1982) *Workers Control and Socialist Democracy. The Soviet Experience*, London: Verso/NLB.
Skinner, Quentin (1993) 'The Italian City-Republics', in: John Dunn (ed.) *Democracy: The Unfinished Journey, 508 BC to AD 1993*, Oxford: Oxford University Press, pp. 57–69.
Slagboom, D. et al. (1996), *Toelichting op het Program van Beginselen van de Staatkundig Gereformeerde Partij*, Den Haag: SGP.
Smith, Graham (2009) *Democratic Innovations. Designing Institutions for Citizen Participation*, Cambridge: Cambridge University Press.
Smith, Graham (2012) 'Deliberative democracy and mini-publics', in: Brigitte Geissel and Kenneth Newton (eds), *Evaluating Democratic Innovations. Curing the Democratic Malaise?* London/New York: Routledge, pp. 90–111.
Smith, Graham and Corinne Wales (2000) 'Citizens' Juries and Deliberative Democracy', *Political Studies*, 48: 1, pp. 51–65.
Smolik, Josef (2011) 'Far right-wing political parties in the Czech Republic: heterogeneity, cooperation, competition', *Slovak Journal of Political Sciences*, 11: 2, pp. 99–111.
Snider, J.H. (2007) 'From Dahl to O'Leary: 36 Years of the "Yale School of Democratic Reform"', *Journal of Public Deliberation*, 3: 1, Article 9, online: www.publicdeliberation.net/cgi/viewcontent.cgi?article=1046&context=jpd (accessed 28 April 2013).
Soboul, Albert (1966) *Paysans, Sans-culottes et Jacobins*, Paris: Librairie Clavreuil.
Soboul, Albert (1968) *Les Sans-culottes Parisiens en l'an II. Mouvement Populaire et Gouvernement Révolutionnaire (1793–1794)*, Paris: Seuil.
Socialist Party (no date) 'Socialism in the 21st century: How could socialism work?', online: www.socialistparty.org.uk/socialism21/ch6.htm (accessed 15 October 2003).
Sozialdemokratische Partei Deutschlands ([1891] 1960) 'Das Erfurter Programm', in: Wilhelm Mommsen (ed.), *Deutsche Parteiprogramme*, Munich: Isar Verlag, pp. 349–353.

Spanakos, Anthony Peter (2011) 'Citizen Chávez: The State, Social Movements, and Publics', *Latin American Perspectives*, 38: 1, pp. 14–27.
Spann, Othmar (1930) *Gesellschaftslehre*, Leipzig: Quelle und Meyer (third edition).
Spann, Othmar (1972) *Der wahre Staat, Band 5*, Graz: Akademische Druck- und Verlagsanstalt (fifth edition since 1921).
Stadt Emsdetten (2011) *Emsdettenkonferenz 2011. Der Stadthaushalt*, Emsdetten: Fachdienst 10 Strategie, Kommunikation, Interne Dienste.
Stalin, J.W. (1954) *Problems of Leninism*, Moscow: Foreign Languages Publishing House.
Stanley, Ben (2008) 'The thin ideology of populism', *Journal of Political Ideologies*, 13: 1, pp. 95–110.
Starr, Amory, María Elena Martínez-Torres and Peter Rosset (2011) 'Participatory Democracy in Action: Practices of the Zapatistas and the Movimento Sem Terra', *Latin American Perspectives*, 38: 1, pp.102–119.
Starr, Chester G. (1990) *The Birth of Athenian Democracy. The Assembly in the Fifth Century B.C.*, New York/Oxford: Oxford University Press.
Stauffacher, Werner (1962) *Die Versammlungsdemokratie im Kanton Glarus. Ein Beitrag zur Geschichte der glarnerischen Landsgemeinde und Gemeindeversammlungen*, Zürich: Zurich University PhD Thesis.
Stern, Kenneth Saul (1996) *A Force upon the Plain. The American Militia Movement and the Politics of Hate*, New York: Simon & Schuster.
Stockton, David (1990) *The Classical Athenian Democracy*, Oxford: Oxford University Press.
Stolz, Peter (1968) *Politische Entscheidungen in der Versammlungsdemokratie. Untersuchungen zum kollektiven Entscheid in der athenischen Demokratie, im schweizerischen Landsgemeindekanton Glarus und im Kibbuz*, Stuttgart: Verlag Paul Haupt.
Surel, Yves (2004) 'Populisme et démocratie', in: Pierre-André Taguieff (ed.) *Le Retour du Populisme. Un défi pour les démocraties européennes*, Paris: Universalis, pp. 95–109.
Sutherland, Keith (2008) *A People's Parliament. A (Revised) Blueprint for a Very English Revolution*, Exeter: Imprint Academic.
Sutherland, Keith (2011a) 'Athenian Democracy Reincarnate', weblog with reactions and rejoinders, online: http://equalitybylot.wordpress.com (accessed 13 October–13 December 2011).
Sutherland, Keith (2011b) 'The Two Sides of the Representative Coin', *Studies in Social Justice*, 5: 2, pp. 197–211.
Taggart, Paul (2000) *Populism*, Buckingham/Philadelphia: Open University Press.
Tálos, Emmerich and Walter Manoschek (1988) 'Politische Struktur des Austrofaschismus (1934–1938)', in: Emmerich Tálos and Wolfgang Neugebauer (eds) *Austrofaschismus: Beiträge über Politik, Ökonomie und Kultur 1934–1938*, Vienna: Verlag für Gesellschaftskritik (fourth edition), pp. 75–119.
Talpin, Julien (2012) 'When democratic innovations let the people decide. An evaluation of co-governance experiments', in: Brigitte Geissel and Kenneth Newton (eds) *Evaluating Democratic Innovations. Curing the Democratic Malaise?* London/New York: Routledge, pp. 184–206.
Tännsjö, Torbjörn (1992) *Populist Democracy: A Defence*, London/New York: Routledge.
Tasman, Coen (1996) *Louter Kabouter. Kroniek van een beweging 1969-1974*, Amsterdam: Babylon-De Geus.
The Shorter Oxford English Dictionary on Historical Principles (1980) Oxford: Clarendon Press, (third edition with corrections).

The World Guide 11th Edition (2007) Oxford: New Internationalist Publications.
Therborn, Göran (1980) *What Does the Ruling Class Do When it Rules?* London: Verso/ NLB.
Thomas, William (1979) *The Philosophic Radicals. Nine Studies in Theory and Practice 1817–1841*, Oxford: Clarendon Press.
Thompson, Dennis F. (1976) *John Stuart Mill and Representative Government*, Princeton: Princeton University Press.
Thompson, Dorothy (1984) *The Chartists*, London: Temple Smith.
Thompson, Michael, Richard Ellis and Aaron Wildavsky (1990) *Cultural Theory*, Boulder: Westview Press.
Thorley, John (1996) *Athenian Democracy*, London/ New York: Routledge.
Thorley, John (2004) *Athenian Democracy*, London: Routledge (second edition).
Threlkeld, Simon (1998) 'A blueprint for democratic law-making: give citizen juries the final say', *Social Policy*, 28: 4, pp. 5–9.
Tibi, Bassam (1998) *The Challenge of Fundamentalism*, Berkeley: The University of California Press.
Tibi, Bassam (2000) *Fundamentalismus im Islam: eine Gefahr für den Weltfrieden?* Darmstadt: Wissenschaftliche Buchgesellschaft/Primus Verlag.
Tieleman, Alex (2012) 'Markt met een hart, meer zit er niet in', *Trouw*, 9 October 2012, pp. 2–3.
Trinkunas, Harold A. (2010) 'The Transformation of Venezuela', *Latin American Research Review*, 45: 3, pp. 239–247.
Tökes, Rudolf (1967) *Béla Kun and the Hungarian Soviet Republic. The Origins and Role of the Communist Party of Hungary in the Revolutions of 1918–1919*, New York: Praeger.
Tomlinson, John (1981) *Left-Right. The March of Political Extremism in Britain*, London/ New York: John Calder/Riverrun.
Tønneson, Kare (1988) 'La démocratie directe sous la Révolution française – le cas des districts et sections de Paris', in: Colin Lucas (ed.), *The French Revolution and the Creation of Modern Political Culture*, Vol. 2, Oxford: Pergamon Press, pp. 295–307.
Twal, Ghazi Odeh (2003) *Königreich Saudi-Arabien und seine wichtigsten Gesetze*, Riad (Ryadh): Star Printing Press.
Tweede Kamer der Staten-Generaal (2008) 'Brief van de Staatssecretaris van Binnenlandse Zaken en Koninkrijksrelaties, 18 April 2008', *Kamerstuk* 117682, The Hague: Sdu.
Ulam, Adam B. (1974) *The Russian Political System*, New York: Random House.
Urbinati, Nadia (2000) 'Representation as advocacy', *Political Theory*, 28: 6, pp. 758–786.
Urbinati, Nadia (2008) *Representative Democracy. Principles and Genealogy*, Chicago: University of Chicago Press.
Van Cott, Donna Lee (2008) *Radical Democracy in the Andes*, Cambridge: Cambridge University Press.
Van der Kolk, Henk and Martha Brinkman (2008) 'Kiezen Voor Een Nieuw Kiesstelsel. Deel 1: de selectie van het Burgerforum Kiesstelsel 2006', online: www.utwente.nl/mb/pa/staff/kolk/bf_verslag_deel_1_versie_3.pdf (accessed 11 October 2012).
Van der Land, Lucas (1962) *Het ontstaan van de Pacifistisch Socialistische Partij*, Amsterdam: De Bezige Bij.
Van Versendaal, Harry (2011) 'In Syntagma Square, some see the dawn of a new politics', *Ekathimerini*, 26 June, also online: www.ekathimerini.com (accessed 29 June 2011).

References

Vatter, Adrian (2008) 'Vom Extremtyp zum Normalfall? Die Schweizerische Konsensusdemokratie im Wandel. Eine Re-Analyse von Lijpharts Studie für die Schweiz von 1997 bis 2007', *Schweizerische Zeitschrift für Politikwissenschaft*, 14: 1, 1–47 [also published in English in the *World Political Science Review*, 4: 2 (2008), Article 1].

Vergne, Antoine (2005) 'Portrait of a Pioneer (English Version)', *Journal of Public Deliberation*, 1: 1, Article 11, online: www.publicdeliberation.net/cgi/viewcontent.cgi?article=1017&context=jpd (accessed 16 April 2013).

Vidmar, Neil (2000) 'A Historical and Comparative Perspective on the Common Law Jury', in: Neil Vidmar (ed.) *World Jury Systems*, Oxford: Oxford University Press, pp. 1–52.

Ville de Pont-de-Claix (2007) 'Rapport d'orientation budgétaire. Conseil Consultatif Budgétaire 2006', online: www.ville-pontdeclaix.fr/data/document/le_ccb.pdf (accessed 12 March 2007).

Voerman, Gerrit (2001) *De meridiaan van Moskou. De CPN en de Communistische Internationale (1919–1930)*, Amsterdam: L.J. Veen.

Von Beyme, Klaus (1982) *Parteien in westlichen Demokratien*, Munich: Piper Verlag.

Waardenburg, Jacques (2002) *Islam: Historical, Social and Political Perspectives*, Berlin/New York: Walter de Gruyter.

Warren, Mark E. and Hilary Pearse (2008) 'Introduction: democratic renewal and deliberative democracy', in: Mark E. Warren and Hilary Pearse (eds) *Designing Deliberative Democracy. The British Columbia Citizens' Assembly*, Cambridge: Cambridge University Press, pp. 1–19.

Weber, Max (1968) 'Politische Gemeinschaften und Wirtschaft', in Johannes Winckelmann (ed.) *Max Weber, Soziologie, weltgeschichtliche Analysen, Politik*, Stuttgart: Kröner Verlag (fourth edition), pp. 80–96.

Werz, Nikolaus (2007) 'Hugo Chávez und der "Sozialismus des 21. Jahrhunderts". Ein Zwischenbericht', *Ibero-Analysen*, No. 21, Berlin: Ibero-Amerikanisches Institut.

Westerman, W.M. (1925) *De zieke staat*, The Hague: Leopold.

White, Damian F. (2008) *Bookchin. A Critical Appraisal*, London: Pluto Press.

Winock, Michel (1973) 'Jean Allemane: une fidélité critique', in: Jacques Rougerie (ed.) *1871. Jalons pour une histoire de la Commune de Paris*, Assen: Van Gorcum, pp. 373–380.

Wintrobe, Ronald (2002) 'Leadership and Passion in Extremist Politics', in: Albert Breton, Gianluigi Galeotti, Pierre Salmon and Ronald Wintrobe (eds) *Political Extremism and Rationality*, Cambridge: Cambridge University Press, pp. 23–43.

Wolin, Sheldon S. (2008) *Democracy Incorporated. Managed Democracy and the Specter of Inverted Totalitarianism*, Princeton/Oxford: Princeton University Press.

Wood, Gordon S. (1993a) 'Democracy and the American Revolution', in: John Dunn (ed.) *Democracy: The Unfinished Journey, 508 BC to AD 1993*, Oxford: Oxford University Press, pp. 91–106.

Wood, Gordon S. (1993b) *The Radicalism of the American Revolution*, New York: Vintage Books/Random House.

Woodcock, George (1963) *Anarchism*, Harmondsworth: Penguin Books.

Worsley, Peter (1969) 'The Concept of Populism', in: Ghita Ionescu en Ernest Gellner (eds) *Populism. Its Meanings and National Characteristics*, London: Weifenfeld & Nicolson, pp. 212–250.

Young, Iris Marion (2000) *Inclusion and Democracy*, Oxford: Oxford University Press.

Zakaras, Alex (2010) 'Lot and Democratic Representation: A Modest Proposal', *Constellations*, 17: 3, pp. 455–471.

Zink, Harold, Howard R. Penniman and Guy B. Hathorn (1958) *American Government and Politics: National, State and Local*, Princeton NJ: D. Van Nostrand.

Zoubir, Yahia H. (1998) 'State, Civil Society and the Question of Radical Fundamentalism in Algeria', in: Ahmad S. Moussalli (ed.) *Islamic Fundamentalism: Myths and Realities*, Reading: Garnet Publishing Limited/Ithaca Press, pp. 123–168.

Zuckerman, Michael (1970) *Peaceable Kingdoms. New England Towns in the Eighteenth Century*, New York: Alfred Knopf.

Zúquete, José Pedro (2011) 'Another World is Possible? Utopia Revisited', *New Global Studies*, 5: 2, article 3, online: www.bepress.com/ngs/vol. 5/iss2/art3 (accessed 15 December 2011).

Index

Aleatoria 116–18, 148, 152, 163
anarchism 25, 34–7, 54–5, 59n2, 72, 82, 87, 119
Appenzell Inner Rhoden (political system) 48–50, 56–8, 60n11, 159
aristocracy 1, 15–18, 21–3, 26–8, 120, 154; elective 5–6
Aristotle 1–2, 6, 11
assembly democracy 54–9, 155, 160–1; *see also* Athens, *Landsgemeinde*, libertarian municipalism
Town Meeting
Athens (political system) 1, 34, 44, 47–9, 56–8, 131, 136–40, 159; Council of 500 (*Boulè*) 45–6, 120, 122, 137–8, 140, 149, 155, 157; juries (*dikastèria*) 45, 138–41; popular assembly 44–6
Aung San Suu Kyi 13, 31n1
autocracy 14–16, 19, 23–4, 28, 31n3, 56

Backes, Uwe 4, 11, 13–15, 154
Barber, Benjamin 8–9, 162–3, 164n1
Berlin citizen panel (*Bürgerjury*) 145, 148
Biehl, Janet 37, 40–1, 43
binding mandate *see* mandate
Bolshevik party 20–1, 78–82, 86, 110
Bolshevik Revolution *see* Russian Revolution
Bookchin, Murray 36, 48, 50, 58–9, 60n4, 119, 149, 155, 158; critics 39–43; ideas 37–9; *see also* libertarian municipalism
Buchstein, Hubertus 134
Budge, Ian 107–8, 111
Burnheim, John 118, 134–5, 149–51, 152n1, 158, 163; critics 120–4; ideas 118–20; *see also* demarchy

California (political system) 104–7, 110, 113n13, 147, 157, 159

Callenbach, Ernest 126–8, 132, 134–5, 149–51, 153n10, 158, 163
Castoriadis, Cornelius (pseudonym Pierre Chaulieu) 87–9, 91, 97, 110
CERES (*Centre d'études, de recherches et d'éducation socialiste*, Centre for Socialist Study, Research and Education) 91–2
CFDT (*Confédération Française Démocratique du Travail*, French Democratic Confederation of Labour) 91
Chartist movement 35, 73–4
Chávez, Hugo 98–101
China 22, 96, 97, 143–4, 163
citizen assembly (British Columbia or Ontario) 145–8, 150–1
citizen jury *see* citizen panels
citizen panels 124, 144–50, 157
Clark, Sherman 107
classical democracy *see* democrats, classical
Cohn-Bendit, Daniel 88, 92
communal councils (Venezuela) 54, 100
Commune (of Paris) 20, 75–9, 81–2, 101, 108–9, 156
Communist party (Russia) *see* Bolshevik party
Condorcet, Nicolas de 65, 68–70, 129
consensus conference 145, 147
conservatism 15–17, 29
Considérant, Victor 72, 74
council-communism *see* council-democracy
council-democracy 21, 29, 97, 101, 110, 112, 156–61; in 1920s and 1930s 82–7; in 1960s and 1970s 94–5; *see also* Pannekoek
councilism *see* council-democracy
Critical Theory *see* Frankfurt School

Index

Crosby, Ned 142, 144–5, 157
cyclical voting 42, 57

Dahl, Robert 4, 6–7, 15, 31n2, 59n2, 121–2, 132
deliberative opinion polls 143–4, 157
demarchy 118–24, 149, 151, 158; *see also* Burnheim, John
democracy: direct 3, 34, 36, 102, 107 (*see also* assembly democracy); parliamentary democracy *see* mixed regime; participatory democracy 25, 92, 98, 101; plebiscitary democracy 101–12, 157, 160–1; proletarian democracy 78–9, 156 (*see also* dictatorship of the proletariat); radical democracy 8, 81, 94–5, 159, 162 (*see also* democrats, classical)
democrats: classical democrats 4, 6–9, 20, 59, 94, 97, 154–5, 157, 162; dialectical democrats 6, 8; elitist democrats 6, 154, 159
dictatorship of the proletariat 19–21, 77–80, 82
Dienel, Peter 142, 144, 157
Dieterich, Heinz 95–9
Dutra, Olivio 52–3
Dutschke, Rudi 94, 97

electoralism 126, 129, 132; *see also* mixed regime
elitism, democratic 6, 154, 159
Emsdetten 145
Engels, Friedrich 19, 73, 76–8, 98
extremism 11–15, 28–31, 126; aristocratic and autocratic extremism 15, 24, 28–31, 154; democratic extremism 7–8, 15, 20, 29–30, 36, 59, 79, 125, 154–9; theocratic extremism 22–5

Fascism 17–18, 21, 28–9, 31n5
Fishkin, James 142–4, 157
Frankfurt School 93, 97
French Revolution 62–5, 67, 109, 140

Glarus (political system) 48–50, 56–8, 60n11, 159
Global Justice Movement 6, 55–6
Godwin, William 34–6, 59n1
Goldwater, Barry 11
Goodwin, Barbara 116–18, 135, 152
green parties: in France (*Les Verts*) 92; in Germany (*Die Grünen*) 94–5; in the Netherlands (*GroenLinks*) 93

Guild Socialism 121, 123

Hitler, Adolf 16, 18–19, 29, 102; *see also* National Socialism
Hoogeveen (forges of) 54, 60n8

initiative, popular or people's initiative 9, 78, 92, 126, 157, 162–3; in California 104–6, 110; in Switzerland 74, 102–3, 110, 113n12; in Venezuela 100
Internet 61, 107, 111, 157
Ireland (medieval political system) 26
Islamism 22–4, 28, 31
Islamic Republic of Iran 23

Jacobinism 65–6, 71–2, 75–6
Jacobins 2, 62, 68, 108, 156; history 63–5
juries 35, 129, 132, 150; in Athens (*dikastèria*) 45, 138–41, 157; in England and US 136, 140–1; *see also* citizen panels

Kabouters (The Netherlands) 54–5
Khomeiny, Ayatollah Ruhollah 23
Kleroterians 122–3, 131

Landsgemeinde (Switzerland) 48–50, 155
Ledru-Rollin, Alexandre-Auguste 71–2, 74
Lefort, Claude 87–8
Leib, Ethan 124, 132–6, 149–51, 158
Lenin, Vladimir 20–1, 95, 98; and Bolshevik party 80–2; and Pannekoek 83–4; about proletarian democracy 78–9, 156
Leninism *see* Lenin; Marxism-Leninism
libertarianism 25–8
libertarian municipalism *see* municipalism, libertarian
libertarian parties 26, 31n8
logocrats 136
Lotreps (allotted representatives) 117–18, 135–6, 151

mandate, binding or imperative (*mandat impératif*) 69, 71–2, 86, 95, 104, 112n1, 156–7; in England (pledges) 73–4, 157; in Paris Commune 76; in Russian Revolution 79
Mandel, Ernest 93
Manin, Bernard 4, 6
Mansbridge, Jane 8, 44, 51–2, 128–9
Marinaleda 55, 60n9, 155
Marx, Karl 19, 73, 76–8, 81, 88, 93, 97–8, 101, 108, 156

Marxism 39, 77, 88, 95, 97–8, 112, 156
Marxism-Leninism 21, 28–9, 40, 88
Mawdudi, Abul Ala 22–4
Mill, John Stuart 74
mixed constitution *see* mixed regime
mixed regime 4, 10, 14, 59, 154–5, 161, 163
municipalism, libertarian 36–44, 58–9, 119, 155–6, 159; *see also* Bookchin, Murray
Mussolini, Benito 17–19, 29; *see also* Fascism

Napoleon Bonaparte (Emperor Napoleon I) 65, 71, 108
Napoleon III (Emperor, Louis Napoleon Bonaparte) 75, 102
National-Socialism (Nazism) 18–19, 21, 27–8, 31n5
neighbourhood assembly 89, 91–3, 95, 97, 112, 162–3
neighbourhood council *see* neighbourhood assembly
Neo-Jacobins *see* Jacobinism
New Left 87, 95, 98, 101, 161; in France 87–92; in Germany 93–4; in The Netherlands 93; in the US 96
NPA (*Nouveau Parti Anticapitaliste*, New Anti-Capitalist Party, France) 92

O'Leary, Kevin 132–6, 150–1, 158
Occupy movement 6, 14, 56
Orange Free State (The Netherlands) 54–5

Paine, Thomas 68, 73
Pannekoek, Anton 89, 109, 156, 158–9; critics 85–7; ideas 83–5; influence 88, 91, 93, 95, 101
Paris Commune *see* Commune (of Paris)
participatory budgeting (*Orçamento Participativo* in Portuguese) 52–4, 159
participatory democracy *see* democracy, participatory
Partido Azar (Chance Party, Spain) 125, 134, 150, 158
Phillips, Michael 126–8, 132, 134–5, 149–51, 158, 163
Pitkin, Hanna 3, 128
planning cells 141–2, 144
Plato 1–2, 6, 47
plebiscite *see* initiative; referendum
polyarchy 4, 31n2
Pont-de-Claix 145
populism 29, 63, 95–6, 98, 107, 109, 157

Porto Alegre 52–3, 56–8, 155; *see also* participatory budgeting
primaries (US) 104–5
primary assemblies 68–9, 72–3, 111
PS (*Parti Socialiste*, Socialist Party, France) 91–2
PSP (*Pacifistisch Socialistische Partij*, Pacifist Socialist Party, The Netherlands) 93, 95, 156
PSU (*Parti Socialiste Unifié*, United Socialist Party, France) 90–1, 95, 156
PT (*Partido do Trabalhadores*, Workers' Party, Brazil) 52

radical democracy *see* democracy, radical
radicalism 9, 13, 81; democratic radicalism 8, 29–30, 63, 75, 101, 109, 156–7, 159; ideology of Radical parties 8, 71–4, 156–7, 159
Rand, Ayn 27
recall 3, 9, 73, 85, 90, 92–5, 109, 157; in California 105; in French Revolution 71, 156; in Paris Commune 76–7; in Russian Revolution 79–81; in Venezuela 100–1
referendum 3, 9, 78, 92, 95, 97, 107–9, 126, 152, 153n12, 161–3; in California 104–6, 110; in France 68, 70, 156; in Switzerland 74, 102–3, 110; in Venezuela 99–100
Riker, William 5, 42, 97, 108
Riklin, Alois 4, 14, 50
Rittinghausen, Maurice 72–4
Robespierre, Maximilien 2, 64, 70–1
Rothbard, Murray 25–7
Rousseau, Jean-Jacques 66–7, 70–2, 74, 86, 108, 113n3, 156, 159
Rühle, Otto 84–5, 95, 156
Russian Revolution 11, 78–81, 156

sans-culottes 2, 64–5, 67, 70–1, 108, 156
Saudi-Arabia (Kingdom of) 24
Saward, Michael 3, 6, 8, 162
Schmidt, Marcus 134–5, 150
Schumpeter, Joseph 5, 97
SDS (*Sozialistische Deutsche Studentenbund*, Socialist German Student League) 93–5, 156
SDS (Students for a Democratic Society, US) 37
SGP (*Staatkundig Gereformeerde Partij*, Calvinist Party, The Netherlands) 22
Sheikh Omar Bakri Mohammed 23, 31n7
Sinn Féin (Ireland) 113n10

Sintomer, Yves 134–5, 142
situationism 88–90, 146, 156
Situationist International *see* situationism
Socialisme ou Barbarie (Socialism or Barbarism, France) 87–8, 156
sortitionism 29–30, 117, 123–4, 126, 132, 134, 136–7, 150–1
Soviet Union 21–2, 81, 87, 97, 112
Soviets *see* workers' councils in Russia
Spann, Othmar 15–16
SPD (*Sozialdemokratische Partei Deutschlands*, Social Democratic Party, Germany) 78, 83–4
Stalin, Joseph 21, 87
Sutherland, Keith 129–34, 136, 149–51, 158, 163
Switzerland (political system) 74, 102–3, 107, 109–10, 157, 159
syndicalism 39, 85

Taliban regime 24
Tännsjö, Torbjörn 95–8, 163
Threlkeld, Simon 124, 134, 149–51, 158
Tibet (political system) 24
Town Meeting (New England) 50–2, 56–9, 155, 159
Trotsky, Leon 20, 22, 87, 92, 101
Trotskyism 22, 37, 87, 92–3

Urbinati, Nadia 3–5, 8, 69, 86, 157

Vatican state 24–5
Venezuela (political system) 98–101

workers' councils: theory 83–9, 108–12, 161–2; in France (1968) 90–1; in Germany 81–2; in Hungary 81–2; in Russia 20, 22, 78–81, 86, 108–9, 156; in Venezuela 101, 109; *see also* council-democracy

Young, Iris Marion 128

Zakaras, Alex 132, 136, 150, 158, 163
Zapatistas (Mexico) 6, 14, 55

Taylor & Francis
eBooks
FOR LIBRARIES

ORDER YOUR FREE 30 DAY INSTITUTIONAL TRIAL TODAY!

Over 23,000 eBook titles in the Humanities, Social Sciences, STM and Law from some of the world's leading imprints.

Choose from a range of subject packages or create your own!

Benefits for you
- Free MARC records
- COUNTER-compliant usage statistics
- Flexible purchase and pricing options

Benefits for your user
- Off-site, anytime access via Athens or referring URL
- Print or copy pages or chapters
- Full content search
- Bookmark, highlight and annotate text
- Access to thousands of pages of quality research at the click of a button

For more information, pricing enquiries or to order a free trial, contact your local online sales team.

UK and Rest of World: **online.sales@tandf.co.uk**
US, Canada and Latin America: **e-reference@taylorandfrancis.com**

www.ebooksubscriptions.com

ALPSP Award for BEST eBOOK PUBLISHER 2009 Finalist

Taylor & Francis eBooks
Taylor & Francis Group

A flexible and dynamic resource for teaching, learning and research.